Studies in Childhood and Youth

Series Editors: Allison James, University of Sheffield, UK, and Adrian James, University of Sheffield, UK.

Titles include:

Kate Bacon
TWINS IN SOCIETY
Parents, Bodies, Space and Talk

David Buckingham, Sara Bragg, Mary Jane Kehily
YOUTH CULTURES IN THE AGE OF GLOBAL MEDIA

David Buckingham and Vebjørg Tingstad (*editors*)
CHILDHOOD AND CONSUMER CULTURE

Tom Cockburn
RETHINKING CHILDREN'S CITIZENSHIP

Sam Frankel
CHILDREN, MORALITY AND SOCIETY

Allison James
SOCIALISING CHILDREN

Allison James, Anne Trine Kjørholt and Vebjørg Tingstad (*editors*)
CHILDREN, FOOD AND IDENTITY IN EVERYDAY LIFE

Nicholas Lee
CHILDHOOD AND BIOPOLITICS
Climate Change, Life Processes and Human Futures

Manfred Liebel, Karl Hanson, Iven Saadi and Wouter Vandenhole (*editors*)
CHILDREN'S RIGHTS FROM BELOW
Cross-Cultural Perspectives

Orna Naftali
CHILDREN, RIGHTS AND MODERNITY IN CHINA
Raising Self-Governing Citizens

Helen Stapleton
SURVIVING TEENAGE MOTHERHOOD
Myths and Realities

Afua Twum-Danso Imoh, Robert Ame
CHILDHOODS AT THE INTERSECTION OF THE LOCAL AND THE GLOBAL

Hanne Warming
PARTICIPATION, CITIZENSHIP AND TRUST IN CHILDREN'S LIVES

Karen Wells, Erica Burman, Heather Montgomery and Alison Watson (*editors*)
CHILDHOOD, YOUTH AND VIOLENCE IN GLOBAL CONTEXTS
Research and Practice in Dialogue

Rebekah Willett, Chris Richards, Jackie Marsh, Andrew Burn, Julia C. Bishop (*editors*)
CHILDREN, MEDIA AND PLAYGROUND CULTURES
Ethnographic Studies of School Playtimes

Studies in Childhood and Youth
Series Standing Order ISBN 978–0–230–21686–0 hardback
(*outside North America only*)

You can receive future titles in this series as they are published by placing a standing order. Please contact your bookseller or, in case of difficulty, write to us at the address below with your name and address, the title of the series and the ISBN quoted above.

Customer Services Department, Macmillan Distribution Ltd, Houndmills, Basingstoke, Hampshire RG21 6XS, England

Childhood, Youth and Violence in Global Contexts

Research and Practice in Dialogue

Edited by

Karen Wells
Birkbeck College, University of London, UK

Erica Burman
University of Manchester, UK

Heather Montgomery
The Open University, UK

Alison Watson
University of St Andrews, UK

palgrave
macmillan

First published 2014 by
PALGRAVE MACMILLAN

Palgrave Macmillan in the UK is an imprint of Macmillan Publishers Limited, registered in England, company number 785998, of Houndmills, Basingstoke, Hampshire RG21 6XS.

Palgrave Macmillan in the US is a division of St Martin's Press LLC, 175 Fifth Avenue, New York, NY 10010.

Palgrave Macmillan is the global academic imprint of the above companies and has companies and representatives throughout the world.

Palgrave® and Macmillan® are registered trademarks in the United States, the United Kingdom, Europe and other countries.

ISBN 978–1–137–32259–3

This book is printed on paper suitable for recycling and made from fully managed and sustained forest sources. Logging, pulping and manufacturing processes are expected to conform to the environmental regulations of the country of origin.

A catalogue record for this book is available from the British Library.

Library of Congress Cataloging-in-Publication Data
Childhood, youth and violence in global contexts : research and practice in dialogue / edited by Karen Wells, Birkbeck College, University of London, UK, Erica Burman, University of Manchester, UK, Heather Montgomery, The Open University, UK, Alison Watson, University of St Andrews, UK.
pages cm
Summary: "The common-sense understanding of childhood as a protected space has led to violence against and by children being understood as spectacular or exceptional. In contrast, this edited collection shows how violence enters into ordinary, routine practices of childhood and children's experiences. It brings together academic and practitioner points of view to understand how violence is enacted against children in infancy, adolescence, in school, in care, at home and on the street. Each topic is addressed in one chapter by an academic and in the next chapter by a practitioner, to draw out and explore the differences and similarities between academic and practitioner perspectives. Wells' and Montgomery's introduction brings these viewpoints together and argues that violence against children can be related to issues of social recognition, particularly at the start and end of childhood and in contexts of poverty" — Provided by publisher.
ISBN 978–1–137–32259–3 (hardback)
1. Children and violence. 2. Violence in children. I. Wells, Karen, 1961– editor of compilation.
HQ784.V55C435 2014
303.6083—dc23 2014020347

Contents

Contributors

Nelly Ali is a PhD student in International Childhood Studies at Birkbeck, University of London and lectures on children's rights, social studies of childhood and human rights research methods. She holds an LLM in Human Rights and is a volunteer Project and Implementation Manager for Hope Village Society. She is also an activist for children's rights and is a member of the Egyptian Coalition on Children's Rights.

Amandine Bollinger works as an HIV specialist with children affected by HIV/AIDS at the UNICEF Regional Office for West and Central Africa. She has been a consultant for TearFund, Save the Children and International Aids Alliance as well as managing a project for HIV-positive children in India.

Erica Burman is Professor of Education at the University of Manchester. As a feminist developmental psychologist and group analyst, she has written extensively on the role of psychology in international development policy and practice, on the politics and affects of representations of childhood (both remembered and depicted), on relationships between women and children, and on transnational issues such as violence and migration as they affect state responses to women and children. Her most recent books *Deconstructing Developmental Psychology* (2nd Edition, Routledge, 2008) and *Developments: Child, Image, Nation* (Routledge, 2008) and co-edited (with Jackie Stacey) issue of *Feminist Theory* in 2010 on 'The child in feminist theory' reflect these themes.

Alma Gottlieb is Professor of Anthropology, African Studies, Global Studies and Gender and Women's Studies at the University of Illinois at Urbana-Champaign. She has also taught and held research appointments at the École des Hautes Études (Paris), Katholieke University of Leuven (Belgium), the Instituto Superior da Ciências Sociais e Políticais (Lisbon), Princeton University and Brown University. She has conducted fieldwork in Côte d'Ivoire and, more recently, with Cape Verdeans (in Africa, Europe and the USA).

Deborah Haines has worked for several years with NGOs and the United Nations supporting education in humanitarian and development contexts. She has worked in Belize, Liberia, Indonesia, Afghanistan, Liberia, Haiti, Lebanon, South Sudan and Kenya. She currently advises the UK's Department of International Development on the regional education response to the Syrian conflict.

J. Christopher Kovats-Bernat is an American cultural anthropologist and the author of *Sleeping Rough in Port-au-Prince: An Ethnography of Street Children and Violence in Haiti* (2006). He is currently Professor of Anthropology at Muhlenberg College, a Research Affiliate with the Faculté d'Ethnologie at the Université d'Etat d'Haiti in Port-au-Prince, Chair of the Executive Committee of the International Society of Small Arms Scholars and a member of the Editorial Board of Childhood.

Trefor Lloyd is the founder of and development worker for the Boys Development Project. In the last three years, his work has increasingly targeted boys in primary and early years and has involved the development of a range of methods and approaches that effectively target and engage boys.

Sylvia Meichsner trained as a sociologist and social science researcher. She has been living, working and researching in Latin America for a number of years. Currently, she is affiliated with the University of Essex and the Open University.

Heather Montgomery is Reader in the Anthropology of Childhood at the Open University in the UK. She is the author of *Modern Babylon? Prostituting Children in Thailand* (Berghahn, 2001) and *An Introduction to Childhood: Anthropological Perspectives on Children's Lives* (Wiley, 2008). She has edited *Local Childhoods, Global Issues* (Policy Press, 2013) and co-edited, with Laurence Brockliss, *Childhood and Violence in the Western Tradition* (Oxbow, 2010).

Claudia Seymour obtained her PhD in Development Studies from the School of Oriental and African Studies, London. She researches how young people cope with and make sense of structural violence and protracted violent conflict. Engaging with resilience theory and political economy analysis, her research is supported by 12 years of child protection and humanitarian experience with the UN and various protection-based NGOs.

Alison Watson is Professor of International Relations at the University of St Andrews. Her primary research interest lies in examining grassroots perspectives and marginalized actors within the international system, and in particular in considering how their incorporation into the IR discourse may change the questions raised within the discipline itself, as well as in its sub-fields. This has included a body of work on the place of children and youth in the international system and an ongoing examination into questions of rights and agency. She is the author of *The Child in International Political Economy: A Place at the Table* (Routledge, 2008).

Karen Wells is Reader in International development and Childhood Studies at Birkbeck College, University of London. The focus of her research is on how global processes and structures interact with practices of childhood in local contexts and how this dialectic between the global and the local impacts on children's lives and on practices of childhood. She is particularly interested in how these processes are represented in visual culture and has published widely on visual representations and global/local dynamics of childhood. A specific focus of her research is on representations of violence and related to this she is interested in how war and other forms of structural and corporeal violence impact on children's lives, e.g. in mobilizing youth migration and youth military recruitment. She is the author of *Childhood in a Global Perspective* (Polity, 2015, 2nd edition).

1

Everyday Violence and Social Recognition

Karen Wells and Heather Montgomery

Introduction

This book is about violence in the everyday lives of children and young people living in poverty. It explores children's experiences of violence in four contexts: early childhood, orphanages, homelessness and war. With the exception of the chapters on early childhood, none of these contexts might appear to readers as ordinary or quotidian spaces and events. However, what is evident from each of these chapters is that many children are living in extremely difficult situations of terror and insecurity where violence is a routine part of everyday life at different scales from the individual to the nation. It is in this sense that we are using the term 'everyday' violence – violence which, in the contexts in which children live, is routine, inescapable and mundane. In contrast to many other books on children and violence, we are not focusing on those forms of violence that, again in the specific sociocultural context within which a child lives, are considered exceptional and abusive. This focus on the quotidian allows us to ask, 'what is the purpose of violence', and given that the experience of living in deep poverty and living with war and political insecurity is harsh and often terrifying for adults as well as children, we ask 'what difference does it make to be a child'? In this chapter, we suggest that 'social recognition' is an important concept that makes sense of the contradiction between the recognition of children as vulnerable persons and the levels of violence that they are subjected to. Although we all are always involved in struggles for social recognition, this struggle is different for children than it is for adults for two reasons: their exclusion from full social personhood and the materiality of their bodies.

Anthropology, violence and childhood

The violence of everyday life has become the focus of much anthropological writing (for an excellent collection of essays on the subject, see Nancy Scheper-Hughes' and Philippe Bourgois' 2004 anthology). While this has not always concentrated directly on children, it has shown the multiple impacts of violence on children and the many forms it can take, including the mundane but concealed forms of violence inherent in structural adjustment programmes and trade embargos (Quesada 1998), poverty (Scheper-Hughes 1992), racism (Bourgois 1998), pollution (Stephens 1995) or hunger (Farmer 2004). Others have looked at the violence inflicted on children within the home, often dismissed by previous anthropologists as socialization or necessary discipline. Such work has often left those who carried it out profoundly troubled. Helen Kavapalu, for example, was one of the first anthropologists to look specifically at children's daily experiences of corporal punishment in Tonga. What she witnessed left her deeply uncomfortable because she found a society in which the beating of children was endemic. Beatings were designed to inflict both physical and emotional pain on the child and to ensure that they were aware of their subordinate status (Kavapalu 1993). As an anthropologist, Kavapalu was well able to explain and understand these beatings and clearly showed how such punishment was used to teach respect, obedience and, importantly, an understanding of social hierarchies and status relationships. Yet her personal response was much more ambivalent, and she found it hard to watch children in distress, being beaten or humiliated without making value judgments and without distancing herself from her own morality and understanding of what constitutes an act of violence against a child.

In order to examine violence against children in such situations, anthropologists have tried to use a structure which emphasizes the importance of local context and have argued that, while various forms of harsh treatment may be seen as totally unacceptable to Western observers, it is hard to label them as violent per se if they are judged fair and reasonable by the society within which they occurred. Anthropologist Jill Korbin (1977; 1981; 2003) has provided such a framework which differentiates between three types of practices that need to be untangled in discussions of violence (her framework refers specifically to abuse but is also useful in wider discussions about violence). The first category she examines is that of cultural practices, such as initiation or beatings, which may seem harsh, unnecessary and even abusive to outsiders but which are deemed culturally necessary and have the full approval of the community. Alongside the corporal punishment described by Kavapalu above, it is not difficult to find examples from many ethnographic accounts of what appear to be extremely painful, and physically and mentally harmful, practices inflicted on children, such as elongating babies' heads, scarification, neck stretching, foot binding, tattooing, ear piercing or other bodily modifications (Montgomery 2009). Although painful and capable of causing long-term damage, few anthropologists would regard these modifications as acts of violence against children. They are carried out to mark membership of a community and culture, and within that setting they are culturally sanctioned.

Korbin's second category is the idiosyncratic or individual maltreatment of a child, carried out against cultural norms and acknowledged as such and likely to cause a child serious harm. Here the important point is not the intensity of the violence but the deviation from the cultural norm. The third type of abuse she identifies is the social or structural abuse of children, where children as a group are targeted, or when they suffer distinctive consequences as a result of poverty, ill health, hunger, social inequality, war, government policy or social neglect. These forms of violence have been conceptualized by others as structural violence – a concept that many of the contributors to this book deploy and which we explore in more depth further on in this chapter.

While this three-part schema is intellectually coherent and useful in many instances, particularly on its insistence of understanding structural violence as fundamental to children's experiences, it also points to two potential, interconnected, areas of conflict between academics and practitioners. The first one concerns cultural relativity and the extent to which academics can, or should, remain as neutral observers when confronted with violence against children, while the second concerns intervention – either to prevent violence against children or to try and improve children's lives after they have experienced violence. Cultural relativity has long been a hallmark of anthropological research, but as Kavapalu's research suggests, it is often impossible to maintain in the field. While understanding and explaining need not lead to condoning or supporting – and today few anthropologists would argue that cultural relativism should be absolute – there is, nevertheless, a thin line and anthropologists have often found themselves in conflict with practitioners over issues such as female genital cutting (or mutilation depending on your viewpoint), child punishment, child prostitution or child soldiers. Increasingly too, they have found that the role of the detached observer is not one they are morally comfortable with and some – such as Kovats-Bernat (this volume), Nancy Scheper-Hughes and Philippe Bourgeois (2004) – have called for and tried to implement a new type of engaged and subjective anthropology which offers critical analysis and explanations but makes no pretence to be detached. Indeed, Scheper-Hughes rejects the idea of the anthropologist as a 'neutral, dispassionate, cool and rational, objective observer of the human condition' (Kovats-Bernat this volume; Nancy Scheper-Hughes and Philippe Bourgeois 2004, 410), believing that anthropology must be politically committed and morally engaged. She believes that cultural relativism, which brings with it moral relativism, is an unsustainable position for modern anthropologists, arguing that 'those of us who make our living observing and recording the misery of the world have a particular obligation to reflect critically' (2004, 416), and must produce 'politically complicated and morally demanding texts and images capable of sinking through the layers of acceptance, complicity and bad faith that allow the suffering and the deaths to continue' (2004, 417). She rejects the idea of an anthropologist as a spectator and argues that they must take on the more active role of witness and in doing so must be accountable and responsible, engaged and empathetic.

This raises the second problem of intervention. In the past the anthropological ideal, as laid down by Malinowski (1922), was that of the researcher as a neutral outsider – watching, observing, even experimenting but not intervening and eventually withdrawing from the situation leaving it unchanged. Although this has been questioned from the very beginning and proved hopelessly unrealistic in practice, there is often a reluctance to get involved, and intervention is still not seen as the proper role of the anthropologist. For practitioners, of course, the situation is very different. While many academics have the freedom to observe and understand violence against children, practitioners, by definition, are trying to prevent such violence and have fewer options to privilege local understandings without the need to intervene. Academics such as Claudia Seymour, writing about children and war in the Democratic Republic of Congo, will inevitably have different perspectives and see their roles differently to practitioners such as Deborah Haines (this volume) whose work with Save the Children aims to restore normality for war-affected children. Here, the humanitarian strategy might be another example, for Seymour, of the obfuscation that non-governmental organizations (NGOs) practice in relation to the gap between children's legal rights and their actual lives.

Yet the situation is not as polarized as this might suggest. All the chapters in this book show that there is much common ground, space for overlap and synergy between academics and practitioners, and the differences between them are not greater than the similarities. Both academics and practitioners working on children have been heavily influenced by the United Nations Convention on the Rights of the Child (UNCRC), which – whatever its faults and deficiencies – has led to a rethink about the role of children within their families and within society and about their roles and rights in relation to violence. Certainly, as children begin to be envisaged as equals or right-bearers and family relationships are idealized less in terms of hierarchies, the issue of violence against children and the question of appropriate and inappropriate use of force become more problematic. Outside the family, there is an increasing acknowledgement of the economic and social roles children play, as well as their agency and ability to participate fully in society. While such thinking may well be a product of Western individualism (Burman 1996; Goodman 1996; Boyden 1997; Twum-Danso 2009), with less relevance outside the minority world, it has still been deeply influential for academics and practitioners alike and is one of the areas where ongoing discussions between them are necessary and urgent.

Structural violence

One area of convergence between practitioners and academics is the attempt to give moral agency to political and economic structures through the concept of structural violence. This concept originates in the Political Scientist Johan Galtung's 1969 paper, in which he argues that '[v]iolence is present when human beings are being influenced so that their actual somatic and mental realizations are below their potential realizations'. This definition rests on an implicit assumption that individuals have 'potential' that is immanent to them but only realized in particular conditions. It is unclear, however, how one would know that an individual's actual somatic and mental outcomes were less than their potential outcomes. Galtung's thesis is not in fact, despite this definition, about the capacities of individuals but of social groups and of the conditions that prevent the full flourishing of the human spirit. It is not Galtung's intention to deploy, say, psychological functioning as a measure of normal (or potential) achievement against which the limiting impact of structural violence can be measured. The purpose is rather to suggest that the constraints and burdens that inequality places on the lives of the poor are a form of violence. It is in this sense that the concept of structural violence is imbricated with or enters into everyday life. Structural violence tries to make visible the 'hidden injuries' of class and racial oppression.

The medical anthropologist Paul Farmer has argued for the efficacy of the concept of structural violence within medical anthropology in explaining the unequal distribution of illness and early death by attending to the 'ethnographically invisible'. This phrase signals precisely that we cannot see what injury violence has caused, or we cannot directly trace the agent of violence to the suffering subject's experience. This is because 'structural violence is violence exerted systematically – *that is, indirectly* – by everyone who belongs to a certain social order' (Farmer 2004, 307, emphasis added). Despite this emphasis on the indirectness of structural violence, Farmer does not want to completely move away from the connection between violence and its impacts on the body. He says that all forms of structural violence 'come to have their "final common pathway" in the material' (2004, 308), that is to say in its impact on bodies.

By contrast, Bourgois and Scheper-Hughes, whose powerful ethnographies of the violence of everyday life (*Selling Crack in El Barrio* and *Death Without Weeping*) have placed them at the centre of anthropological investigations of violence, want to conceptualize violence 'as operating along a continuum from direct physical assault to symbolic violence and routinized everyday violence, including the chronic, historically embedded structural violence whose visibility is obscured by globalized hegemonies'. In this definition, acts anywhere along the continuum should be in their view conceptualized as violence, implicitly, regardless of whether or not they cause bodily harm. For them it is not the act but '[t]he social and cultural dimensions of violence [that]...give it its force and meaning' (2004, 318).

In these renderings, violence becomes a metaphor for the effects of inequalities. There is the danger here that violence against children, who are the least protected from interpersonal violence because of their dependency and physical and social immaturity, is cloaked by the metaphor of structural violence. As a metaphor, structural violence may simultaneously make visible the constraints and psychic injuries on adults of a specific social order and make invisible the direct physical injuries that children are exposed to.

In Bourgois's review of his ethnographic research over the last 30 years, he makes this link by suggesting that the experience of economic precariousness and the often frustrated search for respect lead to domestic violence by men against women and children. He speaks of 'the shift from politicized violence to intimate violence' (2009, 18) and argues that

> [t]he street culture that emerges from the drug economy represents a creative response to exclusion and creates new forums for masculine achievement, such as gang leadership and drug entrepreneurship. It is predicated, however, upon being expressively aggressive, unexploitable, and enmeshed in drugs and violence. Drug sellers must engage in public displays of violence to enforce credibility.
>
> (2009, 29)

Bourgois wants to link the interpersonal (or intimate) aggression of (poor) men toward each other and toward women and children to the effects of the US war on central America and the 'structural violence' of the US labor market (2009, 30). In this way, physical violence becomes the responsibility not of individual protagonists but of structural or institutional forces. Politically one can understand the progressive political urge that lies behind this discursive move, but it is nonetheless very problematic in its inattention to the agency of violent men and the harm experienced by others (including children) at their hands.

Corporeal violence or bringing the body back in

To use violence as a rhetorical concept or metaphor is to relinquish its visceral impact. As Lois Wacquant notes, the concept of structural violence 'collapses forms of violence that need to be differentiated, such as physical, economic, political, and symbolic variants or those wielded by state, market and other social entities' (322). He suggests that nothing is gained by putting together social inequalities like racism and sexism with racial and gender-based violence or poverty with war or genocide (323). He contends that the task of a materialist anthropology of suffering should begin with 'distinguishing various species of violence and different structures of domination ... rather than merging them into one catchall category liable to generate more moral heat than analytical light' (322).

The body has a specific materiality; an assault on personhood may be damaging, but its damage needs to be theorized separately from bodily harm. Bodily harm may simultaneously inflict psychic trauma, and whether or not this is the case or to what extent may well depend on the symbolic order in which it is enacted. Children's bodies are different to those of adults. This self-evident fact has been somewhat obscured by the emphasis within childhood studies on the social construction of childhood and the recognition of children's agency. Children, because of their physical immaturity (their size, the immaturity of their internal organs), are at a greater risk of harm from violence than adults would be if they were subjected to the same level of assault as a child. Like Korbin, Shepher Hughes and Bourgois want to distinguish between 'a violent act or a culturally defined legitimate expression of parental authority and responsibility' (2). This very formulation presupposes that cultural legitimation and violence are mutually exclusive terms. Clearly they are not. What else is it if it is not violence to slam a child against a wall (which is one of the examples they cite)? If that violence is culturally legitimated, it is no less violent for being so.

Social recognition

The injunction against violence against children is now a cornerstone of the international governance of childhood. However, as this collection makes very clear, everywhere children are subjected to forms of violence that they are supposed to be protected against in the name of their universal rights. It is in this context that we ask the question: what does violence do? This is not intended to legitimate the injury of children's bodies. It is rather to suggest that unless we lay bare what in any given cultural context the violence of everyday life accomplishes for the entry of children into the social order, for their recognition as human beings and social persons, we will not be able to make any meaningful progress on instituting the protections that are supposedly already their birthright.

As the above section shows, anthropologists have 'displayed an ambivalence about culturally sanctioned practices that may cause children pain, suffering or harm... [they] have gone to great efforts to explain how such rites, although physically painful and emotionally frightening, fall outside the rubric of "abuse" in that they are collective expressions of cultural values' (Korbin 2003, 434). Korbin points out that 'not only adults who perform and perpetuate the rites, but also children who are subjected to them, view these rites, however painful and terrifying, as having a positive long-term value' (2003, 434). For Korbin the question is how do 'meaning and agency act as mediating forces between violence and its impact' (Korbin 2003, 441). We suggest that one of the meanings attached to many acts of violence is the conferment of social recognition on either the perpetrator or the subject (often, both) and that this social recognition expands the space for agency.

Elaine Scarry in her book, *The Body in Pain* (1997), claims that violence unmakes the world. What we understand her to mean by this is that humans make the (social) world through language and that pain destroys our capacity for symbolic expression and through this our ability to be in and to make the world. However, when this claim is applied to children it loses some of its explanatory power because children are often subjected to pain precisely in order to make the (social) world. Violence against children, particularly against infants, is not usually intended to be an end in itself; it is intended to produce other ends, specifically to incorporate the child into the social world. Everyday violence against children takes two general forms: painful bodily modifications intended to recognize or mitigate children's liminal status (e.g., circumcision) and physical punishment for wrongdoing (i.e., corporal punishment).

Unpacking the often-heard claim that parents hit their children to ensure that they learn how to behave can illuminate the role of violence in making the world. As campaigners against corporal punishment have pointed out, one of the lessons the child logically might learn from being hit is that you should hit people if they behave badly or simply that the more power you have the more right you have to do violence to others. Alternatively, imagine that parents hit their children to assert their right to hit their children. This is not tautology. Through hitting, they may demonstrate to others (and their selves) their control over and their active attempts to shape children into appropriately moral beings. Hitting children conveys social recognition on the child and the parent: 'I hit you and therefore you belong to me' or conversely 'you belong to me and therefore I hit you'. Since the child is marked as belonging to the parent through the parent's rights to him or her, this also means that the child has some social recognition; they are not alone in the world, someone speaks for them and stands between them and the world. At the same time, the (social and legal) right to hit a child conveys social personhood on the parent derived from their rights over people.

Reflecting on the chapters in this book, only Alma Gottlieb's chapter addresses the kind of idealized account of culturally sanctioned bodily violations that Korbin is referring to (Chapter 6). This is perhaps indicative of the dissolution of relatively discrete or intact cultural spaces as the flows and processes of globalization stretch and hybridize cultural practices. In Meichsner's chapter on a religious orphanage in Mexico, the violence that children are subjected to is unremarkable, both in the wider cultural space of this Mexican town and in the space of the orphanage (Chapter 4). However, within the frame of international child protection that the orphanage operates within, the beating and terrorizing of children is not normative, even for the sake of God, and indeed another orphanage was closed by its funders. In the other chapters, we hear of forms of quotidian violence, but these are not culturally sanctioned. The boys in Port-au-Prince and the girls in Cairo find violence unavoidable; they also harm themselves and their peers in acts that the wider culture would not consider normative. In Seymour's chapter on young people coping with violence in the Democratic Republic of Congo (DRC), their narratives of violence are not normative but nor are they abuse, the exceptional has become the routine (Chapter 8). This is the social or structural abuse that Korbin recounts and that we have discussed above as 'structural violence' and which Seymour, in this volume, calls 'structures of violence', emphasizing their 'final common pathway' in the body.

What each of these forms of violence share is their relationship to the struggle of the child to attain social recognition. In Seymour's chapter, she argues that her young respondents deploy narratives about their experiences of violence to attain recognition from a wider public and in doing so find a way through which they can cease to experience violence again (Chapter 8). In the counterpart, practitioner's chapter, Haines suggests that children and their parents believe that education will restore their social position and provide a mechanism through which their children will eventually attain social recognition (Chapter 9). In the Mexican orphanage, violence is done 'for the sake of God', but this moral technology is intended to provide children with social personhood in relation to a wider set of parameters than those offered by their families. In the orphanages, in Bollinger's chapter, violence is directed at children who have lost their tenuous purchase on social personhood, and here violence does unmake their world (Chapter 5). In both the chapters on street children, the children struggle with daily forms of violence that unmake their worlds but are also violent toward one another, using violence to defend their claims to social recognition and to mark out particular forms of abject social personhood (Chapters 2 and 3).

Children's bodies

Central to the concept of everyday life is the sociological task of understanding how we make meaning through interaction. It is through the events of everyday life that we come to understand at a deep bodily level what it means to belong to a culture with a specific history and geography. The young child's insertion into the symbolic order is seen as being concurrent with the entry into language. It is in this moment that Lacan and his post-structuralist followers locate the loss, the 'lack' in Lacanian terms that is coterminous with the necessary insertion into the symbolic order if the bundle of desires and energy, that is the infant, is to be transformed into a culturally recognized person.

In most, perhaps all, cultures the entry into language is not the start of the infant's entry (or indeed the yet-to-be born infant's) into the symbolic order. The infant's body itself and, prior to birth, even the imagination of the infant's body is the site of the child's entry into the symbolic order. This is accomplished not by language but through the cultural imposition – the cultural stamp of a way of life onto and into the child's body. This inscription of culture onto the child's body involves harm, pain, injury that is not generally recognized as harm within the immediate symbolic order but is widely recognized as such outside of the specific cultural context into which the child is born. Strapping a resistant child into a car seat or a pram involves the pushing and holding down of the child: their restraint. This may be distressing for child and parent alike, but few would recognize it as violence. Hitting a child is still legal and almost universally practiced because it is not thought to be violence; indeed, it is mostly understood as a necessary practice in relation to prelinguistic children (or older children who are still seen as below the 'age of reason'). Many parents hit children for their own safety and also to impress (literally) on them the importance of particular ways of behaving: of holding a fork, of sitting, of forms of address, of demeanour. 'Stop crying, or I'll give you something to cry about' was an often-heard and unremarkable refrain of my childhood and is instructive in its insistence that through hitting (something to cry about) the prohibited behavior (crying) could be repressed.

We conceptualize then the kinds of everyday 'unremarkable' violence that children and young people endure or encounter as the infliction of bodily harms that are intended to have specific cultural and social effects. In other words, violence is motivated and to undo violence the place to start is not necessarily with the harm itself, important as that is, but with the motivation or intention that lies beneath acts of violence. Our contention is that, counter-intuitively, the intention of everyday violence against children is not to 'unmake the world' but to make it by incorporating the child into it in specific ways. These modes of incorporation – that is modes that act on the body, the corporeal, for example hitting, circumcision, piercing and various forms of restraint – can be thought of as technologies of domination. At the same time, particularly in the transition to adulthood, young people themselves use bodily techniques or techniques of the self in their own search for social recognition.

In the absence of other resources, the body is deployed as a resource in the struggle for social recognition, and this deployment of the body involves violence. The poor are more likely than other classes to deploy, shape or inscribe their bodies in the search for social recognition, and the young, whose access to material and symbolically valued resources is even more constrained than adults of the same class, are particularly likely to focus on the affordances of their bodies in the search for social recognition.

'Pessimism of the intellect, optimism of the will'

This book pairs chapters from practitioners and academics (although in some cases the authors are both practitioners and academics), all of whom have many years of experience working with children in contexts of everyday or mundane poverty. Yet they have radically different viewpoints, and the divergence between the chapters in this collection written by these different authors brings to mind Gramsci's injunction to exercise: 'pessimism of the intellect, optimism of the will'. The academics, writing within the traditions of anthropology or sociology, strive through their narratives of violence in the lives of children and youth to bear witness to their lives. Thus Christopher Kovats-Bernat's chapter presents an account of the relentless violence of the context in which Haitians live and of the specific and escalating violence that some children enact on one another (Chapter 2). In Nelly Ali's chapter too, the violence that girls experience at home leads them to leave for the streets where they are subjected to more violence at the hands of adults, both men and women, and children, both boys and girls (Chapter 3). A relentless violence pervades their lives. However, where Kovats-Bernat, working as an anthropologist, sees little scope for children finding any protection from this relentless violence, Ali offers 'Hope' (the charity she volunteered with in Cairo) as a space of at least partial redemption or respite. In Mexico, in a town that borders the USA, Sylvia Meichsner recounts how, in the name of religious salvation, children living in orphanages – most of them not in fact orphans – endure beatings and arbitrary force intended to inspire terror 'for the sake of God'. By contrast, Amandine Bollinger recounts how orphanages for children affected by acquired immunodeficiency syndrome (AIDS), also religiously inspired, provide a safe space away from the violence (including witchcraft accusation) and neglect (including abandonment) that children affected by AIDS face in their communities and extended families. Claudia Seymour recounts how in the Kivus in DRC, young people try to exert some control over their lives despite living in what she calls 'structures of violence', that is the tangible, visceral, embodied impacts of 'structural violence'. She cautions that child protection agencies stimulate a kind of valorizing of vulnerability that may fix young people in their violently formed identities – as victims of rape or child soldiers, for example – and notes the extreme gap between a belief in child protection, as set out, say in the UNCRC, and the realities of everyday life in contexts of ongoing political violence. Deborah Haines, ranging across a number of contexts in which she has been involved in working with NGOs to secure educational provision for children in the immediate aftermath of war, insists on the capacity of schools to provide a space for children to explore, imitate and resolve their feelings about the violence and social breakdown they have witnessed. The chapters on early childhood point to how culture (in the specific context of the Beng people, but implicitly, everywhere) makes its imprint on children's bodies often, as here, in ways that can seem harsh and potentially dangerous. Gottlieb suggests that the social isolation that would befall the child and her mother if these practices were not adhered to is more dangerous for the child than the practices themselves (Chapter 6). Trefor Lloyd, in the only chapter on violence and childhood in the Global North, like our other practitioner chapters, is optimistic about the scope for limiting violence in children's lives (Chapter 7). Here he discusses a school-based intervention intended to reduce violence (e.g., bullying) by teaching young boys how to resolve conflict through dialogue.

Many of the academics in this collection practice what Gramsci referred to as the 'pessimism of the intellect'. Meichsner and Seymour are both concerned that the interventions intended to rescue children obscure or elide the continuation of violence and gloss over its persistence. Gottlieb and Kovats-Bernat, both anthropologists, accept that violence persists and hope that an accurate and powerful witnessing of those experiences may have some effect, eventually, in diminishing the violence of everyday life or, perhaps, that simply witnessing is, at this particular moment in the global political economy, the best that we can do. In different ways, both suggest that violence and violation are bound to the effects of living in poverty but can offer few solutions to the endemic violence in children's lives. By contrast, the practitioners (one of whom, Nelly Ali, is also an academic) practice an 'optimism of the will'.

In each of the accounts offered here, the authors are convinced of the ability of small-scale, local interventions to make a difference in the lives of these children in this place. Here too, social recognition is an important concept. In the children's everyday lives, outside of these institutions (schools, orphanages and shelters) they are subjected (i.e., made as social persons) in and through violence. In these institutions, partly as a consequence of the global dissemination of psychologically informed ideas about children's capacities and vulnerabilities, they are offered new ways of gaining social recognition through dialogue and self-reflection. By pairing these viewpoints and contrasting these two ways of looking at and understanding violence in children's lives, this book aims to open up a dialogue between the two positions and to widen our understandings of how both children and adults react to, cope with and possibly overcome the effects of violence in their lives.

Bibliography

Ali, N. (2014) The Pervasive Nature of Violence in the Day-to-Day Lives of Street Children. In K. Wells, E. Burman, H. Montgomery, and A. Watson (eds.) *Childhood, Youth and Violence in Global Contexts: Research and Practice in Dialogue*, Basingstoke: Palgrave Macmillan.

Bollinger, A. (2014) The Role of Residential Homes in the Care of Orphans Affected by HIV. In K. Wells, E. Burman, H. K. Montgomery, and A. Watson (eds.) *Childhood, Youth and Violence in Global Contexts: Research and Practice in Dialogue*, Basingstoke: Palgrave Macmillan.

Bourgois, P. (1998) Families and Children in Pain in the U.S. Inner City. In N. Scheper-Hughes and C. Sargent (eds.) *Small Wars: The Cultural Politics of Childhood*, Berkeley: University of California Press, pp. 331–351.

Bourgois, P. (2003) *In Search of Respect: Selling Crack in El Barrio*, 2nd edition. Cambridge, New York: Cambridge University Press.

Bourgois, P. (2009) Recognizing Invisible Violence: A Thirty-Year Ethnographic Retrospective. In B. Rylko-Bauer, L. Whiteford, and P. Farmer (eds.) *Global Health in Times of Violence*, Santa Fe, NM: School for Advanced Research Press, pp. 17–40.

Bourgois, P. and Scheper-Hughes, N. (2004) Introduction: Making Sense of Violence. In N. Scheper-Hughes and P. Bourgois (eds.) *Violence in War and Peace: An Anthology*, Oxford: Blackwell Publishing, pp. 1–27.

Boyden J. (1997) Childhood and the Policy Makers: A Comparative Perspective on the Globalization of Childhood. In A. James and A. Prout (eds.) *Constructing and Reconstructing Childhood*, 2nd edition. London: Routledge Falmer, pp. 184–215.

Burman, E. (1996) Local, Global or Globalized?: Child Development and International Child Rights Legislation. *Childhood*, 3 (1), 45–66.

Farmer P. (2004) An Anthropology of Structural Violence. *Current Anthropology*, 45 (3), 305–325.

Galtung, J. (1969) Violence, Peace, and Peace Research. *Journal of Peace Research*, 6 (3), 167–191.

Goodman, R. (1996) On Introducing the UN Convention of the Rights of the Child into Japan. In R. Goodman and I. Neary (eds.) *Case Studies on Human Rights in Japan*, Japan Library: Curzon Press, pp. 109–140.
Gottlieb, A. (2014) In K. Wells, E. Burman, H. Montgomery, and A. Watson (eds.) *Childhood, Youth and Violence in Global Contexts: Research and Practice in Dialogue*, Basingstoke: Palgrave Macmillan, pp. 115–134.
Haines, D. (2014) In K. Wells, E. Burman, H. Montgomery, and A. Watson (eds.) *Childhood, Youth and Violence in Global Contexts: Research and Practice in Dialogue*, Basingstoke: Palgrave Macmillan, pp. 173–192.
Kavapalu, H. (1993) Dealing with the Dark Side in the Ethnography of Childhood: Child Punishment in Tonga. *Oceania*, 63 (4), 313–329.
Korbin, J. (1977) Anthropological Contributions to the Study of Child Abuse. *Child Abuse and Neglect: The International Journal*, 1 (1), 7–24.
Korbin, J. (ed.) (1981) *Child Abuse and Neglect: Cross-Cultural Perspectives*. Berkeley and Los Angeles: University of California Press.
Korbin, J. (2003) Children, Childhoods and Violence. *Annual Review of Anthropology*, 32, 431–446.
Kovats-Bernat, C. (2014) After the End of Days: Childhood, Catastrophe and the Violence of Everyday Life in Post-Earthquake Haiti. In K. Wells, E. Burman, H. Montgomery, and A. Watson (eds.) *Childhood, Youth and Violence in Global Contexts: Research and Practice in Dialogue*, Basingstoke: Palgrave Macmillan.
Malinowski, B. (1922) *Argonauts of the Western Pacific: An Account of Native Enterprise and Adventure in the Archipelagoes of Melanesian New Guinea*. London: Routledge and Kegan Paul.
Meichsner, S. (2014) In K. Wells, E. Burman, H. Montgomery, and A. Watson (eds.) *Childhood, Youth and Violence in Global Contexts: Research and Practice in Dialogue*, Basingstoke: Palgrave Macmillan.
Montgomery, H. (2009) *An Introduction to Childhood: Anthropological Perspectives on Children's Lives*. Chichester, West Sussex; Malden, MA: Wiley-Blackwell.
Quesada, J. (1998) Suffering Child: An Embodiment of War and Its Aftermath in Post-Sandinista Nicaragua. *Medical Anthropology Quarterly*, 12 (1), 51–73.
Scarry, E. (1987) *The Body in Pain*. New York; Oxford: Oxford University Press.
Scheper-Hughes, N. (1992) *Death without Weeping: The Violence of Everyday Life in Brazil*. Berkeley: University of California Press.
Scheper-Hughes, N. and Bourgois, P. (eds.) (2004) *Violence in War and Peace: An Anthology*. London: Basil Blackwell.
Seymour, C. (2014) Everyday Violence and War in the Kivus, DRC. In K. Wells, E. Burman, H. Montgomery, and A. Watson (eds.) *Childhood, Youth and Violence in Global Contexts: Research and Practice in Dialogue*, Basingstoke: Palgrave Macmillan.
Stephens, S. (1995) The 'Cultural Fallout' of Chernobyl Radiation in Norwegian Sami Regions: Implications for Children. In S. Stephens (ed.) *Children and the Politics of Culture*, Princeton, NJ: Princeton University Press, pp. 292–318.
Twum-Danso, A. (2009) International Children's Rights. In H. Montgomery and M. Kellet (eds.) *Children and Young People's Worlds: Developing Frameworks for Integrated Practice*, Bristol: Polity Press, pp. 109–126.
Wacquant, L. (2004) Comment on Paul Farmer: An Anthropology of Structural Violence. *Current Anthropology*, 45 (3), 322–323.

Part I

Street Children and Everyday Violence

Heather Montgomery

The following two chapters concentrate on the everyday experiences of very different groups of children living on the streets of Egypt and Haiti. Chapter 2, by Christopher Kovats-Bernat, examines the lives and deaths of young people involved in armed street gangs in Port-au-Prince, Haiti, while Chapter 3, by Nelly Ali, looks at children in Egypt surviving on the streets and the attempts by one particular NGO to offer an alternative to street life. Both offer ethnographic accounts of the role of endemic violence in the lives of these children and point to the difficulties of imagining or realizing the circumstances in which children would be able to grow up without violence being an ever-present feature of their lives.

Much of the earliest literature on street children sought to break down distinctions between children 'in' the street, 'on' the street or 'of' the street and showed how there was no clear separation between home and street life and that these externally imposed discussions were arbitrary and had little relevance to children's experiences. In a similar way, these two chapters suggest the impossibility of categorizing violence in terms of the place in which it occurs. Violence is part of children's experiences at home, in the street, in wider society and even in the institutions specifically designed to protect children. It forms the backdrop to children's earliest experiences and carries on through later life, and without looking at it holistically, or even as the central organizing principle, and one constant, of their lives, it is impossible to understand children's responses to it as they grow up.

On the surface, therefore, these two chapters are linked by their focus on street children – those children who live or work away from their families and who are not subject to, or who contest, adult control. This is a crude definition, obviously, and the different groups of street children explored in these two ethnographies have very different histories, needs and experiences which defy easy categorization. There are clearly great differences between those children in armed gangs in Haiti and young mothers in Cairo trying to raise stigmatized and illegitimate children, but what links both groups is the endemic nature of violence in their lives and its longevity. This is much less about cycles of violence and more about the continual and ubiquitous violence, present from long before this cohort of children were born and likely to extend well beyond their lifetimes. In the case of Haiti, Kovats-Bernat places the violence that these armed gangs experience and perpetrate in a broad historical, cultural and socioeconomic context, linking it to colonialism, poverty, state corruption, natural disasters and the 'ordinary catastrophes' of impoverished childhood, such as disease and malnutrition. Ali instead concentrates on the present and the impact that violence suffered from their earliest days has on children's contemporary lives, and she explores whether it is possible to imagine a future for such children without violence.

Looked at in this way, the link between these two chapters is not so much their overt focus on street children as on the exposure of children to violence from a young age and its pervasive, and also highly intimate, nature. Children are born into a world where adults are already brutalized and inculcated into cultures of violence and where socialization, survival and violence are indistinguishable. Their primary caregivers are those who perpetuate acts of violence, and home offers no respite or protection. Despite the idealization of the family as a refuge – and it is interesting that the NGO used as a case study in Ali's chapter uses the model of a family in their programmes designed to rehabilitate children – the family remains a primary source of violence of a kind which, apparently, children find most difficult to tolerate (Chapter 3). Both chapters suggest that street life is not necessarily a bad alternative to home life, as it is sometimes portrayed, but a chance of escape and even a source of refuge. It can offer opportunities, sometimes for basic survival, sometimes for forms of advancement, at the same time as exposing children to high levels of risk and further violence. In all the academic literature on street children, however, there is still little research on why children might choose to risk violence on the street rather than at home or whether there is, in reality, any qualitative difference between the violence that takes place in these places. As both chapters show, homes and families are physically as well as emotionally unstable and are intrinsically volatile places to be, and both families and individual children can be forced out of them for many different reasons. Homes may collapse or be destroyed by earthquakes or government anti-slum policies, families can be split up through circumstance, choice or state policy, and this instability and uncertainty contribute to the everyday cultures of violence in which children find themselves. While we can admire their agency, and even their resilience, this should not blind us to the overwhelming nature of the factors and forces ranged against them and the very limited choices they are able to make.

Given the everyday violence of their lives, it becomes less surprising that one of the most conspicuous forms of violence is carried out by children on other children. Whether this involves the conscious decision to inflict violence in return for food and shelter, as in Haiti, or if it remains the only resource left to the weak and brutalized, as in the case of the traumatized young mothers abusing their babies in the shelters of Cairo and Alexandria, the level of violence between children remains extremely high and is hard to change. As it takes place in cultures already saturated with violence and where there are no safe spaces or refuges for children, it would take an extraordinary naïve view of childhood, rooted in a form of fundamentalist Romanticism, to expect these children to look out for others, to form affective ties within street families or to submit meekly to rehabilitation by outside agencies. These two chapters examine the difficulties in these children's lives as well as those of the adults around them. They capture the complexity and contradictions of children's lives as they struggle to retain some control over their lives and as they move between the ordinary catastrophes of childhood toward the never ending violence of adulthood.

2

After the End of Days: Childhood, Catastrophe and the Violence of Everyday Life in Post-Earthquake Haiti

J. Christopher Kovats-Bernat

Ordinary catastrophes

It simply fell down.

A three-storey concrete-block schoolhouse in Pétionville, with 500 kindergarten and elementary school students and their teachers inside, simply fell down one day and crushed 94 children to death. This was in November of 2008.

There was no earthquake that day, no tremor, no storm. It wasn't even raining. It was in fact a day as ordinary as any other in Haiti, where for two centuries anything that could have possibly gone wrong – historically, ecologically, economically, politically, climactically, epidemically – has in fact gone very wrong. Horribly, ruthlessly, fatefully, mercilessly, relentlessly, hopelessly wrong.

On that ordinary June day in 2008, a schoolhouse in Pétionville fell down because the mortar used to set the block was mixed with either too much sand or too much water (this remains unresolved) so that the schoolmaster (he was also the builder) could stretch the value of his cement, the price of which has been fixed artificially high for over a decade by the clutch of elite families who hold the 80 percent monopoly share in Ciment d'Haiti. So while the anger of the families of the dead children focused on the schoolmaster's cruel calculus, most others shook their heads with solemn aspersion and indignant acceptance because they knew that those kids died of scarcity not cruelty and under the weight of a world utterly indifferent to human suffering.

In Haiti, one doesn't live life; life is *suffered* as a matter of course.

'Nou sufri lavi, Kwis', they say to me. We suffer this life, Chris.

Five days after the Pétionville collapse, a second school, this one in Port-au-Prince, collapsed around a class of kindergartners, whose dancing and singing during a musical was in part blamed for the buckling of the walls that precipitated the fall. So it was that Providence again shrugged indifferently over the mangled bodies of Haitian children, buried beneath the weight of the world.

'We suffer this life, Chris'. That is what they say to me.

Two months before the schools fell down during that awful November in 2008, Haiti was struck in rapid succession by demons from another quarter: Tropical Storm Fay made landfall in Haiti on 15 August and left ten dead. Hurricane Gustav hit two weeks later on 28 August, a Category 1 storm that left 77 dead. Four days on, Hurricane Hanna pounded into Haiti killing 529. Then, six days later, Hurricane Ike struck, leaving 74 dead Haitians just for good measure. It was, to be sure, a deadly year and one that began with government paralysis, a 70 percent spike in cereal prices, food riots, a rash of kidnappings.

Tragedy, despair and the Haitian calculus

Having devoted close to 20 years of my life to the anthropological study of violence and adolescence in Port-au-Prince, I have come to expect that, when Haitians are struck by tragedy, the customary algorithms used to measure the price that is paid in human lives and suffering are ill-suited to the task. I have learned that it is usually necessary to calibrate the expected tally of the dead and the wounded by multipliers that more accurately represent the tragedy that has always been Haiti...

...Is it a gun battle in the streets of the slum districts? Multiply the reported civilian casualties by about a factor of five, since a bullet fired in the ghettos of Port-au-Prince punch through the cardboard and tarpaulin and particleboard walls of shanties with little effect on either magnitude or trajectory, the round stopping only when it strikes and flattens into the tissue and bone of an unintended victim several hundred yards beyond the intended target.

...Is it a storm? Most will pass over the southern peninsula of Haiti throughout the rainy season, and few Western media outlets regard such storms as consequential enough to track carefully unless they threaten to graduate to hurricane magnitudes. If a sudden deluge overwhelms a rural area of the country near a hillside stripped of trees and therefore subject to erosion, it would not be unreasonable to anticipate a sudden slide of mud over a town or village at the hill's base; a sheet of muck as deep as eight feet or more engulfing a hamlet of a few hundred people in a matter of seconds is likely to suffocate at least a third of the hamlet's population. Over 1000 died this way when a mudslide smothered the town of Gonaïves in September 2004.

...Is it a proper hurricane? If so, then wind speeds matter as much as rainfall, insofar as the majority poor of the country are living in ramshackle hovels that are apt to blow into the sea with wind speeds that barely turn your umbrella inside out. Coastal shantytowns hit by such storms take on casualties that baffle the actuaries of disaster deaths, unaccustomed as they are to the compounded problems of flimsy shelter, unstable sheets of hillside mud and the frequency with which those who seek safe haven in shacks made even partially of tarpaulin are entangled in their plastic shelters and blown out into the sea in a death shroud of blue plastic.

...Has it simply rained heavily in Port-au-Prince? The city is mostly at or below sea level, and sewage is channeled down storm drains and through open canals. The absence of systematic garbage collection means that these channels are almost always clogged with trash and debris, damming up a stew of shit, and piss, and diesel, and carrion and rotting vegetation, all of it churned in a tropically warmed bath of stagnant water rife with giardia and amoebic dysentery, cholera and typhus, parasites and worms, and the eggs and larvae of botflies and mosquitoes. Watch the level of this wastewater rise above the curb, flood the sidewalks and pool in the homes of the poor. Start the death toll here in the hundreds, but be prepared to top a thousand or more if the medical response is slow.

A history of Anguish, a destiny of suffering and a catastrophe lying in wait

Jean-Claude Duvalier, a despot whose rule from 1971 to 1986 was so typically graphic in its brutality and rapacious in its corruption that it really merits no special elaboration here, once quipped that '[i]t is the destiny of the Haitian people to suffer'. Though he may not have intended it to be more than a flip dismissal of the human toll taken by the excesses of his regime, it is this single sentiment that remains perhaps the most pragmatic observation ever made of the human condition in Haiti. Anguish is the thread that is woven throughout the fabric of Haitian history; and that history begins something like this.

In 1491, millions of Arawak-speaking Taíno Indians inhabited the islands of what we today call the West Indies, the largest of the islands that form the northern arc of the Caribbean archipelago. Then in 1492, Columbus and his small but capable flotilla arrived in the Bahamas, the vanguard of what most historians call the Spanish conquest of the Americas. Today we would call it a genocide; within 50 years of Columbus' arrival, nearly every native of the islands was either dead, enslaved or shortly to be one or the other. Guarocuya was among the last of his kind, a Taíno cacique, an aboriginal chieftain on the island known in his native Arawak as *Ayiti*. The name means 'mountainous place', and this is not only an accurate description of the topography of what is today the interior of Haiti but is also suggestive of the geological agitation beneath the island that had forced those very mountains upward in the violent heaves of magma and rock that have roiled beneath this slice of the Caribbean since the late-Quaternary Period, around 500,000 years ago.

Total Spanish conquest over the Taíno of Ayiti was just about accomplished with the treacherous assassination of Guarocuyo's father, also a cacique, by immolation (along with the rest of the indigenous leadership on the island) at what were supposed to be talks of peace with the indigenous insurgents. With the native rebellion effectively broken, the remaining Taíno – including Guarocuyo and his wife Mencía – were subjected to a form of slavery known as the encomienda, whereby the Indians worked, lived and died at the pleasure of their Spanish masters. Guarocuyo labored under Andrés de Valenzuela, a man whose dominance over his encomienda was so total as to entitle him to rape Mencía – wife of Guarocuyo – at his leisure. Denouncing his master and suffering a humiliating and public beating for his insolence, the former cacique appealed to the authority of the Lieutenant Governor of the island, Pedro Badillo, who refused to intervene and in fact ordered the arrest and imprisonment of Guarocuyo. Rallying a band of Taíno followers, he took to the mountains to wage war on the Spaniards in 1520. A bloody campaign against the rebels followed for over a decade, resulting in a stalemate. In 1533, a treaty brokered largely by a Spanish delegation that included Franciscan clergymen and Taíno sympathizers was accepted and Guarocuyo and his men surrendered their arms in exchange for their freedom from the *encomienda*.

Now pacified, Guarocuyo was sent to a monastery in Santo Domingo, studied under the tutelage of Bartolomé de Las Casas and within a year was baptized a Catholic and assumed the name Enriquillo. Lake

Enriquillo, along the Haitian-Dominican border, is named in honor of the site of his capitulation. He died one year after his surrender to the Spaniards, and to their God, in 1534.

For close to five centuries, a succession of cultures would root themselves into the soil of the Taíno. Descendants of the land of the last of the great caciques, each of these settlers would, in turns unique and divergent, preserve in some way the shared belief that the subjugation of Guarocuyo *cum* Enriquillo would somehow, someday be avenged. Stripped of his prestige – witness to the slaughter of his people, his wife raped, his freedom stolen, his rebellion quashed and his dignity drained – the exhausted cacique would, at the last, submit to the otiose God of his conquerors, and perish.

Baptized in the blood of his rebellion, and then in the bitter waters of the God of his conquerors, Enriquillo descended beneath the earthen womb that birthed the first Taíno, beneath the sea whose fish sustained them, beneath the reefs that encircled his lost empire like a palisade now breached. Enriquillo plumbed the long, narrow abyss that ran beneath his island, wedged himself into the breach and seethed.

Mackandal's revolt and the earthquake of 1751

The Enriquillo-Plantain Garden Fault zone (EPGFZ) forms a continuous geomorphic lineament that extends due west from the Haitian-Dominican border near Lake Enriquillo (named in commemoration of the Spaniard's pacification of the last of the island's great caciques), passing beneath Port-au-Prince and along the full length of Haiti's southern peninsula. From there, it cuts due east across the ocean floor and beneath the Blue Mountains of eastern Jamaica, where it terminates at the Plantain Garden River. The EPGFZ effectively defines the southern edge of what is known as the Gonâve microplate (Mann et al. 2008).

The fault line that today bears the name of the once proud then enslaved, humiliated, subjugated, rebellious, conquered, converted and now-dead cacique had already existed as a deep gash beneath the earth, its ragged edges compressing without closing. This deep geological laceration would steadily accumulate a hot, eruptive pressure like an angry pus-filled boil, until eventually, in its own time, it would blow outward in a sudden horrible release of violence – a furious explosion of seismic destruction releasing in a matter of seconds the cumulative stress of centuries of unrelenting pressure.

Until 2010, there had not been a major rupture of the fault since 1751. This was the same year that François Mackandal catalyzed the first full-scale revolt against the French colonists. Mackandal was the charismatic leader of a band of insurgent Maroons – brazen visionaries who fled the plantations for the freedom of the island's mountainous interior. Here they established creole visions of the African villages they had never seen, having themselves been born into servitude in the colony. Mackandal rallied, unified and organized a guerilla army of Maroons, and hatched a plot to poison every accessible store of provisions, cask of wine, barrel of ale and pitcher of water across the entire colony. Amid the death throes of their former masters, Mackandal and his followers planned to torch the plantations and slaughter en masse every French man, woman and child that had not yet succumbed to the poison.

The revolt nearly succeeded. Chaos, panic and fear haunted the French in the weeks that followed the first poisonings as hundreds of planters and their families died slow and agonizing deaths, while bands of rebel Maroons descended from the mountains in terrifying mass attacks on the plantations. The terror wrought by Mackandal's rebellion was so insidiously consuming that it succeeded in overshadowing the calamitous earthquake that shook the island that same year. Enriquillo's collaboration with Mackandal's rebellion collapsed the just-founded town of Port-au-Prince, and then overwhelmed it entirely with a massive tidal sea wall that rushed a full kilometer inland, crushing and drowning Frenchmen by the thousands. The drawback of the tide then pulled the material and human wreckage out and beneath the sea, as scores of sugarcane fields burned and hundreds of slavers were slaughtered at the hands of Maroons. Having seized his recompense for that age, Enriquillo descended again into the gash beneath the island to lie in wait and to seethe anew.

Over the course of the next 200 years, the two geological plates along either side of the Enriquillo-Plantain Garden Fault slowly but relentlessly grinded against one another at a rate of 7mm–20mm per year, a miniscule amount for a single year. But by 2010, two-centuries worth of seismic pressure had accumulated along the fault, enough to cause the kind of catastrophe that would soon defy all descriptions short of the apocalyptic (Merco Press, 2010). Enriquillo, the last of the great caciques, was about to rise again and tear apart the very earth beneath the Republic of Haiti in an eruption of geological rage that would last barely a shade longer than a slow sip of coffee, before the island would be returned to itself once again. Only this time, Enriquillo's wrath would leave Haiti crumpled like wastepaper in the hand of God.

Out of nowhere and from nothing, the end of everything

And I heard, as it were the noise of thunder;
one of the Four Beasts saying, 'Come and see'.
And I saw.
And behold a pale horse;
and his name that sat on him was Death,
and Hell followed with him.

(Revelation 6: 1,8)

It is against the catastrophes of the past that we are apt to judge those of the present. Some of these bygone atrocities, whether the product of human will or natural folly, we regard as touchstones of cataclysmic devastation, the low-water marks of human despair. The three-day incendiary bombardment of Dresden by the Royal Air Force and the US Army Air Force in 1945 claimed an estimated 25,000 lives and destroyed the city center in a magnanimous firestorm, but left the majority of the residential, industrial and military outskirts of the city relatively unscathed. The atomic bomb dropped by the US Air Force on the Japanese city of Hiroshima on 6 August 1945 killed an estimated 160,000 (including 80,000 directly killed in the blast and another 80,000 who died within the year due to blast injuries or radiation poisoning). Sixty-nine percent of Hiroshima was destroyed, and another 7 percent severely damaged. The 2004 Indian Ocean Tsunami claimed the lives of 240,000 people from 14 countries. When Hurricane Katrina struck the Gulf Coast of the USA in 2005, it claimed the lives of over 1,800 people while Federal Disaster Declarations covered 90,000 square miles of the southeastern USA (an area roughly the size of the United Kingdom).

Twenty-Three seconds

And, lo, there was a great earthquake;
and every mountain and island was moved out of their places.
For the great day of wrath is come.
And who shall be able to stand?

(Revelation 6: 12,14,17)

On Tuesday, 12 January 2010, at 16:53 local time, the eschaton was nigh. The End of Days had come.

At that moment, what geologists call left-lateral strike-slip erupted along a 65 kilometer stretch of the Enriquillo-Plantain Garden Fault system, causing a magnitude 7.0 earthquake equivalent to the simultaneous eruption of 35 Hiroshima atomic bombs. The epicenter was less than 15 kilometers southwest of Port-au-Prince, by far the most destitute, volatile, crippled, ramshackle and sordid city on the face of the earth. As many as two-thirds of Port-au-Prince's three million citizens are representative of the country's majority poor who live on less than US$2 a day in metastatic slums flooded by raw sewage, rife with disease and devoid of the most basic of services such as potable water, electricity and garbage collection.

The earthquake lasted only 23 seconds. Enough time to bring Hell unto earth. Enough time to ravage, destroy, crush, consume, annihilate, mangle, despoil, befoul, fracture, extinguish, uproot, demolish, wrack, defile, deface, lay low and lay waste to an entire city. Enough time to kill in legion, to slaughter in droves, to mutilate by hordes and to bring anguish forthwith to multitudes. In less time than it will take you to read this paragraph, the earthquake that befell Haiti on that ordinary Tuesday afternoon in January 2010 claimed the lives of over 315,000 Haitians, maimed 300,000 more, left one million homeless, displaced three million from their homes and left over 25,000 to eventually be classified as 'missing/presumed dead'.

In 23 seconds, all of this was laid low: the Presidential Palace, the National Assembly, the Palace of Justice, the Supreme Court, 13 of the government's 15 Ministries, the headquarters of the United Nations (UN) Stabilization Mission, Port-au-Prince's City Hall, the capital seaport, the control towers and terminals of Toussaint L'Ouverture International Airport, the Central Bureau of the Haitian National Police, the offices of the World Bank, the National Art Museum, the Catholic Cathedral of the Archdiocese of Port-au-Prince. The walls of Haiti's National Penitentiary crumbled, the guards fled, the inmates escaped.

In 23 seconds, 250,000 homes were leveled, 30,000 commercial buildings collapsed and 1,300 primary and secondary schools were destroyed. Thousands of public standpipes from which the majority of the city's denizens draw their water, suddenly went barren as pipes fractured and snapped beneath the buckling earth, bleeding the pressure from pipelines throughout the system. Landline telephones, fiber optic systems, cellular networks, radio transmitters and even satellite communications went offline, down or dead, effectively cutting off seven million Haitians from the outside world. The entire power grid for the city of Port-au-Prince and its surrounding territories crashed and would remain lifeless for weeks to come (though even at its most serviceable, electricity was rarely other than sporadic and dissonant). Within days of the disaster, Haitian, US, UN officials, international relief workers, journalists and many others were speaking openly and in unison of the near-total destruction of Port-au-Prince.

Even the heavens would turn away from Haiti on the first night of her Armageddon, coinciding as it did with January's new moon. The sky deepened from indigo to obsidian, and as the moonless night fell, Port-au-Prince descended into a darkness that would eventually blacken to a viscous pitch.

> *And the moon became as blood,*
> *and the stars of heaven fell unto the earth.*
> *And the heaven departed,*
> *as a scroll when it is rolled together.*
>
> (Revelation 6: 12,14)

While working with a relief team in Port-au-Prince in the weeks that followed the earthquake, I listened as a close Haitian friend spoke of the fleeting moment of absolute stillness that immediately followed those first 23 seconds of the temblor. He described a silence that smothered the entire city for exactly two beats of the heart: a silence so complete, so total and so profound that if he could have listened with his eyes, he would have seen nothing, absolutely nothing at all – a perfect absence of all color, shape, light and form.

He smiled broadly at me after saying this and held it for several moments before he continued.

Just as his heart was about to beat a third time, he told me, the stillness was shattered: '*Li te pèdi*', he told me, '*rèl yo retantir nan fwape a ak dyableman la – moun ki pral nan lapenn moun mouri yo jodi a, men pral gen gwo lapenn pou yo pou tout tan*'..

'Then the silence was lost to the shrill screams of the bereaved and the damned – the ones that will mourn their dead today, but will grieve for them forever'.

The catastrophe of childhood in Haiti

It would be an understatement to say that Haiti did not need this. Even during the best of times, before the earthquake, a day in Port-au-Prince was like a day in New Orleans Ninth Ward during the worst of the

Katrina aftermath. Long the poorest and most volatile country in the Western Hemisphere, Haiti is perhaps the least hospitable place in the world for child development. If there is any place in the world that children have no business growing up, it is in the Republic of Haiti. But grow up – and thrive, live and survive – they do. This is an incredibly young country. Half of Haiti's population is under the age of 18, and 30 percent of them are under five. Nonetheless, the survival rate of children under this age is grim. More babies die in infancy and fewer kids reach their fifth birthday here than in almost any other country in the world. In some parts of the Haiti, the infant mortality rate lays claim to every other child born, and a quarter of those who do survive infancy are moderately to severely underweight and face high rates of wasting and stunting throughout their adolescence.

Sickness, scarcity and physical suffering are ubiquitous, and pediatric infections and nutritional deficiencies are normative. It is not at all uncommon for children here to die of starvation or worse, thirst. Contaminated water and poor sewage management are the primary contributors to child illness and death. Less than half of the adolescent population has access to potable water, and fewer than one-in-five Haitian children have access to adequate sanitation facilities (UNICEF 2011b). Little wonder then that diarrhea, the doppelgänger of child death worldwide, is the number one killer of Haitian children, closely followed by respiratory illness, malaria, tuberculosis and complications resulting from AIDS. Well in excess of 12,000 Haitian children are seropositive for HIV, in a country where antiretroviral drugs are almost nonexistent (UNAIDS 2012). Typhus, malnutrition, dysentery, hepatitis, measles, yaws, elephantiasis, rabies and leprosy claim the lives of tens of thousands of Haitian children annually.

Catalyzed by the negligent handling of human waste at a UN base in Haiti occupied by Nepalese troops who were apparently permitting the drainage of their latrines into rivulets that supplied water for cooking and drinking downstream, and aggravated by the concentration of millions of earthquake survivors into squalid, muddy camps for the internally displaced following the quake and just prior to the floods that accompanied the ensuing rainy season, Haiti was in the grip of the world's largest outbreak of cholera nine months following the quake. (Outbreaks of cholera are historically rare in Haiti, and the particular strain plaguing the country today has been traced to a strain endemic in Nepal). At the time of this writing (November 2013), over 684,085 cases and 8,361 deaths have been confirmed (Centers for Disease Control and Prevention 2012a, 2012b). Children under the age of five years account for at least 78,938 (or 12 percent) of these infections and over 580 or (7 percent) of the deaths overall (Center for Infectious Disease Research and Policy 2013).

Haiti's saturation in small arms and assault weapons over the course of the past decade has had and continues to take a very heavy toll on the country's youth. Armed assault and homicide are the leading causes of death among adolescents aged 10–19 nationwide (Pan American Health Organization 2009), and children under the age of 12 are the second-most frequent victims of gunshot wounds in Port-au-Prince, just behind 'police officers' (Kovats-Bernat 2013a).

The rise of the garrison ghettos of Port-au-Prince

There are a conservatively estimated 250,000 small arms and light weapons in the Republic of Haiti (Agència Catalana de Cooperació al Desenvolupament 2008; Kovats-Bernat 2013a, 2013b; Gun Policy News 2011; MINUSTAH 2005; Muggah 2005). This number is certain to be an underestimate because it correlates most closely to data collected prior to the 2010 earthquake, during and after which tens of thousands more assault weapons disappeared from government arsenals into civil society. The quake broke wide the arsenals of the National Penitentiary, those of the dozens of paramilitaries under state authority and those of police barracks throughout the capital. It is not unreasonable to accept the estimates of scholars like myself who, after tabulating the numbers of known government stocks lost in the earthquake and adding them to the quarter-of-a-million weapons already known to be lost to Port-au-Prince, cites figures in the area of 320,000–350,000 range, and again this is to certainly err on the conservative side.

The primary beneficiaries of the so-called leakage of these weapons into the slums of the capital in the years since the earthquake have by far been the rapidly ascendant youth gangs known locally as 'clans'. Back in 2009, the United Nations Children's Fund (UNICEF) estimated that there were over 1,000 children employed by these clans as messengers, mules, scouts, intermediaries, gun carriers, errand runners, stone throwers, lures, spies and armed soldiers (2009). This is today a laughably low estimate of child participation in gang violence and no longer representative of the nature and operations of the clans. Though there exist no current, reliable quantitative data on child soldiering in the gangs of Port-au-Prince, I am perhaps as well poised as any other to posit a *conservative* minimum estimate of at least 25,000 armed children in the garrison ghettos of the capital alone. The clans are most active in the largest, most destitute and marginal slum communities that make up the majority of metropolitan Port-au-Prince and have utterly substituted the legitimate authority in their domains of influence and effectively serve as de facto governing entities.

The Cité Soleil slum is one such area. Founded in the 1960s on a stagnant floodplain along the Bay of Port-au-Prince and home to over 300,000 Haitians, it is a sprawling, muddy, septic and ever-metastasizing shantytown of the barely living and nearly dead. Basic services such as electricity, access to potable water, adequate sanitation, sewage management and garbage collection are non-existent. Tens of thousands of ramshackle hovels made of wood and plastic and cinderblock and tin form a claustrophobically sprawling warren of serpentine alleys, sewage canals, narrow passageways, debris-strewn trails and rutted footpaths congested with a sucking brown-green mud. Rivulets of greyish water, reeking of shit and the ammonia of piss, trickle alongside of and sometimes through the walls of homes, before fanning out into vast deltas of knee-deep raw sewage clogged with garbage, carrion, botflies, disease and the occasional creole pig rooting amid the flotsam.

Its profound destitution and marginalization have made Citè Soleil rife for exploitation by the youth clans who are believed to be armed with over 200,000 of the country's small arms and assault weapons. They infiltrated the slum like legions of cockroaches in the waning days of the 2004 rebel uprising that succeeded in toppling the Haitian President and plunging the capital into a state of anarchy for months after. Cité Soleil was subdivided among the competing clans into balkanized territories separated by free-fire zones that were frequently the scene of explosive shootouts (Willman and Marcelin 2010). Following a bloody and devastating series of disarmament operations by joint UN-Haitian Police strike forces in 2007–2008 that claimed the lives of score of combatants and hundreds of civilians, a Brazilian UN officer directing the operations announced an end to all UN security operations in Citè Soliel and made an offhand comment that it was 'the most dangerous place on earth'; when asked to elaborate on that sentiment, he simply reiterated the comment in the tone of a formal proclamation, effectively ceding control of the entire district of Citè Soleil to the clans (Kovats-Bernat 2013b).

The extreme poverty of families, the inability to provide children with even a primary school education (even before the earthquake leveled the few schools that stood around Cité Soleil) and the household economic pressures that often compel families to press their young boys onto the street in search of work to support the household are aggravating factors that combine to make such children especially vulnerable to recruitment by the clans (Child Soldiers International 2008; UNICEF 2005). The socializing influences of Cité Soleil – poverty, scarcity, state negligence, political ambivalence, rampant criminality, pervasive violence and a culture of gunplay – conspire to impart a considerable survival value onto brutal and aggressive behavior, making recruitment into the clans an attractive alternative to the social impotence of the unarmed, unaffiliated, impoverished, hungry street children. As they now join the clans in ever-increasing numbers, most are doing so freely and without coercion, having made rationally calculated decisions about the relative value of abandoning the licit work of the street child prior to their affiliation with their new identity as gangsters. The vast majority of Haiti's child soldiers constitute a potential reserve of young and willing labor whose loyalties can be easily costed in proportion to their individual degree of desperation. The complicity of some children in acts most heinous can be repeated over extended periods with the reliable distribution of modest rations of food, sex, amphetamines or power.

Coming of age on the pavements of Haiti: The child and the street in Port-au-Prince context

Though estimates have always varied widely, prior to the earthquake there were as few as 10,000 and as many as 50,000 children living on the streets of Port-au-Prince, Cap Haïtien and other towns and villages throughout Haiti, since the earthquake realistic estimates of 500,000 were reported (Kovats-Bernat 2006, 2008, 2010; Save the Children 2012; UNICEF 1999, 2011a). Though some of these children number among the country's 380,000 orphans, most street kids have living kin and know where to find them. They elect to live on the street. Many are compelled from their homes to work in support of the household economy. Some will spend ever increasing amounts of time away until they stop going home altogether, preferring to support themselves on the street with the money they make rather than take it home and receive a portion of it in return (Kovats-Bernat 2008). For them the street is home.

Since 1994, I have conducted ethnographic research with an ever-shifting population of street children in Port-au-Prince, most of them boys between the ages of 5 and 20. Defining the street child population presents a number of problems because of the almost limitless ways that adolescents might comport themselves to the street, to say nothing of the highly variable amount of time they spend there and the multiplex ways in which they use it (Kovats-Bernat 2008). However these children identify with the street, they rarely call what they do there 'living'. '*Nou sufri lari*', they say; 'we suffer the street'. They run low-grade fevers most of the time and cope with frequent bouts of diarrhea. Their bodies are raked with edge wounds, gouges that reach down into deep tissue. Their frames are bent and broken from breaks and fractures that have gone unset. On the bodies of some are the dented mottle-scars of gunshot wounds. Dogs bite them, flies pester them, rats and roaches swarm them when they sleep. Cars hit them; passersby revile them; and the police kick them, beat them and occasionally shoot them. Always there is the threat of another kid's rock or razor.

The formation of fictive kin relations, extensive networks of kith relations forged through economic exchanges and an overarching ethos of egalitarianism and sharing are what ensures their common survival. Street children work a variety of jobs – shining shoes, selling foraged things, washing cars, stealing, drug dealing – and they usually do this labor alone or in twos or threes. As the sun sets each evening, they return to their respective 'home bases' (*baz fouaye*), where they congregate with perhaps a dozen or so of their closest friends and allies to share what they have pilfered, begged, won or earned from the day: coins and crumpled bills; a mango or an egg; cigarettes half-smoked; tinned fish and some rice; fried plantain in oil-soaked newspaper; candies, to be sure. They pool their net resources and hand them back out again so that each has what she or he requires for the night. They joke and shove and call one another 'my sister' and 'my brother'. It is in this way that they negate their poverty each night with what they share among themselves. When darkness falls, they disperse in even smaller groups to sleep in secret spaces and awaken with the day to suffer the street again.

Street kids and a history of violence, Part I: Ritualization of brutality, conservation of life

Like any population anywhere, street children resort to violence when their physical or economic security is at stake, their dignity is compromised or their lives are threatened. Most of these violent encounters carry little meaning for them beyond immediate utility or necessity, and some even speak with casual indifference about acts of almost indescribable brutality: the beating of a child with a length of lumber in order to steal his radio; the disfigurement of a street boy by a girl who slashed his face with a razor in the haze of a glue-sniffing high; the rape of a prepubescent boy behind a tomb in the National Cemetery. Violent acts like these indeed occur, but most kids living off the street struggle to make an honest living free from conflict and, in most instances, avoid at all costs a potentially volatile encounter with another youth, especially when there is the possibility that such an encounter might interfere with their work. Moreover, many of their individual and group efforts as friends and allies suggest that they peremptorily defend themselves against the eventuality of violent attack by other street youth, particularly at night when they are most vulnerable. They hide themselves when sleeping and do so in groups; they sleep *je klè* ('lightly', 'with one eye open'), prepared to wake easily in order to confront a threat.

But there are times when a child finds herself or himself enmeshed in a protracted conflict with another youth for which there is little effective defense or promise of a compromise. In such instances, animosities erupt in a series of punctuated acts of violence that find no resolution and only promise future altercations. As time goes on, these confrontations escalate in frequency and brutality; fists give way to rocks and then razors. Anger gives way to rage. Vengeance grows insuppressible, and retaliation begets more of its kind or worse. Blood is let once, then again and again – a cracked lip, a busted nose, a slashed forearm. A climate of fear and sickening anticipation descends as both parties are gripped with anxious hypervigilance. The violence becomes a preoccupation, a state of being and a condition of its own reproduction. It grows to be an obsessive fear that interferes with work, sleep, health and one's sense of personal security.

Eventually may come the nighttime attack that the first victim has feared for days or weeks, but now sleeps. It is the opening salvo of a kind of ritualized violence that street kids call *lagè domi*, 'sleeping wars', a systematic series of tit-for-tat attacks between two children with a history of persistent violent encounters that repeatedly fail to find resolution. The sleeping war is believed to be the course of last resort and accomplishes what all of the prior altercations could not: a conclusive end to hostilities. Once the war begins with the first volley of anguish, both actors bend desperately and irretrievably toward an absolute and final solution to their differences.

I first wrote of the sleeping wars in the late 1990s. Then as now, the weapons of choice were typically rocks, melted plastic, chunks of concrete, razors or lengths of lumber used to target the feet, knees and legs of a child adversary as he sleeps unaware until the moment of instantaneous and blinding anguish. The violence, enacted always at night and while the victim sleeps, becomes systemic and cyclical. A child's wounding by his adversary marks a moment of choice. If he so elects, the conflict can end with his own victimization; he may opt to forgo a counter-attack as revenge for his wounds, and so the war ends with a single blow. Or he may opt to continue the war, seeking out his attacker and exacting his vengeance under the cover of night and likewise to his own victimization. His hope in retaliating is to inflict an injury sufficiently painful or debilitating to his adversary so as to deter him from returning the violence. It is the escalating fear on the part of both parties and a mutual desire to put a conclusive end to the terrible tension of what is to come, which ultimately leads the combatants to carry out ever-intensified acts of brutality against one another. Each child so embroiled genuinely believes that the only event that can end the hostilities and the terrible pain inflicted in the dead of night and slumber is the terrorization of his opponent into leaving him alone. That terrorization may come as a profound maiming or a final deathblow, though the latter had almost always been, until recently, an inadvertent consequence of the killer's miscalculation of the ratio of maximal-impact to minimal-harm. Overshooting the mark becomes a likelier outcome as time and fear impel the actors to ever greater acts of morbidity.

Street kids and a history of violence, Part II: Enter the Handgun-for-Rent

The early 2000s saw a mass influx of small arms and assault weapons into Port-au-Prince's slum communities as warring political factions turned the streets of the capital into a battleground. Though the 2004 insurrection lasted all of a few weeks, it marked a shift in the balance of power away from MINUSTAH (the UN Peacekeeping Force in Haiti) and the Haitian Police and its associated paramilitaries. Anti-government rebels with AK-47s and IMI Uzis patrolled the ghettos with impunity and in defiance of UN patrols. Neighborhood strongmen directed squads of fighters brandishing Israeli Galils and South African R4s to launch attacks on the police. SIG Sauer, Taurus, Ruger and Glock semiautiomatic handguns seemed ubiquitous now. Small caliber revolvers proliferated. I found a sharp rise in the production and distribution of so-called creole weapons that had been cobbled together from stray parts of old or damaged firearms or crafted from scratch by local blacksmiths. While these guns are rudimentary and often misfire, I quickly discovered that they were relatively inexpensive to own (they can be had for as little as US$20), are even cheaper to 'rent' from an entrepreneurial owner and can be just as deadly as a factory-manufactured firearm.

It was during a field visit in 2,000 that I first saw the occasional handgun circulating among groups of street kids with whom I was working. The guns were categorically of the 'creole' variety, with the occasional revolver or 9 mm dragging down the waistband of a street child. In one instance, a hand-me-down .38-caliber revolver was inherited by an older street youth from his cousin who had moved on to a semiautomatic model as he rose into the ranks of a drug gang. I watched as he circulated it among a group of boys I knew for their envious inspection and cringed as I saw them dry-fire the weapon at one another's head, seemingly oblivious to the potential consequences of missing the unseen chambered round.

By 2006–2007, I grew unnervingly accustomed to the easy availability of firearms to street kids who could now rather easily 'borrow' or inexpensively 'rent' a handgun by the hour or the day for any number of reasons. Some were simply curious, others had criminal intents and still others simply wanted to flirt with the street prestige that came with carrying a gun in the slums.

Street kids and a history of violence, Part III: The deadly evolution of the sleeping war

It was immediately apparent that the sleeping wars now had an increased potential for lethality, both because of the real possibility that a gun might be had by a child and because of the heightened sense of urgency to put a quick end to animosities as a result. Since 2,000, I have recorded over a dozen instances of firearm homicides among street youth, each at the hands of a fellow street kid. In the six years before then, I had recorded none. In all but two of these instances, the killings were carried out within the context of a sleeping war, usually one so brief as to barely merit the label. The sleeping wars were now starting or very shortly thereafter ending with a fatal deathblow by any means, including but not limited to a gunblast. As small arms increased in prevalence throughout their communities, street kids grew proportionately fearful of being shot to death early in a sleeping war. Some sought to preempt their own victimization by killing their adversary at the very outset of the war as a first and final volley.

I wondered if the proliferation of small arms was changing the fundamental nature of violence among street kids in some way. Could it be that they had given up on restraint and that they would have done so a long time ago had they had the easy access to firearms that they have now? The stigma of killing among street kids has certainly diminished a great deal in the past ten years. They still speak with dread and click their tongues in disapproval when the subject of a sleeping war ending in a fatal gunshot comes up, but no one talks about ostracizing the killer anymore. Many can identify with his desperate measure, even feel sorry for him because now he has to carry the weight of his sin for the rest of his life. Kill or be killed is what they say. It's not like it used to be, when one had more options, when the life of a child was not so cheap.

Toward an anthropology at the unnerving intersection of childhood and violence

I first began my ethnographic fieldwork with street children in Port-au-Prince in 1994, when few anthropologists had ever heard of a specialized 'anthropology of childhood' and fewer still had ever considered an 'anthropology of violence' as viable or even worthwhile. The discipline was, at that time, of the assumption that because they had not yet been fully enculturated and by definition were 'immature' and of 'underdevelopment minds', they amounted to little more than cultural dupes – ignorant and unreliable commentators on the cultural world in which they lived. They were in effect not even actual human beings so much as they were human *becomings* – proto-humans in that they were assumed to be at best proto-cultural. And in 20 years of work with children and adults in the field, I have discovered that it is at least as common if not more so for adults to be grossly misinformed, ignorant, biased and narrow in their understanding and comprehension of their cultural world; they too, like children, have a tendency to embellish, even lie, to make their stories more believable, interesting, self-flattering or at last worth the anthropologist's attention.

So just as American Anthropology suddenly realized in the mid-1960s that half the world's population is women and that maybe anthropologists should start talking to them, it wasn't until a handful of anthropologists in the early 1990s suddenly proclaimed, 'Hey! I'm starting to think that children aren't simply tumors on women, but may in fact be cultural agents themselves!' These anthropologists were Myra Bluebond-Langner, Helen Schwarzman, Patricia Márquez, Helen Morton, Alma Gottlieb, Phil Kilbride, Jill Korbin, Tobias Hecht, Lew Aptekar, David Rosen, Cindy Clark, Donna Lanclos and others; they formed the vanguard of a new paradigmatic revolution in anthropology's ideas about human identity, and in time reconfigured some of our most ardent assumptions of what we believed 'childhood' and 'the child' to be in any cultural context.

As for an anthropology of violence, the problem was far deeper than just the practicalities of dealing with the presumed unreliability and invalidity of adolescent perspectives. Most anthropologists were (and many remain) frustrated with the idea that our charge includes the study of the ephemeral or the abstract. They may say that 'Violence is unquantifiable, unlocatable and defies operationalization'. It cannot be directly observed by the ethnographer, and so by definition could never be the locus of ethnographic analysis without reducing anthropology to little more than an exercise in subjective interpretation of secondary effects. Absurd, I reply. If this is the case, then religion and marriage should also defy ethnographic understanding as much as the study of gravity or biological evolution should defy scientific analysis. Just as I cannot see gravity but I do see things fall to the ground when dropped; likewise, I cannot see the process of biological evolution but I can see the slow and selective increase of adaptations within population. And so though I cannot see religion, I do see devotees pray; and while I cannot see marriage, I indeed can see the cohabitation of specific individuals who reserve exclusive sexual rights for one another (at least in theory), household cooperation and the mannerisms of the relationship.

Something similar can be said of violence, in that I cannot see it, but I can watch it carried out. I can observe the artifacts used to do so. I can see the material and physical damage caused to bodies and things by its deployment. I can hear the dehumanizing lingua franca of the soldier in combat, the needful pejoratives with which he refers to his enemy (a person, a man, a husband, a brother, a father, a son, a friend) to reduce him to a target only. I can see the machete swung, the slug fired, the incendiary detonated, the razor swiped, the rock thrown, the assault rifle discharged. I can hear the screams, see the agony and feel the suffering. I can smell the blood, the wound and the corpse. To be sure, violence is spectacular. It is most apparent as a social act of destruction (of flesh, of body, of dignity, of mind, of personhood, of life, of people, of structures and of things), but it is far more than this.

It was Carolyn Nordstrom, an ethnographer-veteran of all-too-many warzones, who wrote that violence, insofar as it is 'grounded in a *topic* and a *process,* rather than a *place*', is about flux (Nordstrom 1997, 10). Be it the spanking of a willful child, a punch to the face in the course of a dispute, a bullet fired in the interest of vengeance, the torment of extended solitary confinement, the lasting horror of the corpse on display, the rape of a child by a man in the shower of a university locker room or in the sanctum of some house of God, there is indeed a *site* – a *place* wherein these acts of violence occur. But just as importantly there is a *prelude*, an *aftermath,* and a *radiant wave of consequential impact* on the lives of others. This is why Nordstrom goes on to instruct that 'ethnographic analyses should be conducted at the centers, and not just the sidelines, of conflicts' (1997, 8).

When I decided in 1994 to work at the intersection of childhood and violence, I knew that this was to undertake fieldwork at the very methodological, theoretical and ethical brinks of anthropology at the time. But I also knew I was not alone because I knew again that there were already others like me at yet another vanguard of the discipline, doing this unprecedented kind of ethnography, this 'anthropology of violence', in the midst of the crossfire and at the epicenters of war: Carolyln Nordstrom, Jeff Sluka, Antonius Robben, Maria Olujic, Patrick Peritore, Raymond Lee, Philippe Bourgois, Kay Warren, and others.

And now that there is a fortified canon of anthropology based on fieldwork conducted from the front lines of violence and terror and mayhem and that much of this is coincident with ethnographic work with children who are there as well as soldiers, victims, targets, bystanders and witnesses, I have come to the conclusion that above all else what is sorely needed is a new way of writing about children and about violence and about the End of Days.

In my experience, this new way of writing must necessarily be rigorously and fearlessly reflective and must reach beyond the structure, the form, the style, the vocabulary, the rubric and the lexicon of traditional ethnography. We are only now approaching the end of a first generation of the anthropological study of the intersection of childhood and violence. And after the two decades of that generation writing from the frontlines and epicenters about the lives and deaths of children and adolescents, I realize that I must strive for reflexivity to seek meaning in the acts I document because as an ethnographer of childhood and violence, I am a writer of narratives of repugnance – repugnant acts, with repugnant things, in repugnant sites of suffering and fear. Narratives of repugnance within which I waded. But if it is to meet the standards of anthropology, it cannot simply end with a descriptive account of a violent act so presented as to be *explained* or *understood* by others. The narrative of a killing perpetrated by a child, the narrative of the death of a child or the narrative of a child subjected to the daily torments of the street in a Haitian slum – these cannot ever carry so much as a shred of explanation or an iota of truth from which we gain any knowledge, any understanding of the act and place of the violence. But damn if there is not any *meaning* therein, and damn if that is not precisely what I seek to do when I write of child death, of Armageddon, of nihilism and of the End of Days.

I am reminded of a section from Tim O'Brien's memoir of his service in Vietnam, *The Things They Carried*, in which he writes that

> [i]n a true war story, if there's a moral at all, it's like the thread that makes the cloth. You can't tease it out. You can't extract the meaning without unraveling the deeper meaning. And in the end, really, there's nothing much to say about a true war story, except maybe 'Oh'.... A true war story, if truly told, makes the stomach believe (1990: 84).

In order for me to write an ethnographic narrative of children in the throes of violence, it has to first originate from my firsthand witness to the acts and the actors and the artifacts that constitute the *spectacle* of the violence. So I must begin at the epicenter of the horror, must draw on everything at my disposal from that privileged position, to bear witness and take note of the full sensorium of the violence and then proceed to fear nothing – nothing at all – as I reach down inside myself and extract everything that I have internalized as the primary instrument of data collection: from the factual contexts I have researched before I arrived at the frontline; to the empirical facts I documented as jottings in my notebook while there; to my emotive responses as a participant/bystander/witness/target of the violence; to the symbols and metaphors I need to draw upon to articulate that which must be told transcendently, analogically, because 'it' defies all attempts at description; to the existential angst of the aftermath that the survivors will carry with them all the rest of their days, including my own.

The toll it takes: On twenty years of doing anthropology at the unnerving crossroads of childhood and death

This kind of anthropology is simply not of a type for which one can be prepared. Over the course of my life in Haiti, I have been roughed by armed men at roadblocks, held at gunpoint, pinned down at street shootings, roguishly searched, threatened often, tear-gassed, slapped about, suspected of subversion, inches and heartbeats from death, detained and expelled from the country, and on at least one occasion fired directly upon. I have borne witness to the unimaginable consequences of natural disaster and its aftermath. I have slept on the street alongside of its children, swiped at the roaches drawn to the grease of my last meal still on my lips kicked at the rats that sniffed at my boots and wondered how a child can do this night after night after night.

I have slept in the innermost sanctums of Vodou deep in the country's interior. I have danced often with the spirits and have marveled at their possessions. I have swished my fingertips in a calabash of goat's blood before it was offered in sacrifice. I have ingested foul liquids from clay vessels in rituals dedicated to my protection and hoped not to die. I have documented rites of magic that protect the living, curse the livestock, foul the soil and raise the dead.

I have seen the full cycle of gestation to miscarriage or to birth or stillbirth. I have seen the bodies of women and men and boys and girls battered, beaten, slashed, stabbed and shot to tattered ends. I have lain astride boys as they have unleashed impossibly loud bursts of hellfire from automatic weapons at other children and at nothing but the distance. I have heard them scream with fear and cry inexplicably as they did so.

I have dropped to my knees in a paralysis of terror at the deafening sound of a handgun discharged just behind my ear and pulled to safety by the frail arms of two prepubescent street kids.

I have helped to lower the caskets of two adolescent boys into the earth on separate occasions. I have carried away from the funeral party the soaked-with-tears handkerchief of the bereaved aunt of a four-year-old girl blasted through the chest by a large-caliber stray from a gangster's handgun (not sure what to do with it, I walked to the imposingly, black concrete cross that is the cemetery shrine to Baron Samedi – Lord of the Dead and Protector of Children – laid it at the base, and set it ablaze). I have peered into mass graves in the wake of the 2010 quake and retched into them – not because of the stench of death or the spectacle of human rot, but because of what the pigs and the dogs were doing in there as they rooted among the still limbs of infants and beneath the pretty dress of that young girl, legs splayed, face down in ash, so recently deceased as to not yet show a single sign of bloat or decay.

After 13 years, I still cannot rid myself of the guilt I harbor for my inability to muster a single tear over the savage killing of my friend: a 33-year-old American missionary named Maureen who was shot in the face and throat by two assassins in broad daylight as she left a bank on 23 March 2001.

There are still nights in Port-au-Prince that I lie in my bed and stare for hours with stinging eyes at the photographs of my two beautiful children as I wonder this: if I were to be killed in this wretched place, how slowly and unnoticeably I would transform in their memories and dreams from their dead daddy, to the memory of their father, to a painful tug of an image in a photograph.

There were mornings, now long and gratefully in the past, when I drank myself into a state of functional stupor in order to face another day of fieldwork in a country that terrifies me today as much as it did when I first arrived two decades ago. I see someone from time to time who is trained to help me manage the residual effects of half-a-lifetime spent amid catastrophes of everyday life in Haiti – recurrent nightmares, hypervigilance, habituation to the macabre, disordered memories, insomnia, the quiet moments of inexplicable sadness that come and go with a suddenness that leaves me shuddering, the mental 'blank spots' in which I simply cannot recall key aspects of graphically violent events (that sometimes lasted for hours or days) of which I nonetheless have detailed fieldnotes that I drafted as they unfolded in my midst.

I even discovered an emotion I never knew of before: the violent indifference that comes from watching children wasting to death before my very eyes.

I'm still trying to figure out how, but remain certain, that all of what you have read in this chapter – the ethnographic descriptions, the historical accounts, the spinning of a myth of a personified wrath that lies in the black depths of the chasm beneath the island, these 'ethnographic confessionals' I simply have listed above – though little more than fragmentary narratives of acts or events frozen in time and place – will one day be rewritten in such a way that they just might take you by the sleeve and pull you into the canvas so that you are suddenly there, right alongside of me, experiencing it as I have and making of it what you will.

I do not claim that every anthropologist working at the intersection of childhood and violence will find what I have found. But I do believe that any one of them would attest to the fact that the pursuit of such an anthropology can be a deeply affecting experience that mercilessly erodes any attempt on the part of the ethnographer to maintain her purchase on objectivity. The terrain we tread remains largely terra incognita and is fraught with such profound subjectivities that will far more often than not produce little more than narratives of cultural phenomena that may have some degree of meaning, but they are just as likely to leave one with little more to say, except maybe, 'Oh'.

Bibliography

Agència Catalana de Cooperació al Desenvolupament (2008) *Haiti: Country Report*. Catalonia, Spain: AECID.

Centers for Disease Control and Prevention (2012a) *Outbreak Notice: Cholera in Haiti*. 29 August. http://wwwnc.cdc.gov/travel/notices/watch/haiti-cholera. Accessed 12 November 2013.

Centers for Disease Control and Prevention (2012b) *2010 Haiti Cholera Outbreak: Dynamic Map of Cumulative Cases* (as of 15 July 2012). http://www.bt.cdc.gov/situationawareness/haiticholera/Flash/bt/atlas.html. Accessed 12 November 2013.

Center for Infectious Disease Research and Policy (2013) *Cholera Has Struck More Than 6% of Haitians*. 9 January. http://www.cidrap.umn.ed/news-perspective/2013/01/cholera-has-struck-more-6-haitians. Accessed 13 November 2013.

Centre for International Governance Innovation (2011) *Security Sector Reform in Haiti One Year after the Earthquake* (drafted by Isabelle Fortin). Security Sector Reform (SSR) Issue Paper No. 1 (March).

Child Soldiers International (2008) *Child Soldiers Global Report 2008 – Haiti*. 20 May. http://www.unhcr.org/refworld/docid/486cb10528.html. Accessed 11 November 2013.

Cockayne, J. (2009) Winning Haiti's Protection Competition: Organized Crime and Peace Operations Past, Present and Future. *International Peacekeeping*, 16 (1), 77–99.

Delva, J. G. and T. Brown (2010) Gangs Return to Haiti Slum after Quake Prison Break. http://www.reuters.com/article/2010/01/17/us-quake-haiti-gangs-sb-id USTRE60G0CO20100117. Accessed 5 November 2013.

Dolan, J. F. and P. Mann (eds.) (1998) Active Strike-Slip and Collisional Tectonics of the Northern Caribbean Plate Boundary Zone. *Special Paper 326*. Boulder, CO: Geological Society of America.

Dziedzic, M. and R. Perito (2008) Haiti: Confronting the Gangs in Port-au-Prince. *Special Report* 208 (September). Washington, D.C.: United States Institute for Peace.

Gun Policy News (2011) *Haiti – Gun Facts, Figures and the Law*. http://www.gunpolicy.org/firearms/region/haiti. Accessed 12 November 2013.

Hammond, G. (2012) *Saving Port-au-Prince: United Nations Efforts to Protect Civilians in Haiti in 2006–2007*. Washington, D.C.: The Henry L. Stimson Center.

Igarapé Institute (2012) *Haiti's Urban Crime Wave? Results from Monthly Household Surveys, August 2011 – February 2012* (drafted by Athena R. Kolbe and Robert Muggah). Strategic Note No. 1 (March).

Immigration and Refugee Board of Canada (2012) *Haiti: Security Situation, Including Criminality, Measures Taken by the Government and Other Actors to Combat Crime (2010–2012)*. Document Reference # HTI104083.E (28 May).

International Crisis Group (2005) Haiti's Transition: Hanging in the Balance. *Latin America/Caribbean Briefing* No. 7 (February), Port-au-Prince/Brussels.

International Crisis Group (2006) Haiti after the Elections: Préval's 100-Day Challenges. *Media Release* (May), Port-au-Prince/Brussels.

International Crisis Group (2011) Keeping Haïti Safe: Police Reform. *Latin America/Caribbean Briefing* No. 26 (September), Port-au-Prince/Bogotá/Brussels.

Kovats-Bernat, J. C. (2006) Factional Terror, Paramilitarism and Civil War in Haiti: The View from Port-au-Prince (1994–2004). *Anthropologica*, 48 (1), 117–139.

Kovats-Bernat, J. C. (2008) *Sleeping Rough in Port-au-Prince: An Ethnography of Street Children and Violence in Haiti*. Gainesville: University Press of Florida.

Kovats-Bernat, J. C. (2010) Haïti Chérie. *Childhood*, 17, 426–429.

Kovats-Bernat, J. C. (2013a) The Bullet Is Certain: Armed Children and Gunplay on the Streets of Haiti. In B. L. Hewlett (ed.) *Adolescent Identity: Evolutionary, Developmental and Cultural Perspectives*, New York: Routledge, pp. 186–202.

Kovats-Bernat, J. C. (2013b) No Balm in Gilead: Childhood, Suffering and Survival in Haiti. In M. Hashemi and M. Sánchez-Jankowski (eds.) *Children in Crisis: Ethnographic Studies in International Contexts* (Routledge Advances in Sociology), New York: Routledge, pp. 61–81.

Mann, P. et al. (2008) *Enriquillo-Plantain Garden Strike-Slip Fault Zone: A Major Seismic Hazard Affecting Dominican Republic, Haiti and Jamaica*. Paper presented at the 18th Caribbean Geological Conference. http://www.ig.utexas.edu/jsg/18_cgg/Mann3.htm. Accessed 12 November 2013.

Merco Press (2010) Haiti Sits on Two Seismic Fault Lines and a Major Disaster Was Expected. 15 January. Montevideo, Uruguay: South Atlantic News Agency. http://en.mercopress.com/2010/01/15/haiti-sits-on-two-seismic-fault-lines-and-a-major-disaster-was-expected. Accessed 12 November 2013.

MINUSTAH (2005) *Public Information and Sensitization Strategy for the DDR Process in Haiti*. Mimeo. Port-au-Prince: MINUSTAH.

MINUSTAH (2011) *Fact Sheet: MINUSTAH's Post-Earthquake Activities*. 10 January.

MINUSTAH (2012) *MINUSTAH Fact Sheet*. January.

Muggah, R. (2005) *Securing Haiti's Transition: Reviewing Human Insecurity and the Prospects for Disarmament, Demobilization, and Reintegration*. Geneva: Small Arms Survey.

Nordstrom, C. (1997) *A Different Kind of War Story*. Philadelphia: University of Pennsylvania Press.

O'Brien, T. (1990) *The Things They Carried*. New York: Penguin Books.

Pan American Health Organization (2009) *Haiti*. Washington: PAHO Basic Health Indicator Data Base.

Ponsar, F. et al. (2009) Mortality, Violence and Access to Care in Two Districts of Port-au-Prince, Haiti. *Conflict and Health*, 3 (4), 1–6.

Rosen, D. M. (2005) *Armies of the Young: Child Soldiers in War and Terrorism*. New Brunswick, NJ: Rutgers University Press.

Save the Children (2012) *State of the World's Mothers Report: 2012*. Westport, CT: Save the Children.

Small Arms Survey (2011) *Small Arms Survey 2011: States of Security*. Geneva: Small Arms Survey.

UNAIDS (2012) *HIV and AIDS Estimates (2011)*. http://www.unaids.org/en/regionscountries/countries/haiti/. Accessed 12 November 2013.

UN Human Rights Council (2008) *Child Soldiers Global Report 2008 – Haiti*. 20 May. Available at: http://www.unhcr.org/refworld/docid/486cb10528.html. Accessed 10 November 2013.

UN Human Rights Council (2010) *Report of the Independent Expert on the Situation of Human Rights in Haiti, Michel Forst*. A/HRC/14/44 (3 May).

UNICEF (1999) *Haiti Faces Major Education Challenge*. http://www.unicef.org/newsline/99pr19.htm. Accessed 2 November 2013.

UNICEF (2005) *'Xchange' Helps Children Escape from Cycle of Poverty and Violence* (14 October). http://www.unicef.org/infobycountry/haiti_28817.html. Accessed 10 October 2013.

UNICEF (2009) *UNICEF. 2009. The State of the World's Children 2010: Child Rights.* New York: UNICEF.

UNICEF (2011a) Residential Care Centre Provides a Refuge for Street Children in Cap-Haitian. *Special report* (15 February). http://www.unicef.org/infobycountry/haiti_57670.html. Accessed November 2013.

UNICEF (2011b) *The State of the World's Children 2011: Adolescence – An Age of Opportunity.* New York: UNICEF.

UN Office on Drugs and Crime (2011) *2011 Global Study on Homicide: Trends, Contexts, Data.* Vienna: UN Office on Drugs and Crime.

UN Security Council (2007) *Report of the Secretary-General on the United Nations Stabilization Mission in Haiti.* S/2007/503 (22 August).

Willman, A. and L. Marcelin (2010) 'If They Could Make Us Disappear, They Would!' Youth and Violence in Cité Soleil, Haiti. *Journal of Community Psychology*, 38 (4), 515–531.

Wolf, Eric. (1982) *Europe and the People without History.* Berkeley: University of California Press.

3

The Pervasive Nature of Violence in the Day-to-Day Lives of Street Children

Nelly Ali

Hope Village Society (HVS) was registered as a legally recognized non-governmental organization (NGO) in 1988, in Cairo, Egypt. It was set up by an Englishman, Richard Hensley, who was the headmaster of the Manor House Language School, where many affluent families sent their children. Hemsley told the people he worked with at the time, many of whom still work with the NGO, that he decided to work with this marginalized group of street children because he found that the available help and sympathies in Egyptian society were directed solely to orphans and the elderly – two groups who already received financial and social care from the state and other sources and who had homes and alternative care centers set up for them. He went on to establish a home that provided services and shelter, in the first instance, to eight street boys he had got to know on the street. When Hemsley passed away, he left his assets to the NGO, and today the charity is home to 200 children who have come off the street and it has provided assistance and services to over 50,000 street children.

The NGO begins its work with street children through an outreach initiative in the form of mobile units. It has specially designed buses to accommodate a range of HVS personnel, including three social workers: a psychologist, a cook and a nurse or doctor. These buses park in areas where street children are known to congregate – the spots chosen on the basis of research by the outreach workers as well as in response to reports from concerned members of the public that children have begun to beg, play and sleep around certain areas. Mobile tables and chairs are set up once the children in the area are found, and posters are put up around the bus and tables. The children are offered a free hot meal and a free medical examination and first aid if needed. The idea of the mobile units is to act as a first point of contact between the NGO and the children. During the meal, medical check up or while the social workers are discussing the posters with the children, staff will speak to them about the NGO and the services available at the drop-in day-care centers. They are encouraged to visit the centers and spend a few hours there to escape any possible hardships they are facing on the street and find a safe space there to play, shower, get medical attention, speak to the social workers, attend awareness sessions or get a few hours uninterrupted sleep.

Visits from the mobile units, along with word of mouth recommendations, are two of the most important factors that encourage children to make use of the day-care facilities. During a child's first visit to the drop-in center, they have a file opened for them where their particular case is examined. During this process, the reason for the child being on the street is established, and a plan is set up on the basis of this information. This can include attempts to mediate with the child's parents so that he or she can be reintegrated within the family or, where the child has escaped an abusive household, alternatives are offered.

One such alternative is the HVS temporary shelter. The shelters are offered to the children who would like to have a few days respite from the streets. These shelters become temporary homes to the children where they can spend a few days, weeks or months enjoying the services that the shelter offers, including literacy and numeracy classes, art and drama, therapy, care during periods of illness and shelter from other street children or adults posing a risk at that particular time. It is here where their case plan starts to take shape. Negotiations with their parents start or – if returning to their parents is not a viable option – the children are encouraged to become part of a daily routine at the shelter for the next six months. Once this period is over and staff have ensured that the children are ready and want to be off the streets, they are transferred to HVS permanent shelters.

The permanent shelters become alternative homes for them. Here they are encouraged to live as brothers (if in the male shelters) or sisters (in the shelters dedicated to female care). The children are able to attend school, are taught a craft and, unlike other NGOs or governmental institutions, are not asked to leave at the age of 18, but they are allowed to stay until they are independent and able to live alone, get married, work and provide for themselves. HVS staff aim to maintain the relationships they have built with the children so that they act as lifelong parents to them should they need any assistance in their adult life, just as a biological or adoptive family would.

There are also two other shelters in Cairo and Alexandria for young 'street mothers', which are a new addition to HVS. These special shelters were set up in response to a gap identified in services provided by both government and NGOs. To date there is no other organization that deals with children or young women who are unmarried, live on the street and are pregnant. The young street mothers' shelter has provided pregnant street girls with antenatal care as well as support through child birth and afterwards, and both mother and child are able to stay at the shelter until the mother is married or is able to look after her child independently through practicing one of the crafts or trades taught to her during her time at HVS. These shelters were established in conjunction with a national advocacy campaign taken on by HVS that aimed to change the law that affected the children of street girls who were born outside marriage. Previously, as soon as a street girl had given birth, the child was taken away from her and registered as an illegitimate child of unknown parentage (both mother and father registered as unknown). The child would be separated from his/her mother, put into an orphanage and the mother would be charged with prostitution. According to her age, she would either be sent to prison, or – more likely – she would be transferred to a state correctional institution for those children whom the law refers to as 'vulnerable to delinquency'. HVS strongly opposed this law and, in 2008 after a successful campaign, the law was changed to enable mothers to keep their children and have their own names on the child's birth certificate. The child, however, is still legally referred to as illegitimate and described as being of 'half-known parentage'.

Violence and the family

It is difficult to call all the children spending time alone on the streets of Cairo 'street children'. Some of these children have accompanied their families who have migrated from the suburbs and other cities in the hope of an increased income, and they live on the street with their families. There are also children playing and working on the streets in front of the blocks of flats where their parents work as *Bawabeen*.[1] Some are out working on the street and return home (whether that is in Cairo or another city) at the end of the day or the week. Studies of street children elsewhere have found similar situations, suggesting that the relationship between children and the street is a complex one and that 'home' and 'street' are not mutually exclusive (Aptekar 1991; Hecht 1998; Ennew 2000). Children who work on the street do not necessarily live there full time, and while some children are estranged from their families this is not necessarily true in all cases. Therefore, there is an array of circumstances and definitions of street children, but this chapter will use the term street children to refer to those children who spend significant time on the street without parental care; although, as some of the case studies show, this is not definitive.

What is not in dispute, however, is that the children who access the services provided for street children by HVS have all turned to the street following some type of violence by their primary caregivers. Violence in the lives of these children has been the norm, and it is the one common thread that runs through their stories. A number of surveys and research projects have found that violence – whether at home, in the street, by employers, at school, at the hands of the police, from the community, or directed at the self – tops the list of risks that street children face (Hussein 2005; Ammar 2009; Souza et al. 2010). Researchers also found it was under-reported and downplayed because it was assumed to be the norm (Berman 2000; Ribeiro and Ciampone 2001; Karabanow 2003; Smith 2008). The World Health Organization (WHO) classifies violence by type (e.g., self-directed, interpersonal or collective) and by the nature of violent acts (e.g., physical, sexual, psychological or neglect), and this chapter uses this framework to describe how each classification of violence is addressed by the NGO.

In Egypt, before moving to the street a child experiences a range of different types of violence, including verbal abuse, psychological and emotional abuse, genital mutilation, rape, battery, prostitution and economic deprivation (Anam 1999). The files for each of the children who have sought shelter with HVS also indicate that perpetrators of this violence include a variety of people: parents, stepparents, siblings, employers and schoolteachers. The records also indicate that violence against children with some sort of mental or physical disability is common. Even before turning to life on the streets, violence is endemic in many Egyptian children's lives and they are often exposed to physical violence such as bruising, burns and rape and non-physical violence – including verbal humiliation, rejection, neglect and bullying. The evidence of these violations is evident on both their bodies and behavior, and it is noticeable that once on the streets children often carry razor blades and hide them in their mouths or clothes in case they were attacked at night by others.

This problem is not confined to Egypt, and elsewhere it has also been reported that children have fled to the streets because of violence and physical, verbal, sexual and emotional abuse at home (Bibars 1998; Hecht 1998; McFadyen 2004; Karabanow et al. 2005; Smith 2008; Butler

2009). As Panter-Brick puts it, these children live 'harsh and violent lives, abused by relatives, police, shop-keepers, passers-by, and gangs of older youth or peers' (2004, 90). There has been no published work however, either academic or NGO-based, which has asked children directly about how conscious a choice they made between leaving behind the known violence and abuse at home and risking different forms of violence on the street. If the process of arrival on the street is a gradual one – as the children tell us – then they have seen and understood the violence on the streets, and it would be useful to understand how they weighed the benefits and decided that the violence on the street was a better option to that which they faced at home. When asked directly about this, some staff at HVS suggested that the children's choice was based on idealized conceptualizations of family and that while children can accept strangers being violent toward them, they cannot accept or forgive their primary caregivers for being abusive.

Dr Abla El-Badry has worked with HVS for the last 16 years and told me that

> from the moment they are born, the children see violence in the home, usually acted out by the father towards the mother, and then the child experiences it first hand by the father or mother, and then between himself and his or her siblings, and then from the step father or mother.

The majority of children with whom HVS comes in contact have turned to the street as a result of violence they have experienced at home, either in the form of discipline or abuse. This is usually paired with a secondary reason, like poverty or deprivation, or being forced to do certain things that the child found dangerous or disgusting.

Some of the children told HVS that their guardian told them to go out and come back with a certain amount of money, and how the child got the money was not their concern. Mahmoud El Sheikh, HVS Operations Manager who has been working with street children for over 17 years, says that from the years he has spent at the shelter, he thinks that non-physical violence leaves deeper scars on the children than other reported abuse. He claims that the non-acceptance that they suffer from their primary caregivers is the first thing the charity tries to counteract in their dealings with the children. According to El Sheikh, if this step is successful, then the rehabilitation program has a much higher chance of being successful. When training new street workers, therefore, there is a fundamental focus on acceptance, regardless of behavior. El Sheikh says that lack of acceptance at this point is the biggest contributory factor that stops children feeling able to move into the permanent shelter.

At best, the violence the child is subjected to in the home is done with the intention of discipline – at worst it is abuse. However, children who decide that they can no longer tolerate this violence and turn to the street cannot access permanent shelter without gaining the signed consent of their legal guardian. This is, of course, problematic not only because the child is escaping violence from that person but also because there is still a stigma against institutions in Egypt. Many parents refuse to sign the consent forms, claiming that it is less damaging to their honour for the child to be on the street than for their neighbours and family to know that their child is in an institution.

Violence in public

On the street, children are faced with many different types of violence. It is important to understand that once arriving on the street, the street child does not live as an individual unit and that the groups of 'street families' have their own rules and culture which, if they are not adopted and respected, result in violent sanctions, especially for the girls. On the street, there is a long list of those exercising violence toward the children – including street leaders, other street children, drug dealers, those who run prostitution rings, shop keepers, street vendors, drivers, hospital staff, correctional institutions staff, the police and society at large. The streets of Cairo have known criminals operating on them, and sexual abuse, trafficking, theft of body organs and the trading of blood by force are all practices that street children report at HVS. There are also subtler forms of violence to which children on the streets are subjected, and at any busy set of traffic lights passersby can witness this violence. The children, who are usually begging, often see drivers swear or push them away. The same children are then seen walking by cars scratching them with their coins or rusty nails and have told the social workers that this is their way to get back at those who humiliate them at the traffic lights.

HVS considers the non-acceptance of street children by the wider society and the stigma it places on former street children as one of the most difficult forms of violence to which street children are subjected. It is disheartening to work hard with children and see them accept the rehabilitation program and stick to it, only to be turned away from jobs when prospective employers find out the history of the children or see that they are of unknown parentage. Often, during meetings when this is discussed, the staff will bitterly joke that it is society that needs rehabilitation and not the children. It is important, therefore, to prepare the child for this, to engage in wide media campaigns to raise awareness of the plight of these particular children and the importance of acceptance.

Violence exists in many other arenas – including inside police stations, where violence toward both adults and children is rife in Egypt. HVS found that the police feel justified in their violent dealings with street children because they think that the children have committed crimes, and therefore that they deserve to be treated in this way. The term 'vulnerable to delinquency' is often attached to children who have committed no specific crime but which can be used to put them in detention. HVS has worked with the United Nations International Children's Emergency Fund (UNICEF) on a series of awareness sessions for the police in an attempt to counteract the violence the children suffer at their hands, but currently this does not seem like a priority either for funders or for the police who also hold street children responsible for most of the violence associated with recent protests and demonstrations.

Violence at the hands of the police is a constant feature across the literature available on street children and is mentioned by many children interviewed as a major problem (Aptekar 1991; Green 1998; Kovats-Bernat 2000; Fahmi 2007; Salazar 2008). The street children not only feared police abuse and violence but also had to deal with the police stealing from them or forcing them to share their loot (Hecht 1998) or pay them bribes to set them free (McFadyen 2004). Along with institutional acceptance of violence against children (Khair 2001), sexual abuse was also found to be rife by the police. Many of the street children claimed in interviews that sexual favours were either demanded or given for getting themselves released from custody (World Vision 1995; Ammar 2008; Aransiola et al. 2009). Even if they are released, they are then sent to governmental correctional institutions that suffer from an acute lack of resources and are run by staff who have not been trained to deal with street children.

The problem with violence from the police is similar to the problem with violence from parents; they are both a source of supposed protection yet fail to live up to this expectation and cause confusion and disappointment which are very detrimental to the children. This has an impact when these children come to the shelter because they are not able to trust that the staff there will not become another source of violence for them. The children have become used to sexual and other types of violence from their family and the police and see it as a way of life. Some children get used to these violations, and this complicates the rehabilitation process because they see violence as a way of getting things done or as a method of self-protection.

Even if the police themselves do not perpetrate violence toward street children, then the adult inmates with whom children are detained are often very violent toward them. One of the biggest problems that HVS has found in dealing with the police who arrest street children is the placing of children with adults in police cells. HVS has worked with other organizations and advocated for the need to accommodate children separately from adults after they have been arrested. As a result of this campaign, all police stations are now supposed to have a separate cell for children to prevent assault by the other prisoners, and this change made a significant difference to the number of children that came to the HVS centers seeking help over this matter. Nevertheless, HVS has still had to deal with several cases of children being raped, having their money stolen or being forced to give sexual favours in return for protection or for release in custody. When one of these stories was relayed to staff at HVS, the shelter manager went with the child to the station and had the matter officially investigated, and a case was filed; although, it was quickly shelved.

Children's violence toward one another

The violence that HVS finds most challenging occurs between the street children themselves. As mentioned previously, the street leaders are violent toward the younger or newer street children so that they can maintain their control. There have been cases where a street child accesses the shelter because the street leader has withheld food from the child as a form of punishment. However, not all cases of child on child violence involve street leaders. The girls at the shelter often hit each other so violently that one falls off her chair and gets back up ready to hit the other girl back. While this is supposedly done in jest, it appears to be highly aggressive. Unfortunately many of the children respond to the violence they have been subjected to by becoming aggressors, either toward children more vulnerable than they are, such as their babies in the case of some of the street girls or toward themselves in the form of self-harm.

The children's reflections on violence are illuminating and to work with street children is to know that they are 'far more likely to die at the hands of their peers than as victims of death squads' (Hecht 1998, 123). Fahmi notes, 'most violence takes place in-group and is directed against members of the group, seldom against outsiders' (2007, 104). Many street children direct harm toward themselves in an attempt to hurt the people they are dealing with. This is a very sensitive issue for HVS. When El Sheikh was managing the Sayeda Zainab branch of HVS, a boy was told he was not allowed to go on a trip as punishment. The boy then took out a blade from his mouth and started slashing his scalp. He later admitted doing this to hurt El Sheikh, whom he knew would be desperately upset to see the boy, to whom he was close, hurt in this way.

To a large extent, what governs the risk of violence is the time spent on the street. Children who have only just arrived on the street are not usually violent immediately, having been a victim of it themselves, but after a few months on the street they are increasingly likely to turn to violence as a survival strategy. HVS works to contain the violence at its early stages. Their policies assume that there is a line of progression. If the child is on the street for, say, ten years, in the first year the child will not be violent, by the second year he or she may use some violence but by the tenth year, he or she will be very violent – sometimes practicing violence for its own sake. In general, the longer a child has been on the street, the more knowledge and experience he or she has of how to exercise violence. HVS can speak to a child who has been on the street for a week about the risks he or she can face and, as a result, the child might decide to return to his or her family. After a longer period of time, however, the street child has much more information and experience of the risks they face than the staff dealing with them, and this is one more difficulty the staff at HVS confront in trying to find ways to deal with the violence expressed and experienced.

Case studies: Violence in and around the young street mothers' shelter

'Break a girls rib and she will grow twenty-four'. This is a popular saying among poor families in Egypt where hitting a girl is seen as a form of discipline that will do her more good than harm and is therefore beneficial. This cultural acceptance and expectation of violence toward girls make it very difficult for NGOs such as HVS to raise awareness about issues of violence and to campaign for enforcement of child welfare laws that aim to protect children. One member of staff at HVS complains that she hears her neighbours beat their son every night, and there is nothing she can do but bang on the doors and shout until the abuse stops. It was due to a lack of law enforcement that HVS was unable to stop one young mother, Maya, taking her daughter away from the shelter when she left in a moment of rage, even though staff had evidence that she had abused her daughter.

As mentioned previously, the motivation for some street girls leaving home is sexual abuse, often from their stepfathers. Of the ten girls currently at the shelter, one 14-year-old has been sexually abused by her stepfather since she was nine years old. On discovering this, her mother took her to hospital for a virginity check after her husband denied the abuse. He, however, paid the hospital staff to issue a fake report and, in Cairo, subjected her to another virginity test. The report issued after this stated that she was no longer a virgin, and as a consequence she was admitted to the Cairo shelter. Thirteen-year-old Howayda was raped by both her mother and father and has a one-year-old daughter, Mira, who she leaves at the shelter. However, she regularly returns and takes her for 'family visits' after which Mira comes back, a few days later, naked and with lice and skin infections. Perhaps, one of the most severe cases HVS is currently dealing with is of Heidi, a 14-year-old girl whose uncle had chained her in shackles for three months and raped her daily. He only let her go when she promised to join his prostitution ring in which his sister, her mother, was working. As soon as he unlocked the chains, she threw herself out of the window and broke her back. Passersby took her to the police station where she was then referred to HVS.

Sexual violence at home is only the start for many girls, and on the street the threat of rape and other forms of sexual violence continues so much so that rape and sexual violence toward girls are almost synonymous with being on the street. Most of the girls at the shelter bear a curved scar on the side of their face or under their eye because once a girl is raped for the first time, she is then deeply cut – usually by a pen knife or a piece of glass – to mark that she is no longer a virgin; subsequent rapes are recorded by smaller cuts across her face. This is the same if a boy has been raped. Administering first aid at one HVS day-care reception center, the shelter manager records that this type of violence is the most common type they deal with and one that they record more than once a day.

One girl seeking refuge at the shelter saved her face but received 16 stitches on her back as she tried to run away from her attackers. Another girl asked me whether I could buy her a cream from London that would 'make it go away'. Although I could not do this, I did arrange for one of the girls, Taghreed, to see a cosmetic surgeon who offered his services for free. Three operations later and Taghreed's scar is not one she can see in the mirror. I had assumed, however, that this would be something that all the girls would like but one girl told me, 'I'd never think of getting rid of it, if I didn't have it, I'd scar myself, you are far less attractive to the rapists when you have this scar, most of them are after the virgins, this scar protects me'.

HVS and its volunteers like myself have learnt how to respond to each incident of violence that penetrates the private lives of street children through trial and error. Despite having worked at the shelter for over ten years, most staff do not have an agreed way on how they deal with violence, whether it is violence directed by the children at themselves, at adults or at other children. The following incident at the shelter is an example of why one response which had initially seemed inappropriate in terms of advocacy and change was very quickly adopted, and why I came to understand it better.

I found it difficult at first to understand HVS's decision to separate virgin street girls from street mothers once the children moved into permanent shelters and I was, at first, a strong critic of the decision to keep the virgin girls at a separate shelter in Cairo and mothers, or those girls who had been raped, at the Moqattam shelter. However, having witnessed an incident at Moqattam, I came to understand why this decision had been made. An exception to the rule had been made in order to allow Leila, a 17-year-old virgin, to stay at the Moqattam shelter because she was much older than the girls at the Cairo shelter. Yet the young street mothers had reacted with hostility to her presence and took offence at everything she said and interpreted her presence to mean that she thought that because she was a virgin she was better than them. A few days after Leila's arrival, one of the young street mothers, Maya, who had just turned 17 and who had suffered an incredible amount of violence in her life since the age of three, stood up in a group therapy session and said she would 'destroy' Leila and 'break' her so that she became like the rest of the girls and no longer thought she was better than them. It transpired that Maya and the rest of the girls had arranged for Leila to be kidnapped and for some street boys and an adult taxi driver to rape and scar her and then to 'stamp her' in order to let everyone know she was just like the rest of them. Yet the violence in this instance was not only directed at Leila – during this incident of rage, Maya took a razor out of her mouth, slashed her stomach, swung her nine-month-old daughter by the wrist across the room, cut the psychologist's arm, came to attack me as I crouched over her baby in the corner of the room and, when things had calmed down, decided to leave the shelter. This was not an unusual event; the staff at the shelter dealt with incidents of this sort on a daily basis. During the feedback session on what had happened that day, it was pointed out to me that this was the reason management had made the virgin/non-virgin segregation and it was decided after an emergency meeting that night to send Leila away so that she was safe.

Maya is perhaps one of the most complicated cases the organization has dealt with to date. She has been using the services for ten years. Her mother and father separated when she was three years old, and her father remarried. Her stepmother drew a circle in front of the bathroom where Maya was to sleep, play, eat and urinate. At the age of six, her stepmother decided she was allowed out of the circle to serve her new sisters who went to school, unlike Maya. One day, Maya burned the rice and her stepmother cracked Maya's skull with a garlic crusher. When Maya ran to her father crying, he stripped her naked and beat her for trying to cause problems at home. He then covered her body in honey and tied her up, leaving her for three days on the rooftop. It was soon after this, when she was only seven that Maya decided to get on a train to Cairo. A few weeks later, four men raped her for the first time and she was referred to HVS.

It took six years to convince her father to sign the consent forms to allow her to live permanently at the shelter. During this time, Maya was in and out of police stations, correctional institutions and on the street. The day before her father had given his consent, Maya was arrested for a mugging attack for which she took the blame in order to gain status in the street family she had recently joined. Faking her age and identity, Maya was sentenced to three years in an adult prison even though she was only 13. One year after she had served her sentence, Maya married a man whom she had met during his visits to HVS, where his son was being kept. This man often beat her and then went on to be sentenced to a ten-year sentence for selling drugs. Maya is a chronic self-harmer and subjects her baby to an incredible amount of daily violence. Despite the shelter's efforts to control the violence, they have few options for protecting the baby from the violence Maya inflicts on her. For a few months while Maya was interested in my positive praise, she treated baby, Summer, with great tenderness and love, but this quickly wore off and with every perceived injustice at the shelter, the baby was often on the receiving end of her frustrations.

Other forms of abuse and neglect of very young children by their own mothers have also been reported at the shelter. HVS sent one of its staff on a nine-hour bus ride to a part of upper Egypt after a call from one of the former street children, 14-year-old Mirna, who had, at times, displayed signs of schizophrenic behavior. She called to ask the NGO to save her daughter who had been locked up in a den with the chickens for three days by her parents who claimed that she had bought the family shame. Mirna spent most of her pregnancy at the shelter and was hoping that once she had the baby, her parents would accept her and her child. This has not happened, however, and Mirna tells staff that having to live separately from her daughter is the worse type of violence that her parents have inflicted on her.

One HVS shelter, for the under-fives, has been set up to cater for the babies born to street girls who have spent their pregnancy at the Cairo Shelter. These children have been left by their street mothers but are often taken away on family visits. The staff know that these visits mean the toddlers and babies will be used as begging tools by their parents and brought back to the shelter having been physically abused and suffering from lice, skin rashes and displaying difficult behavior. Four-year-old Reem is often taken for these visits by her father. Her last visit lasted three months. When she returned and was asked how her time away was, she told staff:

> Heba dropped a glass and so daddy tied us up and he hit me here [she pulls up her T-shirt to show the bruises covering her back]. He stopped hitting me when I wet myself, but then he started hitting my mum. When I grow up I want to be a policewoman – I want to kill my dad.

One of the greatest difficulties the NGO faces is dealing with street leaders who lose a significant source of income, when the street girls move to the shelters. Calling the police – during and after attacks on both the children and the staff, when the street leader finds that a girl has gone missing and comes to take her by force – is an everyday occurrence at the day-care centers. Girls, more than boys, are used by older street children for both begging and prostitution and are a significant source of income for those who offer the girls protection in return for their loyalty and obedience. Because they are usually submissive to the street leaders, HVS notes that girls are usually not muggers on the street but can be used as pickpockets and petty thieves. The girls will rarely physically harm or kill someone but may be used as accomplices and props for such crimes. They often have been threatened before they agree to take up this role. The only exception to this is prostitution, where HVS have dealt with girls who encourage and coerce other girls into it.

Perhaps nothing is more telling of the violence that the street girls have suffered than their reaction when the door to their bedroom is opened by one of the social workers. When this happens the girls jump out of beds into the corner of their rooms and crouch over their babies. This and the way their children flinch at any sudden movement is very difficult to deal with. It is the NGO's aim to help these children 'sleep with both eyes shut', as Dr El-Badry, General Secretary for HVS, always says.

Conclusion: The challenges and successes of HVS's response to violence

There are still many challenges facing HVS, and the NGO is realistic in its claims of being able to protect weaker children from violence and also to reach the many children who need its assistance. Its work necessarily involves compromise so that, for example, the younger and weaker the child the NGO is trying to protect, the more they are a source of income to the street leaders. Receiving these children at the center upsets the leaders, and they come and fight at the shelters and threaten both the staff and children with their violence and, on many occasions, the children have been taken out by force. There have been incidents when full gangs have come to the shelter trying to break in and hurt those who work there. This is where the NGO finds no other solution but to collaborate with the police. They keep the area safe in exchange for information about the adult street leaders.

There is a large section of society that denies the very existence of children on the streets of Cairo and the reasons that have pushed them to it. Society's denial of the problem, particularly with street girls, is another challenge that faces HVS. Street children remain a low priority, compared with orphans, in fund-raising and awareness campaigns. The political conflicts of recent years have also posed particular challenges, and the current political situation leaves NGOs working with street children troubled. The laws that were changed before the fall of the Mubarak regime are considered illegitimate and are under threat of being rescinded; staff are worried that laws relating to a street child's parentage may be included in the sweeping away of the old laws and that they will have to refight this particular battle.

The staff at HVS is also aware that they need to change attitudes toward violence among the children themselves. Their lives have been such that the girls and boys that access the services of HVS rarely find anything extraordinary in the fact that they have been subjected to such serious violence. Several staff members comment that violence is against their ethical principles so they would never use it on children and also that, even if they did, it would be ineffective. They argue that the children's bodies have become so used to the physical expression of discipline, punishment and abuse that the children can no longer feel the significance of it.

Building trust between the staff and the children and forging long-term relationships and effective rehabilitation is the ultimate goal for HVS when dealing with the violence in children's lives. As soon as a child accesses any of the HVS services, they are taught about their rights and told what their expectations of the services should be. They are encouraged to believe that the shelter, whether they are there temporarily or permanently, is a home to them and that the people working there are being paid to work toward making their lives easier and better. The charity's outreach work is the first step in building this relationship. The charity considers the outreach workers to be those with the most difficult jobs, and it is their skill that determines whether they can win the street child's trust or not. This is important because everything goes by word of mouth on the street: if the child is unable to trust the organization, or if they do so and that trust is betrayed, HVS have lost its access not only to that child but also to the other children with whom he or she is in contact.

Yet working with such children is not easy, and another challenge facing HVS is the high staff turnover at particular shelters where the children practice violence toward each other and/or the staff. If the staff do not have a very firm belief in the cause and in the need to build trust and acceptance, then it is difficult to retain them. When a staff member works with a street child at the beginning, the child tends to assume the worst about that person and to believe that he or she is going to be abusive and violent toward them, like so many other adults in their life. It is therefore very dangerous if there is any incident where a HVS staff member betrays a child's trust or uses any form of violence because this staff member is a symbol of the NGO and is seen as representative of all the staff. The biggest problem, therefore, is recruiting staff who genuinely believe in the cause, whatever background or religious belief they have. Some staff think that working with the street children will be easy, others that the children do not deserve the help they are given and have access to more than they deserve. A number of staff have been fired after hitting a child and, in order to undo some of the damage done, the children have all been made aware of the repercussions for the person who acted in this way.

Despite these ongoing challenges, there have been successes and HVS has established effective ways of working with street children. HVS has made a conscientious effort to incorporate strategies on how to deal with violence within its own branches and shelters, and a copy of these policies is hung on the shelter walls. Such policies were developed in collaboration between HVS and UN agencies, and they address all the types of violence and abuse that a street child has been or might be subjected to in the course of his or her life. Staff are trained on how to achieve and adhere to these policies and also on the principles of protection in any institution in which children live. The HVS policies cover the procedures for reporting abuse and violence and give advice on where and how children can get help inside or outside the organization. A representative from the UNICEF gave the HVS staff training on these issues for three consecutive years until the staff of HVS felt confident enough to develop their own training manual on dealing with street children. They now share this with other charities that have been established to work with street children.

El Sheikh has codified the rules and regulations of HVS, in his capacity as operations manager, in order to ensure that children's rights to provision, prevention and rehabilitation are respected. The importance of prevention is strongly highlighted because, as he argues,

> if you carry on working with cure alone, you will find that the child is exposed to violence, and you treat him, [he is] re-exposed and you treat him and the circle will never end and so it is necessary to work on both together and this is the general policy for all branches and shelters. It is easier to implement this policy in the permanent shelters because of the amount of control the staff have and the children are living with us. It is more difficult to deal with a prevention program in the reception centres of the mobile units because as soon as the child is no longer in the presence of HVS staff, they are exposed to all sorts of violence again.

He uses the phrase: 'it is like digging in water'.

Over the last ten years, HVS has been able to use the older street children who have 'graduated' to help them reach out to those still at risk on the street and in doing so gain credibility with the children and in the outside world. The older ones from the shelters are called street mentors and come out with HVS in the mobile units, thereby giving social workers the benefit of their experience. HVS has had great success with this method and has been the only NGO capable of working in this way, due to it having existed long enough to see some of the children leave its care and go on to lead productive lives. It is hoped the street children are able to see the street mentors' success and are offered a real-life example of what life can be like away from the streets. When they see someone they once knew, now older, unafraid and uninvolved with violence, they are able to visualize different futures.

There are, of course, no easy or simple solutions to such complex and entrenched problems. However, HVS has been at the forefront of new and innovative ways of tackling some of the difficulties of everyday violence on the streets. In doing so, they have attempted to address both the obvious and not so apparent effects of violence in children's lives, drawing attention to the physical, emotional and social causes of violence as well as its all pervasive impact on such children. Their work challenges the view of street children that '[v]iolence is an aspect of identity as tragically indelible as the scars that crisscross their bodies' (Hecht 1998, 45).

Note

1. Every block of flats has a 'bawaab' – a man or woman who can be called on to run errands, clean the flat and ask visitors whom they are visiting.

Bibliography

Ammar, N. H. (2009) The Relationship between Street Children and the Justice System in Egypt. *International Journal of Offender Therapy and Comparative Criminology*, 53 (5), 556–573.

Anam (1999) *Situation Analysis and Need Assessment of Street Children with Disabilities in Dhaka City*. Dhaka: Centre for Services and Information on Disability. Available at http://www.disabilityrightsfund.org/files/street_children_with_disabilities_in_bangladesh.pdf. Accessed 14 June 2013.

Aptekar, L. (1991) Are Colombian Street Children Neglected? The Contributions of Ethnographic and Ethnohistorical Approaches to the Study of Children. *Anthropology and Education Quarterly*, 22 (4), 326–349.

Berman, L. (2000) Surviving on the Streets of Java: Homeless Children's Narratives of Violence. *Discourse & Society*, 11 (2), 149–174

Bibars, I. (1998) Street Children in Egypt: From the Home to the Street to Inappropriate Corrective Institutions. *Environment and Urbanization*, 10 (1), 201–216.

Butler, U. M. (2009) Freedom, Revolt and 'Citizenship': Three Pillars of Identity for Youngsters Living on the Streets of Rio de Janeiro. *Childhood*, 16 (1), 11–29.

Conticini, A. and Hulme, D. (2007) Escaping Violence, Seeking Freedom: Why Children in Bangladesh Migrate to the Street. *Development and Change*, 38 (2), 201–227.

Ennew, J. (2000) *Street and Working Children: A Guide to Planning*. London: Save the Children Fund.

Fahmi, K. (2007) *Beyond the Victim: The Politics and Ethics of Empowering Cairo's Street Children*. Cairo: The American University in Cairo Press.
Godoy, A. S. (1999) 'Our Right Is the Right to Be Killed': Making Rights Real on the Streets of Guatemala City. *Childhood*, 6 (4), 423–442.
Green, D. (1998) *Hidden Lives: Voices of Children in Latin America and the Caribbean*. London: Cassell.
Hecht, T. (1998) *At Home in the Street: Street Children of Northeast Brazil*. Cambridge: Cambridge University Press.
Hussein, N. H. (2005) *Street Children in Egypt: Group Dynamics and Subcultural Constituents*, Cairo Papers in Social Science No. 2. Cairo: American University in Cairo Press.
Iqbal, M. W. (2008) Street Children: An Overlooked Issue in Pakistan. *Child Abuse Review*, 17 (3), 201–209.
Karabanow, J. (2003) Creating a Culture of Hope: Lessons from Street Children Agencies in Canada and Guatemala. *International Social Work*, 46 (3), 369–386.
Karabanow, J. et al. (2005) *Getting Off the Street: Exploring Strategies Used by Canadian Youth to Exit Street Life*. Available at http://www.halifax.ca/qol/documents/GettingofftheStreet.pdf. Accessed 14 June 2013.
Khair, S. (2001) Street Children in Conflict with the Law: The Bangladesh Experience. *Asia-Pacific Journal on Human Rights and the Law*, 2 (1), 55–76
Kovats-Bernat J. C. (2000) Anti-Gang, Arimaj, and the War on Street Children. *Peace Review*, 12 (3), 415–421.
Lusk, M. W. et al. (1989) Street Children of Juarez: A Field Study. *International Social Work*, 32 (4), 289–302.
McFadyen, L. (2004) *Voices from the Street: An Ethnography of India's Street Children: A Case Study of Delhi*. Gurgaon: Hope India.
Oyeniyi Aransiola, J. et al. (2009) Proliferation of Street Children in Nigeria: Issues and Challenges. *Journal of Social Work*, 9 (4), 371–385.
Panter-Brick (2004) Homelessness, Poverty, and Risks to Health: Beyond at Risk Categorizations of Street Children. *Journal of Children's Geographies*, 2 (1), 83–94.
Ribeiro M. O. and Trench Ciampone, M. H. (2001) Homeless Children: The Lives of a Group of Brazilian Street Children. *Journal of Advanced Nursing*, 35 (1), 42–49.
Salazar, G. (2008) Second-Class Citizens in the Making: The Rights of Street Children in Chile. *Latin American Perspectives*, 35 (4), 30–44.
Smith, H. (2008) Searching for Kinship: The Creation of Street Families among Homeless Youth. *American Behavioral Scientist*, 51 (6), 756–771.
Souza, R. et al. (2010) Outcomes for Street Children and Youth under Multidisciplinary Care in a Drop-in Centre in Tegucigalpa, Honduras. *The International Journal of Social Psychiatry*, 57 (6), 619–626.
Tierney, N. L. (1997) *Robbed of Humanity: Lives of Guatemalan Street Children*. St. Paul, MN: Pangaea.
World Vision (1995) *The Commercial Sexual Exploitation of Street Children*. London: World Vision.

Part II

Institutional Care

Karen Wells

The following two chapters offer very contrasting accounts of violence and institutional care of children. In Chapter 4, Sylvia Meichsner describes a routine of harsh discipline and frequent and arbitrary punishment legitimated within a religious (Protestant) ideology. This orphanage contrasts with Amandine Bollinger's account of three orphanages in different countries, each inspired by a religious commitment, in which children who have experienced violence from their communities and families because of their own or their parents' seropositive status find in the orphanage a place of acceptance and care.

As Bollinger points out, institutional care is often seen as the least protective environment for a child to be raised in, and the global shift is toward family care. While she does not advocate for institutional care, she suggests that whether or not it is the best place for a child to grow up depends on how well resourced the institution is; what its ethos is; and what conditions the child would face outside of the institution. As with many chapters in this collection, the practitioner is more optimistic than the academic about the possibilities for protecting children from violence and even enabling them to flourish.

Meichsner's analysis suggests that the religious ethos of the orphanage lends legitimacy to the idea that there is good violence (the physical punishment of children) and bad violence (the surrounding milieu) so that no further justification is needed from the point of view of the institution to justify the cruel and unusual and mostly arbitrary punishment that the children face. Although on the face of it there is no method to the arbitrary and cruel punishment meted out to children, it is also clear that the arbitrary nature of the punishment ('sometimes I break my own rules') and the lack of fit between the offence and the punishment (e.g., kneeling for hours) is intentional. If God's will/the will of the orphanage (director) are offered as identical to one another (as the author suggests), perhaps faith requires subjection not because rationality demands it but because faith requires it (even in or perhaps precisely because of continued suffering.)

Chapter 5 by Amandine Bollinger is also about religious orphanages but in Democratic Republic of Congo (DRC), Cote d'Ivoire and India. In these orphanages, corporal punishment is forbidden – not least because the children in both DRC and Cote d'Ivoire have experienced violence at the hands of the Pentecostal church leaders who have tried to exorcise them or beaten them following accusations against the children of being witches. The governors of the orphanages want to teach them that their God is not violent and cruel but loving. This not only contrasts well with the Mexican orphanage but also highlights a global issue with the increasing influence on ideas about children's capacities and vulnerabilities of Pentecostal churches in developing countries.

Bollinger's chapter (Chapter 5) also draws attention to the emergence of a crisis of care in Sub-Saharan Africa as a consequence of acquired immunodeficiency syndrome (AIDS). Although evidence on this crisis is very mixed (see e.g., Cheney, forthcoming) and suggests that families, particularly maternal grandparents, have continued to provide care for children who are HIV positive or whose parents have died from AIDS-related illnesses, it is clear that children who are AIDS-affected are stigmatized and that this stigma exposes them to violence and abandonment.

4

A Hard Hand for the Sake of God: The Distinction between Positive and Negative Violence in Faith-Based Childcare

Sylvia Meichsner

The attractiveness of 'negative' violence

This chapter seeks to explore violence against children and adolescents in the context of faith-based residential care and to unpick how religion can be used to legitimate it. The rationale is that this type of childcare integrates violence against children in the form of punishment as part of a broader educational concept seeking to fulfill God's will in the sense that the institution is conceptualized as helping the children cared for to become what is understood as good Christians. However, since it is nowadays widely acknowledged that violence against children damages them in a way that is not immediately evident but has multiple and long-term consequences for the individual concerned (Greven 1977, 1990; Miller 1987; Bitensky 2006) the question arises how can violence against children possibly be justified.

It aims to provide a detailed description that helps to understand how some of the people exercising violence on children in care homes, and coercing others to do the same, understand themselves. It is not meant as an assessment of residential care homes in general or of those founded and maintained by religious groups because the ways care homes are run and also how Biblical principles are translated into educational practices both vary greatly.

The research in this chapter is based on an in-depth case study in an orphanage that shared as many features as possible with other similar institutions in the area. It had, for example, a gender-mixed resident population from a wide variety of backgrounds, and it is not an institution focusing narrowly on a specific social problem such as children of imprisoned parents, drug addicts or migrating children. It is hoped that the general characteristics of this orphanage allow valid inferences to be made to other, similar institutions in similar settings.

The case study was part of extensive fieldwork in a Mexican-American border town in 2007–2008.[1] At that time, the urban agglomeration had a firm reputation for being a corrupt, dangerous place – a reputation that had gradually built up over many years due to historic developments. These include US legislation in the early 20th century that prohibited the production and commercialization of intoxicating liquors as well as gambling, boxing, horse races and other similar activities ('Ley Volstead') (Félix Berumen 2003, 80) which lead to these then criminal, but nevertheless quite profitable, activities – moving to the Mexican side of the border where legislative regimes were different. This went along with a moralizing campaign against vice and profane pleasures in California (Campbell 2005, 17). The negative reputation is further strengthened by the specific cross-border commerce occurring at present, such as human and drug trafficking, as well as an ongoing lively leisure industry targeting American tourists that is based on cheaply available sexual services, drugs and alcohol. The combination of both, supported by lurid media reports, has led to the public perception of the entire area on the Mexican side as a deviant subculture wherein social and moral order has long since dissipated. The orphanage under observation was at the time of the fieldwork located within a couple of square blocks in the immediate vicinity of the border fence, right in between the city's red-light district and a busy border-crossing point. Here violence is ever present in daily life as shoot-outs, kidnappings and detentions frequently occur. In addition, the then Mexican president had deployed the army in order to combat organized crime which led to fully armed soldiers appearing regularly and in large numbers in the streets.

Such an environment has attracted, among others, a variety of religious groups mainly stemming from the United States who seek to impede social and moral decay by engaging in charitable activities in the area. They are typically white middle-class Americans affluent enough to be able to cross the border at their own expense on a regular basis in order to dedicate themselves to missionary activities that fill the gaps left by state welfare, including the provision of health services, education, housing and sanitation. Target groups are primarily the most vulnerable segments of the population – such as the lower income strata – and sectors of society perceived as troublesome–such as sex workers, drug addicts and children living on the streets. Residential care for children and young people in at-risk situations is one important strand of these missionary activities, resulting in a density of orphanages within the urban agglomeration and its immediate surroundings – that is, with an estimated over 80 institutions – well over average compared to the rest of the country. The exact numbers of orphanages operating in the area cannot be provided as many are clandestine. However, there are so few in the rest of the country that the disequilibrium is obvious. As a consequence, the orphanages in the area appear as organisms adjunct to the patchwork of bars, brothels, and small-scale drug production sites that are nourished by the unique environment of the border zone. Interviews with staff from some of these institutions made them appear as firmly dedicated to the control of individuals through childcare: on the one hand to control the children through the care they receive and to lead them to adopt the beliefs, values and behavioral norms that are promoted by the respective institution; on the other hand to reach out to the children's parents and relatives through their education and to use them as a vehicle to instil behavioral changes in these adults.

The orphanage

The orphanage under observation was founded by an elderly couple of conservative evangelical Christians from the United States after the wife received what she perceives as a call from God to do so. Prior to the foundation of the orphanage, the female director had attracted public attention as an active member of the Republican Party in California where she was, as a fervent anti-abortion activist, a single topic candidate. When sentenced for causing damage through picketing an abortion clinic, her lawyer explained to the court that she did what she felt was required by the law of God. As, in her view, this overrides worldly laws at any time, her behavior was considered by her to be 'law-abiding'. Her engagement for orphans and children in need is, according to her own words, a continuation of this activity as an anti-abortion activist by other means. She hopes that pregnant women who do not want their child would rather decide to give their child into residential care if suitable places are available rather than having it aborted if they feel they cannot care for it.

The founders have remained directors of the orphanage ever since with the wife playing the more active role and setting the tone of the institution, which she attends almost every day. The husband remains more in the background, taking care of a variety of practical tasks. They are supported by local staff hired from among the urban poor and particularly women with little or no formal education. Most of the workers entered the orphanage after having had experiences in their life that would make it very difficult to get a footing in the formal labor market: such as long-term drug addiction, periods of imprisonment or involvement in sex work. These women are not considered as employees but as volunteers who have the opportunity to live in the orphanage with the children they are in charge of and to improve their life situation by working toward a recommendation letter that enables them to move on to another occupation at a later stage. They also have the opportunity to raise their own biological children who are cared for by the institution like any other child. While they do receive a small compensation for their efforts, this is not intended as a salary and they are not protected by labor rights. In addition, volunteers who come from the United States for short- and long-term stays in order to help with repair work or engage in leisure activities with the children play an important role due to the practical and financial support they provide and the emotional bonds they form with the inmates. There are no systematic selection criteria for the international volunteers to spend time with the children in the orphanage, and therefore they vary greatly in age, educational background and profession and even in their respective values. They are not trained prior to interacting with the children and are not told in detail how the institution works, but they pick it up over time from the children. They are not given specific instructions on what or what not to do either ('Just hang around with the kids...'), and so they often train each other through confidential conversations during overlapping stays. While the Mexican government does carry out irregular visits to monitor the performance of the orphanages in the area, these visits are rare and irregular. The US government is not involved in any formal way.

The orphanage as a 'moral technology'

The concern for the life of unborn babies, the director expressed, combines with evangelization as the main goal of evangelical Christians. The intention is, according to the director, to reach out to adults via the children's education according to Christian values. This can be illustrated by the example of four-year-old twin sisters whose vocabulary and behavior suggest their familiarity with the nitty-gritty of prostitution. Their father gains his daily bread through involvement in the trafficking of adolescent girls to work in a large strip bar just around the corner from the orphanage. The tacit expectation is that the daughters pick up on religious values and pass them on to their father so that he eventually takes on another breadwinning occupation and becomes more responsible for his daughters. To put this in more general terms, the strategy to modify the behavior and attitude of adults who are perceived as not doing the right thing is an attempt to gain control through their children over layers of society that are not normally accessible to missionaries.

The wider context framing this attitude is that the mission pursued by the founders of the institution is, according to the orphanage's promotional material and former website, 'Changing Mexico – one life at a time'. This slogan captures the directors' overarching goal to educate future leaders according to Christian values as they understand them. Such values are supposed to initiate yet undefined changes for the betterment of the Mexican society once the youth in question reach adult age. This places considerable pressure on both the children and the educational success of the orphanage as the implicit message is that the perceived downward spiral of Mexico will continue should the children fail to develop the character and abilities that the orphanage aims for. To produce valuable members of society whose deeds are clearly guided by religious values is meant to be achieved through the inmates observing a given set of rules and regulations. These include regular Bible lectures and prayers, regular attendance at church services, active participation in household tasks and respecting other children's belongings. That the children meet these expectations is assured through a broad range of punitive measures that are applied in case of perceived deviations from these rules. In this way, the orphanage contributes to moulding the children's character and value systems in a similar way to conventional schools (Wells 2009, 110). While norms and values are inculcated with the help of joint Bible readings and prayer, as well as through Christian media such as themed DVDs and the Internet site 'Godtube', punishment serves to hasten the process of the children adopting the orphanage's moral framework and to achieve long-lasting results as it generates pressure to capture expectations toward them quickly and to alter their behaving accordingly.

The logic of 'positive' violence

An inverse reading of the proposition discussed above that the orphanage's children will save the nation as long as they receive the right kind of education might be that the children are perceived as a threat to society as long as their habits and manners are not efficiently corrected. In other words: in trying to 'normalize' (Rose 1999, 134) the behavior of the children and young people through incorporating them into the institution and leading them to adopt practices the orphanage's directors consider appropriate, not only the children are protected from possibly harmful external influences but also the Mexican society is prevented from further deterioration and set up to function in the future in a way that is more agreeable to God.

Both interpretations of the relationship between the children's education and the overall situation in Mexico suggest, nevertheless, that social change is merely a question of how individual behavior is managed. This brackets out other factors so that the underlying economic and political structures leading to inequality and social problems remain unchallenged. Inequality even becomes enacted through rules, norms and practices in the institution, as shown later on in this chapter. Furthermore, the prospect of the children contributing critically to the benefit of their nation offers a narrative that allows staff and inmates alike to find some meaning in their respective social positions, which is then less likely to appear as a source of discontent. Both aspects contribute to reinforcing the existing social order (Bourdieu 1991, 6, 31, 33). A by-product of the educational procedures the children undergo in the institution, which is not explicitly mentioned as part of the directors' agenda, is that a labor force is produced that is both skilled and compliant enough to fit, without major difficulties, into the prevailing economic system (Rose 1999, 126; Wells 2009, 96). This also has a reinforcing effect on the existing structures well beyond the boundaries of the institution.

This approach toward residential care for children and young people also implies two key conditions: firstly, that the orphanage needs children to care for in order to accomplish its mission of raising future leaders; secondly, that the values and principles of conduct brought forward need to be communicated efficiently. In what follows, how these conditions are met and how different interpretations of violence come to bear are explored.

Helping children to become good Christians

At any given time the institution shelters about 90 children of both sexes and within a presumed age range of 0–19 years. (The precise age of many children cannot be verified due to the lack of, incompleteness or otherwise unreliable personal documents). The channels through which the children arrive at the orphanage include the following: being put forward by government social services, being deposited by relatives or neighbors or being attracted by siblings already living in the institution. Most of the inmates are not actual orphans – as the notion of 'orphanage' might suggest – but the offspring of drug addicts, sex workers or individuals otherwise involved in the local drug economy who are, for whatever reason, unable to raise their children themselves. This implies that some children have suffered mistreatment, sexual abuse or abandonment. Some have migrated from other areas, others have grown up in the location of the orphanage where they either witnessed delinquent activities or became involved in them. Some of the children cared for their younger siblings when the parent they lived with was high on drugs, contributed significantly to the household income, or both. For some of the children, exposure to substances in the maternal womb and years of poor alimentation have led to limited intellectual capacities. Due to their living circumstances before entering the orphanage, school education remained fragmented and educational attainment low. In general, the children find it difficult to respect set rules, to follow a fixed schedule and to cooperate with others. Many of them have socio-emotional problems such as a rather limited capacity to manage individual impulses or to pay attention to something for an extended amount of time.

The original aim of the orphanage directors was the transformation of these traits and while the children are presented toward external visitors and childcare agencies as 'normal kids' who have the potential to achieve great things in life ('they just need to be given a chance'), the main expectation toward children is obedience. This is in line with conservative Protestant writings who emphasize that the Bible asks that children respect and obey the authority of their parents without questioning it (Ellison and Sherkat 1993, 132). Consequently, in the orphanage being obedient is discursively equaled with being good Christians. Parents, in turn, are requested to pass their faith-based values on to their children and can be expected to be held accountable for failure to do so (Ellison and Sherkat 1993, 133). In accordance with conservative Protestants' encouragement to apply physical punishment, a rigorous education based on a variety of punitive measures is considered necessary and sufficient for children to become good Christians. The orphanage's directors take on the role of substitute parents thus acting out the punishment on the children on behalf of their parents. This perception of violence as inevitable and necessary resembles the 17th century Puritans' principles of child rearing that, based on the assumption that children are genuinely evil, requires firm discipline and control as part of education so as to purify them of original sin (Kellet et al. 2004, 28). It also recalls the outlook of 18th century British Methodists who explicitly asked parents to 'break the will of your child' in order to achieve submission under the parental will and later under the will of God (Hendricks 1997, 35).

Variations in punitive measures observed within the institution or reported by children and staff include having to sit silently and immobile on either bed or chair, in a corner or cradle for a time span of anything between ten minutes and several weeks; having the mouth forcefully washed with soap or dishwashing liquid; having to sit as a small child on top of a large fridge without being able to get down; smacking, spanking and slaps in the face; deprivation from benefits others enjoy – for example, having to eat beans when others eat ice cream or being forbidden contact with friends and family members from outside the orphanage[2]; not being allowed to attend the nursery school or set meetings with the psychologist; exclusion from leisure activities ('when they don't obey, they can't have fun'); additional cleaning tasks such as scrubbing the floor in the large communal area tile by tile with a tooth brush; kneeling motionless for several hours; having to accomplish kitchen duties in addition to their regular share.[3] Behavioral transgressions potentially generating these sanctions span a wide range and include violating the demands of a faith-based life in the broadest sense of the term and, more specifically, causing harm to somebody else, stealing, taking drugs and showing signs of sexual interest. The latter is an absolute taboo and may attract sanctions up to expulsion from the orphanage as it is supposed to distract the children from what the director perceives as their purpose in life ('we want to help them that they really give their life to the Lord'). What is of particular importance, though, is anything related to religious rites. This might be indicative of the intention to impregnate a 'religious habitus' (Bourdieu 1991, 22) into the children and adolescents that contributes to the shaping of thoughts and actions in tune with the religious norms and values promoted by the institution. This way they are internalized so that the individual reaches a point where they are adhered to without further thought. This form of violence is seen as positive as it is meant to help children to reach their supposed goal of living a meaningful, God-pleasing life. It is carried out against the backdrop of violence, encompassing the particularities of the border area described above and some of the experiences a child might have made prior to entering the institution – for example, where they suffered parental mistreatment. Consequently, the child is discursively constructed as not only worthy of but also in need of protection, and the mission the orphanage has is conveyed as rescuing the children from a negatively violent environment and a sinful life.

The next section explores how the intention to help children to become good Christians shapes educational practices as well as their features and their meanings.

Specific features of punitive measures

The disciplinary techniques play an important role in correcting and preventing what is perceived as misbehavior and lack of compliance. What strikes first and foremost is that the application of these techniques is arbitrary. This can be illustrated by the following example: after starting to rock backward and forward on his chair due to becoming unsettled during a long church service, a seven-year-old boy was punished for this by being forced to sit on his bed in silence for several hours while the other children went to the beach. The rationale was that being able to remain quiet during church services is considered as an important part of what makes a good Christian and, therefore, as something that needs to be taken seriously. A four-year-old girl, however, who had been laughing during church services, had to sit on her bed for five consecutive days for the same reason. The unequal responses to what amounts to similar behavior suggest not only that comparable levels of punishments are not necessarily applied but also that no indulgence can be expected toward misbehavior in younger children who are still less capable of informed reasoning. That there are no set guidelines clearly stating what kind of sanction should follow a particular kind of misbehavior inspires everybody to follow his or her own judgment which makes the orphanage environment rather unpredictable for the children. This is even more so as the background of staff and volunteers varies widely as already shown, both between and among each group, so that everybody's way of assessing a child's behavior in a given situation is likely to vary broadly. A further source of confusion is that any punishment applied by the same person is not necessarily consistent over time. The founding director, for example, admitted frankly that 'I sometimes break my own rules'.

The arbitrary way of punishing children combines with a gendered approach. Boys, for example, usually cease to respect rules once they are about 14–15 years old. Some of them are actually no longer children but grown-up men exhibiting corresponding masculine bodily features – a small detail that unfolds its own dynamics in terms of intimidation of some and the physical attraction of other children and adolescents of both sexes. These young men live in the orphanage as 'children' to be cared for due to the above-mentioned difficulties in reliably establishing their age. While they make the most out of the opportunities they are offered during their stay in the orphanage, such as free housing and education, they only tune in to the daily routines of the institution to varying degrees. Some of them engage in regular cleaning tasks and look after the younger children, whereas others don't eat at the usual hours together with children and staff but enter the kitchen when they want and help themselves to food. As this is something the inmates are not normally encouraged to do, it points to the boys who are doing so as enjoying privileges that other inmates do not have. Some of these lads broke into the carefully decorated in-house nursery school one night to hold a party, leaving it in disorder and partly destroyed – behavior which remained, much to the chagrin of the nursery school teacher, unpunished by sanctions. It is not clear, though, what is at the root of this gendered punishment scheme – whether it is that the male adolescents are feared due to their visible physical strength or stereotypic interpretations of gender roles at work that concede more liberty to males and demand more docility from females. The punitive measures applied in the orphanage do tend to confirm conventional gender roles, though, and do so in multiple ways. Some of the older girls are led to identify with a rather maternal role, carrying out a remarkable amount of household tasks such as distributing food or preparing the smaller children's items for school. This also entails them managing the younger children through threats of punishment and by speaking to them in a tone as if they were actually their own children ('...or I have to punish you...'; '...I don't want to shout...'). In these types of micro-interactions traditional gender roles are copied and the older girls' role as carer and childminder is endorsed. In addition, the boundary between carrying out care work and becoming a perpetrator of coercion oneself is somewhat blurry and each melts into the other. However, this is not confined to female inmates but is also the case with the adolescent son of the orphanage's deputy director who overlooks the dormitory of the older boys. Several interviewees who claim to have an intimate knowledge of the orphanage say that he regularly coerces the younger children into doing him favors such as running errands, serving him food out of hours and handing over their pocket money to him ('He's the mafia...'). He is said to force them to remain immobile on their knees for several hours should they not comply. This would especially be the case on days when the directors are not present as there is an increased demand for the remainder of the staff to watch the children and to attend to their needs. However, as long as they are immobilized through punishment, the children require less attention which suggests that punishment also comes to bear as a matter of convenience. The allegations made seem to be confirmed by the younger boys who usually keep a safe distance from their adolescent dorm supervisor. Here the role of the authoritative father who does not tolerate any contradiction is performed. That the boy does so in exchange for a small remuneration, but the girls looking after smaller children don't but do it 'cause I love young children' socializes not only them but also all those to whom they are role models into the assumption that it is fine for women to do unpaid care work.

What both examples also show is that the punishment culture in the orphanage has repercussions on the relationships between inmates, here through the generation of hierarchical structures among the children and adolescents as a consequence of the power imbalances that result from inmates taking on staff roles which offers space for becoming perpetrators of violence themselves. This results in the division of the inmate population into those who have the power to punish others and with this to establish and reinforce rules and those who do not but have to follow these rules or, in other words, the applied punitive measures contribute to the stratification of the institution on the basis of the power to punish others. This confirms Goffman's observation (1961) that institutions are not composed by fixed structures but rather constantly created and recreated through ongoing microinteraction which is informed by the demands of every situation an individual may encounter. The boy overseeing the boys' dorm, for example, is expected to establish and maintain order in this area whereby the punitive measures he applies are accepted as a means to this end.

Reminiscent of Foucault's interpretation of torture as a spectacle to be seen by others (Foucault 1977, 34), chastised children often have to endure their punishment in public so that others see what can happen to them any time if they chose not to behave. As a side-effect, the punished children are often made fun of by others, which weakens their position in the social hierarchy inherent to the orphanage. For example, when a ten-year-old girl was sitting at a table in the dining room without being allowed to speak, an 18-year-old boy, who happened to be around, teased her and tried to make her talk. When she was eventually at the point of crying, he laughingly took a photo of her with his mobile phone. The public character of many punitive measures regularly leads to the humiliation of the child in question. One example for this is children who are already too old and too large to fit into it having to sit silently in a cradle. Children with learning difficulties or otherwise affected intellectual capacities appear to end up more often than others in this kind of situation. This and the humiliating character of the punishment appears to foster the institutional stratification as it offers opportunities for some children to accommodate themselves in a position superior to and more powerful than others through ridiculing them on the basis of their punishment. This is particularly the case as sons and daughters of staff members appear to be frequently on the side of those who laugh than on the side of those who are laughed about. This brings us back to the previously mentioned arbitrary character of punishment prevailing in the orphanage as the offspring of the sons and daughters of staff members appear to enjoy some sort of immunity and are exempt from punishment in spite of obviously inappropriate behavior. The daughters of the deputy director, for example, who also live as inmates in the orphanage, often give orders to other children thus imitating their mother's role in the institution to a certain extent in the interaction with their peers. Also, they are known for hiding in their mothers' bedroom when their dorm mates are busy with routine cleaning tasks that all are expected to share. That this remains without sanction speaks to their having a more comfortable position within the institution's hierarchy due to their family relationships than other children. The same applies to the daughters of one of the helpers who regularly take the toys of the other children away or intimidate them and the adolescent son of the deputy director who frequently ridicules other children when sitting still for being punished. Neither of them is punished for this behavior.

What was not meant as a punishment measure in the strict sense of the term, but which actually played out as violence, was that a handful of drug-addict adolescents living on the streets were invited to use a separate building at their leisure. They were then shut in this building during the first year of their arrival in order to both force them into a detoxification process and acquaint them with the rules and values of Christian life to support it. While the local health authorities are skilfully circumvented so as to prevent them from becoming aware of this unlawful endeavor, no feelings of doing something inappropriate had been expressed by any of the persons responsible, but rather the imposed limitations to the personal autonomy and private choices of these young men are deemed as part of what carrying out God's will requires.

These examples show that the sanctions applied in the orphanage are not isolated occurrences but follow an ideologically underpinned rationale that partly disregards their legally constituted rights and/or violates their Human Rights.

The applied sanctions function as a hinge between the director's hegemonic moral attitude and the perceived problem of children in need of education. The director of the orphanage presents herself as a 'moral entrepreneur' (Becker 1963, 147) who measures with her own yardstick what is deviant and what is acceptable behavior, and ultimately what responses are appropriate for each. With this, she engages in 'practices of judgment and normalization' (Rose 1999, 131). The Christian ideology employed to justify the violence against the children transforms it into an 'instrument of salvation' (Bourdieu 1991, 27) and also veils it by directing attention to the higher goals that are meant to be achieved through punishment.

However, variations in punitive measures as well as their unpredictability make it difficult for a child to relate the sanction to the misconduct that it generated so that the children do not always know why they are punished. An example of this is the occasion when 15 girls aged four to ten years were sitting immobile and in silence on their beds as punishment and none of them knew why this was happening. As a consequence of the imposition of sanctions without clearly discernible patterns no stable conditioning of the children takes place, but they accept it as something similar to fate that just happens once in a while and which cannot be influenced by them like, for example, changes in the weather. This suggests that the punitive measures are likely to miss the goal of a sustainable alteration of a child's undesirable behavior which, in turn, leads to the question of how the violence the children experience can be justified – unless durable changes in behavior were not the goal or, at least, not the only goal.

Crown jewels to the feet of the Lord

The main reason given for the children's more or less constant punishment is that a successful behavioral adjustment to the life of a Christian requires targeted support. Obedience is considered as paramount as the directors represent the children's parents who, in their turn, represent the authority of God (Ellison and Sherkat 1993, 134). Considering that absolute subjection to God's will is required by good Christians, it appears then consistent when the director of the orphanage demands the children to obey her. Discursively establishing that God and the directors of the orphanage operate on the same level implies such a profound legitimization of their demands on the children and adolescents that they are hard to challenge because, after all, who wants to mess with God?

To facilitate this complete subjection, the arbitrary punishment is intended to break the child's will and sense of self in manifold ways. However, depending on the living circumstances the children had prior to entering the orphanage, it takes more or less time and more or less intensive punitive measures to achieve this, which is why some children appear to be punished constantly. In spite of the often violent attempts to streamline the children's behavior, rearing them is permeated by a discourse of 'love' that is reminiscent of the concept of parental love as the children are told they can grow up in the orphanage regardless of whatever they might have done prior to entering it because the directors love them as does God. This discourse also embraces the imposed sanctions as it is explained to the children that they are punished because they do matter to the directors and they want the best for them, which is also the case with God. To endorse the violence the children experience in the institution on the basis of its being God's will is a powerful tool to rebut critique that can hardly fail to work. It also allows the children and young people to frame their experiences within a narrative that allocates them meaning which is likely to increase their acceptance of their punishment. The punishment practices in the orphanage are not uncontested, however, as frictions between the director defending them and volunteers who find the treatment of the children too harsh are reported. To this the fact can be added that a local NGO that previously supported the orphanage through logistics and donations severed all ties after considering that the way the children and adolescents were treated was too violent. When touching upon the harsh punishment practices in conversations, the director seeks to convince with the argument that her own biological children received a strict education also encompassing physical violence that 'did not do them any harm' but helped them to overcome inappropriate behavior and personal shortcomings. She sees it as proof for the success of the way she educated her offspring in that they are now all responsible adults who work in their respective professions and have their own families. The logic with which the punishment is applied and defended aligns with the institution's overarching goal to help the children to become good Christians and respectable persons. The rigor with which this help is provided is deemed as necessary, perceived as God's firm will and part of the female director's efforts to be a good Christian herself and to accomplish with what God expects from a good Christian parent ('These children are the crown jewels that I will once bring to the feet of the Lord . . . ').

Bourgeois philanthropists and the global South

The director's point of view suggests an interpretation of the violence applied within the orphanage as a 'positive' and thus desirable form of violence. It is perceived as one tool among several for the accomplishment of the orphanage's mission and is – while building on the assumption that a child is a being in the making and something that needs to be formed – perceived as the type of violence a child needs to be exposed to become a better person, similar to the proverbial 'crooked wood' that can only be straightened with the help of fire.

This, however, is in sharp contrast with the perception of the violence the children are surrounded by in their wider living environment of the border zone as 'negative' and as in need of being eradicated in order to make the world a better place in accord with God's plans. Faith-based values are intertwined with the narrative of an environment damaging to children while damage to children through violent education is denied. The risk of violence being carried forward to the next generation is downplayed as is the emotional and psychological damage resulting from frequent hazardous, humiliating punitive measures that are going to inform relationships later on, especially with the children's own children.

In this way violence appears as a binary concept with the values of good and evil, depending on the perpetrator's intention and normative framework. This notwithstanding, both interpretations of violence relate to the orphanage's intention of missionary activity. On the one hand, through extracting children from a family environment that is perceived as unsuitable and as having detrimental effects on their health and well-being in order to integrate them into the orphanage, the institution takes stock of 'material' that can be fashioned for serving God's purposes. On the other hand, by educating the children rigorously according to Christian values as understood by the orphanage's founder, the institution corresponds to what is perceived as its divine mandate.

The founding director of the orphanage arduously pursues this. To that behalf, she ascribes herself the legitimacy to interpret the Gospel in a specific way and the authority to assess both the social, economic and cultural life in the border area and the conduct of the children in her care against this interpretation. That her moral position appears as non-negotiable confirms this. By advocating vehemently for educational principles such as being 'hard on the kids' in spite of obvious signs of disapproval, she continuously appoints herself to a position of power from which she defines what the transgressions of boundaries are and what the adequate responses to this should be. By educating the children with the help of violence with the intention of changing Mexico in the long run into a country that she imagines would be more to God's liking, she suggests not only that the children's uncorrected behavior is deviant but also that the entire Mexican population lives and behaves in an unacceptable, problematic way. The assumption that children can be converted into leaders of society at a later stage builds on the tacit assumption that children are malleable and that they have a specific set of abilities that makes them the right persons for this mission and more suitable than adults. The narrative that Mexico's destiny is dependent on the success of forming valuable members of society through a strict education turns the orphanages into an extended arm of foreign ideological forces intervening in the children's education. On the basis of her faith, the director performs as an expert who 'knows' how to distinguish between the normal, desired behavior of a child and that which is abnormal and pathological (Rose 1999, 133–134).

This morally authoritative attitude strikes a chord with her previous anti-abortion activities that were also aimed at liberating the world from an evil identified in the light of the norms and values she shares with like-minded people such as fellow Christians who adhere to similar interpretations of the Gospel.

That God's will is communicated directly in prayers to privileged individuals such as the director of the orphanage gives her the air of a 'prophet', who leads the way in the extraordinary situation of the perceived decline of Mexican society that needs to be halted via the appropriate education of members of the next generation (Bourdieu 1991, 35). This occurs with the help of the moral framework and the instructions for good conduct that the orphanage seeks to implement in order to prevent and correct undesired behavior and that it reinforces with the help of sanctions. It also locates the director's undertakings in the broader context of a personal crusade with evangelical and moral shades.

That white 'bourgeois philanthropists' (Rose 1999, 156), such as the directors of the orphanage, set up ethical and behavioral norms and enforce their respect from children stemming from deprived backgrounds through the use of punishment, and with the intention to change a country of the minority world as they consider appropriate may be seen as a reflection of the typically rather paternalistic relationships between Western industrialized countries and countries of the global South.

Notes

1. In order to protect the researched, anonymity will be preserved and therefore no information is provided that could allow for tracking back the research site or the researched individuals.

2. The frequency and quality of these outside contacts, when they are not being punished, vary from child to child due to variations in their social and family background.
3. Accounting for the difficulty in separating single components of these techniques neatly from each other, the terms 'violence', 'punishment' and 'sanction' shall be used interchangeably. In this way often commonly accepted forms of violence, such as bullying and deprivation that are used as punishment measures in the orphanage are also subsumed under the umbrella term of 'violence'.

Bibliography

Becker, H. S. (1963) *Outsiders: Studies in the Sociology of Deviance.* New York: Free Press.

Bitensky, S. H. (2006) *Corporal Punishment of Children: A Human Rights Violation.* Ardsley: Transnational Publishers.

Bourdieu, P. (1991) Genesis and Structure of the Religious Field. *Comparative Social Research*, 13, 1–44.

Campbell, F. (2005) La frontera sedentaria. *Letras Libres.* Año VII, 83, 16–19.

Ellison, Ch. G. and Sherkat, D. E. (1993) Conservative Protestantism and Corporal Punishment. *American Sociological Review*, 58 (1), 131–144.

Félix Berumen, H. (2003) *Tijuana la horrible. Entre la historia y el mito.* Tijuana, B.C.: El Colegio de la Frontera Norte.

Foucault, M. (1977) *Discipline and Punish: The Birth of the Prison.* Harmondsworth: Penguin.

Goffman, E. (1961) *Asylums: Essays on the Social Situation of Mental Patients and Other Inmates.* Harmondsworth: Penguin.

Greven, Ph. (1977) *The Protestant Temperament. Patterns of Child-Rearing, Religious Experience, and the Self in Early America.* New York: Alfred Knopf.

Greven, Ph. (1990) *Spare the Child: The Religious Roots of Punishment and the Psychological Impact of Physical Abuse.* New York: Alfred Knopf.

Greven, Ph. (1997) The Protestant Temperament Revisited. In R. Hoffman, M. Sobal, and J. Teute (eds.) *Through a Glass Darkly: Reflections on Personal Identity in Early America*, Chapel Hill: The University of California Press, pp. 349–369.

Hendricks, H. (1997) Constructions and Reconstructions of British Childhood. An Interpretative Survey, 1800 to the Present. In A. James and A. Prout (eds.) *Constructing and Reconstructing Childhood: Contemporary Issues in the Sociological Study of Childhood*, London & Bristol, PA: Falmer Press, pp. 33–60.

Kellet, M., Robinson, C. and Burr R. (2004) Images of Childhood. In S. Fraser et al. (eds.) *Doing Research with Children and Young People*, London: Sage, pp. 27–42.

Miller, A. (1987) *For Your Own Good: Hidden Cruelty in Child-rearing and the Roots of Violence.* London: Virago.

Rose, N. (1999) *Governing the Soul. The Shaping of the Private Self*, 2nd edition. London; New York: Free Association Books.

Wells, K. (2009) *Childhood in a Global Perspective.* Cambridge: Polity Press.

5
The Role of Residential Homes in the Care of Orphans Affected by HIV

Amandine Bollinger

Introduction

There is a general recognition in the international development community that children in situations of vulnerability – particularly if orphaned – should remain in their extended families or communities. Placing children in residential care should be a 'last resort' solution (UNICEF 1989, 2007; OAU 1999). This is to protect them from the negative outcomes observed in residential care, including abandonment of the child, reliance on access to food and education and restricted emotional development (Morantz and Heymann 2010; Van Vilsteren et al. 2011). The 1989 United Nations Convention on the Rights of the Child 'recognises the critical role of the family in the development, care and support of the child' (UNICEF 2006). The 2003 Stockholm Declaration on Children and Residential Care advises '*institutional care only as a last resort and as a temporary response*' (Knorth et al. 2007 citing Anglin and Knorth 2004, 141, emphasis in the original). While this policy is sensible and is used to guide many community support development programs, there are circumstances where a child can face abuse and rejection from exactly those from whom love, nurturing and support is expected.

Despite this injunction against residential care, a sort of 'mushrooming' of residential care for children affected by HIV and AIDS is happening worldwide (Meintjes and Pinkerton 2011; Richter and Norman 2010; Mann et al. 2012). Little research has been done on the reasons why children affected by HIV end up in these places and on what is happening inside them (Knorth et al. 2007). As a result, these institutions have become taboo in the programing of international non-governmental organizations (NGO) working with children, especially since program funding relies on the application of recognized international good practice (Delpeu 2011). No frameworks structuring or guiding these institutions are in place, which implies that the quality of care is generally left to the responsible individuals' management and knowledge (Delpeu 2011). Residential institutions are all the more criticized where they specialize in the care of children living with HIV since international policy recommends mixing children living with HIV with HIV-negative children to maintain the anonymity of the children's HIV status and avoid increasing stigma (UNICEF, UNAIDS, USAID 2004).

This chapter looks at the work of three residential institutions specializing in the care of abandoned orphans, mostly living with HIV, in three countries in Africa and Asia: Ivory Coast, the Democratic Republic of Congo (DRC) and India. These three countries were selected on the basis of the work experience of the author as a project manager of a residential care home for orphans affected by and living with HIV in Bihar – one of the poorest states of India – and as a consultant in DRC and in Cote d'Ivoire on projects caring for children affected by HIV. Data were obtained through discussions with families, children, caretakers and NGO workers.

This chapter does not seek to defend or encourage the institutionalization of children. Rather, it intends to inform international thinking around HIV-specialized institutional care and to bring into focus the issue of family rejection of orphans living with HIV so that it is better addressed in HIV programing. Most data on the topic are empirical, and there is a general agreement that more research within residential institutions is needed (Mann et al. 2012). This chapter is an opportunity to testify to what is happening in these centers so that appropriate policy can be applied. It contextualizes the level of community violence to which children can be subject and describes how, under these circumstances, care institutions can be beneficial to children who might otherwise simply die. It is also a call for relevant support to extended families that are often overwhelmed with challenges of their own (poverty, disease, debts, malnutrition, promiscuity, etc.) and ignorant about HIV-related issues.

Defining violence

Violence is defined by the World Health Organization (WHO) as 'the intentional use of physical force or power, threatened or actual, against a person, or against a group or community, that either results in or has a high likelihood of resulting in injury, death, psychological harm, maldevelopment or deprivation' (Krug et al. 2002). This covers a range of manifestations of violence (from threat to actual act, from physical force to the use of power) and of consequences (from physiological to psychological harm). The WHO also identifies three categories of violence (Krug et al. 2002): self-directed violence, collective violence and interpersonal violence. The latter involves violence within the family and/or the community and will be the one of principal concern in this chapter.

The principal manifestation of interpersonal violence for children is maltreatment. That is, 'all types of physical and/or emotional ill-treatment, sexual abuse, neglect, negligence and commercial or other exploitation, which result in actual or potential harm to the child's health, survival, development or dignity in the context of a relationship of responsibility, trust or power' (Butchart et al. 2006). Child maltreatment has been categorized into four types: physical, sexual, emotional/psychological and neglect (Krug et al. 2002). These four aspects of violence against children are all present in the data presented in this chapter.

There has been little formal research conducted to assess the level of HIV-related interpersonal violence children experience (Abadıa-Barrero and Castro 2006; Lockhart 2008). Drawing on the studies of Bourgeois (1998, 2003a, 2003b), Farmer (2003), Green (1999), Scheper-Hughes (1992) and Walter et al. (2004), Lockhart (2008) explains that an ethnographic definition of violence should include 'processes that contribute to social oppression and assaults on human rights and dignity'. He draws particularly on Farmer's concept of health crises as a form of 'structural violence' (Farmer 1992, 1995, 2003 cited in Lockhart 2008, see also Wells and Montgomery, this volume) and its close interrelation with 'underdevelopment, poverty, racism and the spread of AIDS'. Therefore, in order to understand HIV-related vulnerability and violence, it is critical to address 'social inequality and severe poverty' (Lockhart 2008).

The intersection between structural violence and HIV is also raised by Abadıa-Barrero and Castro (2006) who note that violence is triggered by HIV-related stigma and exacerbated by structural factors such as poverty and by promiscuity. They explain that 'stigma leads to discriminatory processes with harmful consequences to the person's well-being'. Stigma may be defined as 'an attribute which is significantly discrediting and which serves to reduce the person who possesses it in the eyes of society' (Goffman 1963 cited in Parker and Aggleton 2003).

HIV-related stigma relies on social fear, lack of knowledge, denial, shame, taboo and ignorance, among other factors (Abadıa-Barrero and

Castro 2006). The negative judgments associated with HIV (punishment, otherness, drug use and sexual misconduct) and AIDS images of skinny, dying people, feed into AIDS-related social fear (Abadıa-Barrero and Castro 2006). Stigma may be understood as the ideology behind attitudes to HIV and discrimination (status loss, internalization and social withdrawal) as the practice (Deacon and Stephney 2007). Children affected by HIV face various types of stigma, which have high impact and consequences – including violence – at different levels of their lives (Deacon and Stephney 2007). They face violent actions due to the 'fear of their infection', whether they are living with HIV or not (Abadıa-Barrero and Castro 2006). This is what Deacon and Stephney (2007) define as 'courtesy stigma'. It is closely linked to secondary stigma and self-stigmatization. Secondary stigma is the attachment of stigma to other things such as disease, objects and practices. Deacon and Stephney in their review of the literature on stigma, children and HIV (2007) found that 'children whose parents are ill with AIDS or who have died of AIDS ... report being marginalized and isolated from other children, being teased and gossiped about, being presumed to be also HIV-positive, and not receiving care'. Self-stigmatization describes how living with HIV may have a devalued social perception of the self, which could lead to self-directed violence.

School is a significant place for discrimination and rejection: due to ignorance about transmission, most parents refuse to let their children play with HIV-positive children in case an accident happens. As a result, children living with HIV are often excluded from schools (Deacon and Stephney 2007). Although in reality, the risk of HIV transmission between children is negligible, teachers tend to isolate or exclude a child if they know that he or she is HIV positive, and children themselves can be cruel toward a child who is living with HIV or whose mother (or father) has died of AIDS (Chase and Aggleton 2001).

These situations of rejection, isolation and discrimination are frequent as a lack of awareness and ignorance about HIV are still predominant. All children in the residential care institutions studied below have faced HIV-related stigma at some stage in their lives. In many cases, the children have been coping with the double stigma of orphanhood and HIV.

Children affected by HIV

Children affected by HIV are defined by United Nations Children's Emergency Fund as 'children and adolescents under 18 years old who are living with HIV, or/and have lost one or both parents due to AIDS, or/and are 'vulnerable, i.e. whose survival, or/and whose well-being or development is threatened or altered by HIV' (Smart 2003) because they live in HIV-affected households and communities (UNICEF 2011, 6). They can alternatively be called 'Children affected by AIDS' (CABA or CAA), 'AIDS orphans', 'Orphans and Vulnerable Children' (OVC), 'Children in distress' (CINDI) and more recently (PEPFAR 2012) 'Children in Adversity'.

The categories in which these children now sit have become so broad that many organizations have started to include in their HIV programs children who are not affected by HIV but are made vulnerable for other reasons such as trafficking and disability. Gender is a key factor as all inequalities tend to be accentuated where HIV is concerned. The epidemic is reaching more women (58 percent of people living with HIV in Sub-Saharan Africa are women, UNAIDS 2013) and girls are more likely to be subjected to sexual violence (UNICEF 2006). In most places, boys are the victims of beatings and physical punishment more often than girls, while girls are at higher risk of infanticide, sexual abuse, neglect and being forced into sex work (Deacon and Stephney 2007).

HIV has multiple impacts on children. They may be living with a person living with HIV, caring for a person living with HIV, may have lost one or both parents to AIDS-related illnesses, may themselves be living with HIV or may be simultaneously living in all of these circumstances.

We are here focusing on children orphaned by AIDS – those who have lost at least one of their parents to AIDS-related illness and who have been abandoned by their extended families and communities and are themselves living with HIV.

Among children affected by AIDS, orphans are particularly likely to experience psychiatric problems such as depression and anxiety. They face a double stigma – that of orphanhood and of HIV. They are more likely than other children to have economic, legal (inheritance rights), nutrition, health and education issues. They have to adjust to bereavement (Deacon and Stephney 2007). All the children in the residential care that will be described below are orphans who have had to face all of these issues. The problem of inheritance is particularly worrying in India, especially in the case of boys whose father was the eldest of the family.

Not all children born of a HIV-positive mother will themselves be born with HIV. Roughly one child in three will be HIV positive where the mother is not under treatment; otherwise, the incidence is below

1 percent (Von Linstow et al. 2010). All children in the residential care studied below acquired their HIV status through their mother.

The impact of HIV on the children starts before the death of one of their parents. Children living with parents who are living with HIV witness parental sickness, may care for their ill parent and have to cope with housework and financial difficulties (Deacon and Stephney 2007). It is therefore critical to take into account the context in which these children might have lived. In addition, while stigma against caregivers – particularly mothers – can be high (Deacon and Stephney 2007), violence against mothers living with HIV is also a problem in many places (Chase and Aggleton 2001; Hale and Vasquez 2011) and manifests as rejection, being thrown out of the house, blame, loss of property and inheritance rights, social and economic isolation and so on. All the children from the residential care in the cases discussed here have lost their mothers and have been through similar experiences.

HIV status can itself be thought of as a form of violence to the child both at the physical level (through the harmfulness of medication) and at the psychological levels (through disclosure and secrecy).

While in Western countries children are diagnosed for HIV within the first four months of their life, in Sub-Saharan Africa the HIV diagnosis often occurs after two years of age as there is limited access to infant diagnostic tests and rapid tests are underutilized (de Baets et al. 2008). Most children in the residential care studied below were diagnosed quite late, when the children were three or four years old and started developing related illnesses.

The most common symptoms due to the weakness of the immune system in children are lung infections, tuberculosis, diarrhea, ear infections and fungal diseases. All of these infections can further mark the children apart, cause them to suffer and damage them psychologically. All children in the residential care studied have had opportunistic infections.

A late diagnosis can be problematic as the child's immune system might already be compromised. De Baets et al. (2008) demonstrated that disease progression, particularly in children, can be rapid in developing settings where environmental factors such as early high infection exposure, malnutrition and limited use of preventative measures (drinkable water, bednets and medication) are prevalent.

Most children brought to the residential institutions arrived in poor condition: they had developed opportunistic infections and had low CD4 counts (a type of white blood cell that fights infection), the level of which in the blood serves as an indication of when to start Anti-RetroViral (ARV) treatment. Opportunistic infections may lead to AIDS (defined as the development of five opportunistic infections) and eventually to death.

The side effects of ARVs on the body of a child are severe and violent. They include diarrhea (resulting in dehydration), poor absorption of nutrients and drugs, weight loss and fatigue, nausea, headaches, rashes, lipid abnormalities and lipodystrophy (losing or gaining body fat). Lipodystrophy is often disfiguring and stigmatizing. It can result in sunken cheeks, prominent veins on the limbs, shrunken buttocks, the appearance of breasts in boys and of prominent bellies in girls. In India, the Stavudine drug was until recently systematically given to children and adults living with HIV as it is locally produced, despite its strong and long-lasting deformative side effects. In 2010 the WHO recommended the phasing out of Stavudine because of its known side effects, and in 2012 the Indian National Aids Control Organization filed an affidavit in the Supreme Court phasing out the use of the drug following a petition to the Supreme Court by a group of NGOs and patients (Anand 2012). Many of the children at the residential institution in India below were taking Stavudine.

There are also many side effects that have not been assessed but are frequent such as bad headaches and terrible nightmares. In the case of children, it is particularly difficult to assess whether these manifestations are the result of the side effect of the drugs or caused by other reasons such as psychological distress or simply not wanting to go to school. Nightmares can be problematic in children who then fear bedtime; this was particularly true for one of the girls in the Indian residential care institution who had problems at school but was also on medication – the identified side effects of which include bad headaches and nightmares.

Children living with HIV need to undergo regular blood tests, check-ups, scans and so on. Their frequent sicknesses cause them to miss out on school and to need regular hospital visits, which can be a burden on their carers and single them out as being different. At least three of the children in the Indian residential care home were sick every other week and missed out on school as a result. In Ivory Coast, a young girl was sent home by her teacher who ignored her HIV status and thought she had a contagious skin disease. She was asked to come back after it got cured. Her rash had been present for eight months and had still not cleared up at the time of the interview.

Many children do not want to take their medicine as they are made to understand that they have to take it everyday for their whole lives. ARV timing and dosage are of critical importance – failure to respect a strict treatment regime (e.g., at the same hour everyday, before or after eating depending on the drugs) can lead to the development of resistance and the failure of the treatment. If the treatment fails, the child can be put on second or third line and beyond treatments, but they are very expensive and not always available in developing countries (this is certainly the case in DRC and Cote d'Ivoire). In India, only the Clinton Foundation provides second-line treatment. As timing is essential, the children within the residential care studied below all take their medicine at the same time across all three countries – usually 6 am and 6 pm, before and after school. The same has been observed in other orphanages.

Access to ARVs – and to preventative treatment (cotrimoxazole) – can be problematic because of difficult access to healthcare centers and potential stock outs. In the state of Bihar, where the Indian residential care home mentioned below is situated, there is a particular concern with ARV shortage and corrupt health staff who ask patients to pay for the drugs which are given for free by the State.

In addition to the physical trauma caused by the medication and the related emotional violence from not knowing or understanding why they are ill, children experience social violence in the medical environment from doctors, surgeons, nurses and health workers (Deacon and Stephney 2007). HIV-related stigma among health practitioners is surprisingly still high. Those who should know best are often perpetrators of unequal treatment and prejudicial attitudes. In DRC and in India, breach of confidentiality is often an issue. The HIV status of some of the children in residential care had openly been revealed in waiting areas. Some doctors had refused to examine or operate on them for fear of HIV transmission. Nurses had avoided touching them or had talked to them in a rude and aggressive manner to keep them at bay. Some children had witnessed workers whispering about them 'this one has AIDS'. Others have been shouted at for not having taken their medicine as prescribed, generating strong feelings of guilt and poor self-esteem. Negative staff attitudes have also been described by Yeap et al. (2010) as being an important factor influencing the uptake of HIV care and treatment among children.

Defining residential care, extended families and reasons for placement of HIV-positive children

Residential care is defined as 'places of safety for emergency care, transit centres in emergency situations, and all other forms of short and long-term residential care facilities, including group homes' (UN 2010: Article29a[iv]). This definition goes beyond the term orphanages and includes places called children's villages. In the present study, all three residential care homes call themselves Children's Homes or 'One Stop Centres'.

According to Deacon and Stephney (2007), orphans are more likely to be older and poorer than other children and are more likely to be in households with non-biological caregivers and of course are dealing with the psychosocial impact of the death of their parents.

The majority of the children placed in the institutions described below have lost both of their parents to AIDS-related illnesses or were abandoned at birth. Only a very small proportion of them still have their fathers, and where they do, the fathers are either too sick to care for them or have abandoned their family when the mother started to show signs of sickness. The children are therefore all orphans who were either directly referred to the centers of the present study or were placed in extended families who could not cope.

Abadıa-Barrero and Castro (2006) argue that the HIV-affected children they studied in residential care homes in Brazil encounter several types of discrimination: being orphans, living in an institution, living with HIV, racism and coming from poor families. Children in the residential care discussed in this chapter also have to face similar multiple stigmas, including poverty, orphanhood, living in institutions, gender discrimination, HIV status and being from a low caste or minority ethnic group.

Children end up in residential care homes for multiple reasons. Abandoned children with no known extended family are referred there by various institutions, as described below. In the case of children with family, several scenarios have been observed including children being moved from one household to another with little life stability (Ford and Hosegood 2005), which has an impact on their treatment uptake, on their education and on their emotional stability (Hejoaka 2014).

However, in the three places studied below, the main reason for children's placement was a mix of HIV-related status implications (e.g., secrecy within the family, ignorance around HIV transmission, inability to cope with medical appointments) and overburdened families struggling with poverty, unemployment, alcohol abuse, promiscuity and so on. In most cases, children arrive in these centers critically ill and emotionally disturbed. Many have lived on the street, undergone violence, neglect and abuse in previous places where they lived. Others are placed in the care homes due to fear of violence in case their HIV status is discovered within the extended family.

This is similar to the experience of other care homes – for example, in Brazil Abadıa-Barrero and Castro (2006) found that the majority of AIDS-affected children in care homes reported 'various forms of physical and emotional violence such as neglect, abuse, mistreatment or abandonment'. In Morantz and Heymann's (2010) work on institutional care homes in Botswana, the reasons for placement of HIV-affected children were – in order of priority – orphanhood, neglect, poor health of parents, access to education, destitution, abandonment, abuse and illness.

The WHO (2002) indicates that a child's vulnerability to violence can be increased when she or he is raised by a single parent or by very young parents. This is frequently the case for children affected by HIV. Other risk factors are household overcrowding and the presence of other violent relationships in the home. It is also suggested that child abuse is related to poverty and to the lack of 'social capital' or social networks that can protect children. In the case of HIV, this is particularly true since families tend to remain hidden due to fear of HIV-associated stigma.

Desmond (2009) identifies six components which are key to assess the level of family care for AIDS-affected children. These are intentions (which can be altered by gender, age and other forms of discrimination), power relationships, human resources, financial resources, bonds and access to services. These six aspects are reflected in the difficulties cited by extended families when placing children in the residential care homes described below.

Once the status of the child has been known by other members of the family or of non-HIV-specialized institutions, children are reported being discriminated against, having to eat from separate plates, being laughed at, abused, blamed, having heavier workloads and being generally neglected. This is also described by Deacon and Stephney (2007) in the literature they reviewed. They describe children having to endure the 'provision of separate eating utensils, isolation from other members of the household, greater expectations of work contributions, and lack of care, emotional support and attention' (2007, 31). This situation is partly explained by the great poverty in which these households live (Deacon and Stephney 2007). Poverty is a factor identified as a constant stressor in children's vulnerability (Akwara et al. 2010). Abadıa-Barrero and Castro (2006) argue that economic and social stress are the main convector of HIV-related violence within extended families, which is why it is important to look at stigma through a structural violence lens. In the context of this chapter, this is all the more relevant given that most children placed in the residential care below are from poor and crowded family homes.

The three case studies that follow show how, in the context of HIV, stigma is the starting point for community-based violence. Indeed, children living in extended families are at risk of abuse such as aggravated punishments, physical abuse, overload in domestic tasks, internal competition with children of a similar age and having food withheld (West and Wedgewood 2006).

Three countries were chosen as case studies for this chapter: two postwar African francophone ones and one in Asia. This comparative framework is useful since most HIV best practice is rooted in African experiences (Delpeu 2011). What emerges from the study is that despite differences in culture, location, language and governance, orphans living with HIV tend to face similar situations and challenges.

DRC, orphans and community violence

The DRC is one of the world's poorest countries and is coming out of one of the deadliest conflicts since World War II. Women and children have been particularly affected: sexual violence has been used as a weapon of war by armed groups, and children were enrolled not only as soldiers but also as porters, spies and sex slaves. There are an estimated 40,000 children living and working on the streets – one-third of them are orphans (MINAS 2009).

HIV is a major social issue. The 2007 United Nations General Assembly Special Sessions National Monitoring Report estimated that over a million adults in DRC are living with HIV, including 142,970 pregnant women and 110,120 children under 14 years (IFRC 2009). AIDS is the leading cause of death in the working age group 20–49 years. It impoverishes families and decimates the labor force. The DRC has a very religious social framework, which is often judgmental and in which discussions about sex and sexuality are generally taboo. The level of stigma is extremely high, pushing people to remain underground and to go through their HIV diagnosis in secrecy and total isolation.

I obtained data on the placement of orphans living with HIV in DRC as I worked there as a consultant for a project caring for children affected by HIV. In this capacity, I was able to interview mothers living with HIV, their children, social workers and people from relevant ministries who all testified as to the level of HIV-related community violence against children. This violence is characterized by religious, emotional and physical abuse. Most orphans I met lived in extended families in small overcrowded dwellings. Alcohol use and unemployment are common. All these factors contribute to the state of neglect in which orphans are being raised. Children who were still living with their mothers were living in extreme poverty, often on the street. All children, particularly those living with HIV, reported episodes of verbal abuse and accusations of witchcraft.

Data were also collected through a priest (who is a well-known psychologist) who had campaigned with another Catholic sister activist, Sister Isabelle Tschipulula, against child abuse in religious contexts, for example accusations of child witchcraft, child exorcism and institutionalization, all perpetrated by self-appointed priests. Sister Isabelle set up a one stop center for street children called La Samaritaine, which is a Catholic orphanage managed by the congregation of the Sisters of Saint-Teresa of the Child Jesus in Kinshasa (Ndjili district). The orphanage takes only girls, most of whom have lived on the street. Their approach is to try to reintegrate them socially and to reconcile them with their families.

Many of the children brought to La Samaritaine are orphans of parents who have died of AIDS-related illnesses. In the case of children themselves living with HIV, they are referred to the Sisters of Calcutta (Teresa of Calcutta) in Kinshasa – an institution specializing in the care of children living with HIV, which provides medical care, school access, nutrition and emotional support.

This section contextualizes the type of community violence that surrounds the orphans brought to the Sisters of Calcutta's orphanage. The information on the orphanage was gathered by means of phone and email conversations.

The Sister's of Calcutta's orphanage is called Don de Marie (Mary's gift) and was set up in 2004, initially to care for the poorest and those rejected by society. There are about 40 children, most of them HIV positive and aged between four months and 13 years. The children are brought to the orphanage by community members, police, other orphanages and by parents for temporary care. They are brought because they have mental or physical disabilities or because they are sick with malnutrition, tuberculosis and other AIDS-related illnesses. Most of them have been accused of witchcraft and have been ill-treated for that reason. They arrive in poor physical condition with low CD4 counts, skin diseases and other infections. The type of community violence observed here is therefore predominantly neglect, abandonment and abuse.

Accusations of witchcraft are officially banned by the law. Most children and parents interviewed explained that orphans are often feared because it is believed that parents have died of supernatural causes and that a child who has prematurely lost his or her parents is responsible for their death and is therefore a witch. Members of the extended family are usually the first ones to blame children for the death of their parents, and sometimes parents themselves will accuse their own children of practicing witchcraft. Adults fear that the child might cast a spell on another member of the family, putting anyone in contact with the child at risk of death.

The situation is worse in the case of children living with HIV and having lost at least one parent. In addition to almost certainly being branded as witches, they face HIV-related stigma as described above. Lukela from RNOAC (a national network of community organizations of people living with HIV) comments that 'Stigma remains high with many people being ostracized by their families after they test positive for HIV, and others turning to churches for "healing", rather than seeking medical help'.

The accepted way to 'treat' a child witch is to place them in the 'hands of God' – a principle which has become a source of gold for New Churches, Sects and Churches of Revival ('Eglises du réveil'). Self-proclaimed pastors, who are often poorly educated, seek financial gain and find ways to put the blame for early death on the weakest – that is, children.

Exorcism has become a very profitable business. Orphans are often locked in a room with no food or drink until they show signs of remorse; they are forced to swallow a toad or chemical products and are only exorcised if they vomit; they are submitted to traumatically loud noises (speakers at high volume) magical prayers; they are accused of almost anything ('you have eaten your mother/your father!'), are forced to dance and are shaken and pushed around late at night among crowds of congregants to encourage them to confess the 'truth' and get the devil out of their bodies. Priests sexually abuse them to 'clean' their bodies and they are often burnt when they keep on denying their pact with the devil. Many children have died this way. A representative of the Ministry of the Family whom I interviewed explained that sometimes families do not even bother to go to Pastors as this can be costly. They formally declare the child a witch, put them in a car tyre, douse them with petrol and set them on fire to get rid of them.

Many churches (including the Jehovah's Witnesses in Kinshasa) also say that they can cure a child of HIV just through intense prayer and that treatments are detrimental to children's health and faith. Many children (and adults) have died as a result.

This is the situation most children who arrive at 'Don de Marie' have faced. They have also often been living on the street before coming to 'Don de Marie'. Discussions conducted with social workers in the field have shown that most children were abandoned and rejected by their own families – most commonly by their stepmothers. Neglect and eventually abandonment of orphans by their extended families is a frequent type of violence that has to be faced in Don de Marie. Family reconciliation is a real challenge and there is no actionable legal basis to support children.

Community workers reported in interviews that the loss of 'traditional African family values' (see Dahl 2009 for similar claims made in Botswana), poverty, over-crowding (families often live all together in one or maximum two rooms) and the rise in alcohol use explain why children affected by HIV and placed in extended families are often abused, exploited as servants, beaten up and verbally abused. This point was also mentioned in the MINAS (2009) report that indicates that the average size of Congo households is 5.4, two-thirds live in a three-room dwelling and 15 percent of households care for orphans. Many orphans reported being discriminated against, being treated differently from the biological children of the family, especially with regards to access to food or basic social services. This behavior is accentuated with regard to children whose parents died of AIDS.

Extended families often refuse to take responsibility for children, as their own economic situation is often already too precarious. Children who are abandoned or rejected end up living on the streets having to steal and to join local gangs to be able to survive.

Sister Isabelle Tschipulula says that many street children were actually born on the street and are descendents of parents, sometimes even grandparents who grew up on the street. Their physical environment is very insecure. They sleep under stalls on market places if they can, get high on *bangi* (cannabis) and drink cheap alcohol sold in plastic bags. Many children brought to both orphanages were raped by guards employed to protect the streets, exploited by small businesses for a plate of food and were regularly sexually abused at night.

Don de Marie provides medical care, food, spiritual support through talks and conferences and psychological help where appropriate. The ultimate aim is to make children feel loved and accepted. As in other orphanages, most children have been badly abused and have faced all sorts of trauma including being regularly beaten up, deprived of food and shelter and so on. This violence is often replicated between the children. Rebellion, bad habits and lack of confidence are common behaviors.

The orphanage receives little support from other organizations. Their only partner is Medicins San Frontiers (MSF), which provides adequate medical and psychosocial support. There are about ten staff who do not have specific training but are being taught to act as mothers to the children. Some of the staff are also people living with HIV. The children all attend school, though many of them are underachieving because of the trauma they have experienced.

The biggest challenges anticipated for the children in the future are difficulties in finding a partner, in forming a family and in finding a job. These are common worries for children living with HIV throughout the world. The orphanage insists on providing love and understanding – another common point of importance for institutions caring for children living with HIV as described below.

Côte d'Ivoire (Ivory Coast)

Long regarded as one of the most stable and prosperous countries in Africa, Côte d'Ivoire suddenly fell into political disarray on the death of its President of thirty years, Felix Houphouet, in 1993. The 1999 military coup led to further political confusion and a rise in violence, which slowly turned into ethnic and religious divisions dividing the country between the rebel-occupied north and the south. Elections were finally organized in 2011 after ten years of military disorder and led to contested results with two presidents in power. After several months of military turmoil in which France took an active part, the preexisting president was deposed. The country remains politically and socially fragile.

Ivory Coast has for much of its recent history been an economic magnet attracting various international businesses, regional migrants and sex workers from neighboring countries (Liberia and Ghana), and it has been particularly affected by HIV. Côte d'Ivoire has one of the highest HIV prevalence rates in West Africa – with an estimated 3.4 percent of adults living with HIV in 2009 (UNAIDS/WHO) and 440,000 children orphaned to AIDS, out of which 63,000 are living with HIV. Its epidemiological context is marked by high prevalence among exacerbated by an increase in post-conflict sexual violence.

Chigata is a center that takes in orphans living with HIV rejected by their extended families. Chigata is not really recognized as a case for good practice because of its emphasis on children living with HIV (as opposed to HIV-positive and HIV-negative children living together). However, as it was set up by a group of women living with HIV, it could be described as an example of international good practice since the involvement of people (especially women) living with HIV in HIV programs is a key principle.

It is located in one of the most politically heated, poor and highly populated districts of Abidjan called Yopougon. Though it serves as a residential care center for abandoned children, it also closely works with adults living with HIV – for example through support groups to address stigmatization, disclosure, treatment adherence and confidentiality issues.

Data were collected as I was working in Abidjan as an HIV consultant. I visited the center, interviewed the manager and one of the women who set it up, spoke with the carers – some of whom also live with HIV – and with the HIV pediatrician at the local hospital where the children go for consultations.

The center is a house which has been transformed into an office and a community center, together with a small dwelling at the back where the children live. It is extremely simple. I was struck by the poverty of the place. The children sleep on simple mattress on the floor. There are no wardrobes or any child-friendly decoration or items, the walls are bland and old. The bathrooms are extremely basic. The children watch the television in the courtyard; there is a garden with many games but the atmosphere is simple and quite familial. Children were not interviewed, as it would have been too sensitive given that they did not know me.

Chigata organizes regular and discreet home visits to ensure that people living with HIV are well integrated and are in a caring environment. Through these home visits they have identified that children living with HIV are often extremely stigmatized – having separate dishes, bedding, clothes and so on – and are left alone to take their medicines. One of Chigata's roles is to address this situation and explain actual modes of HIV transmission.

Abandonment is frequent. Many children are referred to Chigata by other orphanages or state institutions for children that fear HIV transmission. Cases of children placed in adoptive families, which then refuse to keep them when they learn about their HIV status, are quite widespread. Chigata mentions the case of a four-year-old girl who was abandoned at birth, placed in an institution that had to close down, then placed in a fostering family that gave her their family names, then placed in a second fostering family who abandoned her when she started to develop opportunistic infections. Eventually she was placed with Chigata at the age of ten. She is 13 today.

Neglect is another reason why children are cared for by the center. Most children arrive in very poor health. They mostly have CD4 counts below 350 while being already on second-line treatment. The organization tries to avoid relieving families of their responsibility for children and often refuses to take on children, favoring a home visit support system so that the children are kept in their home environment. But there are situations where not taking a child in results in the death of the child. Whenever the children are well enough, they are then put back into their family environment.

Chigata gives the example of a grandmother who had to travel out of Abidjan and did not know where to put her grandchild while she was away. The child should have been kept a month only, but the team realized that his foot was nearly rotten and that he had a high fever. He was taken into hospital. The grandmother came back in the first few months to check on her grandson and then disappeared. This kind of abandonment is quite frequent.

Another example of neglect of responsibility is the case of a child whose mother had died and whose father could not reconcile working hours with hospital visits. The child was in such poor condition that Chigata agreed to take care of him, especially since the father seemed genuinely overwhelmed but of good will. The child stayed three years at Chigata and then went back into his family but then the father came to ask again for help. Chigata found out that the father had remarried and was refusing to accept his responsibilities. The solution chosen was to provide organizational support and sibling involvement through home visits. Though these situations are frequent and seem sensible, the actual well-being of the child and the trauma this rejection represents can be a source of difficulties and self-recrimination.

In addition, many children who come to stay for school breaks in the center then refuse to return to their own families. Many relate that they have been beaten up, insulted and accused of witchcraft. As in DRC, problems frequently occur when one of the parents has remarried. Cases of violence between children happen, but it has been identified that it is usually linked to the fact that the family slowly disengages with them and does not care for them after some time.

Most children at Chigata come from poor families, not exclusively from Abidjan but also from all over the country. Most of the children are girls. All of them attend school and benefit from home support. The organization works closely with the local hospital. Many children are abandoned by their village as there are low levels of literacy and little education on HIV in rural environments.

In the case of children living with HIV, difficulties stem from neglect and displacement. Accusations of child witchcraft also exist, although not with the same prevalence as in DRC. Since the war, there has been a renewal of New Churches and Revivalist Churches.

It is not rare that children are accused of having killed their parents, are feared, rejected and abandoned in religious centers where they will be deprived of medicine and food. Chigata gives the example of a child whose only carer was an aunt who eventually died leaving him in the responsibility of his two uncles who refused to care for him – one for financial reasons and the second for fear of HIV transmission. The child was placed in a prayer center where he remained for one year without any treatment before Chigata heard of him. He is now on second-line treatment and is developing tuberculosis and other opportunistic infections. In these cases, the Church denies responsibility and blames it on various spiritual reasons. There is no way to use the law against them.

Another important aspect described as being detrimental to the child is the lack of disclosure of their HIV status. The doctor interviewed at the local hospital explained that often adults do not know how to talk about HIV with young children and fear the child's traumatic response. Yeap et al. (2010) confirm that the main reason for children to refuse to take their medicine is that they do not understand why they are taking it, which leads to treatment adherence issues and ultimately challenges the health of the children.

In reality, not knowing about their own HIV status can be more traumatic for children as they tend to imagine all sorts of bad reasons for their illnesses and often develop feelings of guilt and low self-esteem (Abadıa-Barrero and Castro 2006; Deacon and Stephney 2007; Hejoaka 2014). Hejoaka's (2014) study of HIV-positive children's drawings reveals the social isolation and the negative images children have of themselves and of their parents' illnesses. She also describes the violence of children's suspicion of their own HIV status through their symptoms (especially skin rashes), their daily pill taking and the 'witnessing of revealing facts' by which adults speak about HIV around the child as if they were not present. This suspicion leads to misconceptions and guilt, to uncertainty and further secrecy and gives the impression that the child is 'growing up in the shadow of death and stigma' (Hejoaka 2014).

Similar drawings, self-deprecating writings in personal notebooks, auto stigmatization and the issue of suspicion were also witnessed at Chigata. Interestingly, as in Hejoaka's study (2014), while children suspect their own status, they pretend not to be aware of it and live in secrecy; all of which has further deteriorating consequences on the child's psychological balance and isolation.

Hejoaka (2014) also describes how HIV disclosure – usually by a non-biological caregiver – can be violent and emotionally disruptive to the child. Violent words, often referring to death, are used to encourage the child to take their medicine, both by caregivers and by healthcare staff. The Director of the center related how many of the children had been threatened by their families to take their pills on a regular basis and told they 'were going to die' if they did not. Chigata worked with psychologists to explain to the children what HIV is, how it is transmitted and why it is important to take the treatment. The organization makes a point that all children staying in their care know their HIV status. As some of the carers are also HIV positive, the children identify themselves with adults in good health, which brings them psychological health benefits.

The war has also had a strong impact on the children. For those who stayed at Chigata, it has been quite traumatic because they witnessed home searches, night robberies, gunfire and street violence. They often draw armed men in their pictures; they fear men in uniform and jump whenever they hear a noise. The district of Yopougon was particularly affected during the war.

A year after visiting the center, I had the opportunity to talk with one of the key women activists who set Chigata up. She informed me that she was about to close the center, that she could not pay the rent anymore, that she had placed most of the orphans in foster families – all except two whom she was worried about – and had received indirect pressure from major donors through the government to stop her activity, as it was making HIV workers uneasy. She herself had concerns:

> I'm not sure what we did was good, maybe we could have done it differently as some of our children have been stigmatised because they were identified as being in the 'AIDS place'. The ministries contradict themselves: on the one hand they say maybe children should be left in their families, and on the other they say you are doing a wonderful job. They also say orphans should stay in other general orphanages where AIDS is not identified but in reality those orphanages do not want to take in children living with HIV. What will happen now to those that no one wants to care about? I'm also worried for all the children we had. What they miss the most is love. Families need a lot of support and counselling.

India

While DRC and Ivory Coast are regarded as high-prevalence countries because of the high percentage rate of people living with HIV, India is perceived as a low-prevalence country with a HIV rate of 0.30 percent. Yet, because of the size of its population, India is effectively the third country most affected by HIV worldwide with 2.39 million people affected – 39 percent female and 3.5 percent children. Its epidemic is highly concentrated among truck drivers, migrant laborers, sex workers, men who have sex with men, injecting drug users and pregnant women.

India is also the country that saved generations and allowed a real democratization of health in developing countries, particularly in Africa, through the creation of generic drugs in the late 1990s.

As India faces a high level of poverty, the fate of orphans and vulnerable children is often left to 'the will of the Gods'. However, there is a proliferation of orphanages caring specifically for HIV-positive children. Among them, Naz Foundation in Delhi is particularly well known because it is international and fights for the rights of people living with HIV as well as addressing gay and transgender issues in India.

This chapter looks primarily at the work of the Tara Children's Project (TCP), a Buddhist residential care home for orphans and vulnerable children based in Bihar, which works in close partnership with Naz Foundation.

Bihar is one of the poorest states of India with 46 percent of its population living on the equivalent of 26 US cents per day. The state is characterized by poor infrastructure, high rates of poverty and illiteracy. A large male migrant labor force means that HIV is often brought back to wives and children.

I have been able to observe that the situation of the children at TCP is very similar to that of other orphanages specializing in the care of children living with HIV around India – for example, in Delhi, district of Bagalkot, Tamil Nadu and Kerala – and in fact, the rest of the world according to conversations with colleagues working in this area. I worked as a project manager of the center for a period of about two years and lived there with the children and the carers during several months. The account which follows is drawn from my observations, training of local staff and conversations with the children and families over this period.

In 1991, Root Institute – the Buddhist organization behind the project – started a Home for the Destitute, which gradually evolved into the Shakyamuni Buddha clinic. Today, the clinic runs a very dynamic healthcare program with gynaecology, physiotherapy, HIV counselling and health education. It has a special emphasis on gender issues. The clinic started to work with HIV-positive patients in 1995. It reaches out to hundreds of patients on a daily basis, both on its premises and through a mobile clinic that offers health services to six rural centers.

The TCP was conceived as they came to identify, through the work of the clinic, the needs of local children affected by HIV: in 2009, a five year-old girl was brought in by her extended family after her parents had died after a car accident. Her father, a migrant worker, had been diagnosed with AIDS in hospital before he passed away. The child was also found to be HIV positive. Her extended family did not want to look after her, and she had never been to school. From that beginning, the TCP grew.

The philosophy of the TCP is based on Buddhist-derived principles and values. On a day-to-day basis, the children are taught to live by the Six Guidelines given by the Tibetan Lama who inspired the TCP: to practice Kindness, Patience, Forgiveness, Courage, Rejoicing and Apologizing.

The carers are poor women from local villages, widows, HIV-positive mothers and abandoned mothers. The TCP tries to provide them with education and financial support so they can in turn support their families.

There are almost no organizations working on HIV in the region because Bihar has not been identified as a high HIV prevalence state. This is a mistake given that migrants regularly migrate to and return from urban centers where HIV is predominant.

There are no other care homes in Bihar for children affected by HIV. The aim is to provide love, medical and educational support, ensuring that all the children are not discriminated against and are integrated into the mainstream society. All the children attend school locally and are provided with uniforms, materials for school and additional after-school tuition and activities.

Children who arrive in TCP are in extremely poor health. Their CD4 counts are generally much lower than the standard for starting an ARV treatment, they have started developing opportunistic infections and they are undernourished. Most of the children are from local rural families who are too poor to support them. All of them have lost their mothers, some still have their father who is often in too poor a condition to care for them (e.g., suffering from AIDS, alcoholism or behavioral problems) or they have itinerant jobs, such as driving trucks. Many of the children have been referred by other orphanages who felt that they did not have the capacity to care for them.

The children brought to the residential home have undergone at least one if not all aspects of social violence as defined by WHO: neglect, emotional and physical ill-treatment, sexual abuse and commercial exploitation. They have also had to endure the physical trauma of living with HIV.

Neglect is immediately visible given the poor condition of health and hygiene that the children arrive with. Most children show signs of physical violence from previous orphanages, street life or from their families. It manifests in the way they interact with each other, often with fists and verbal abuse before any other means of communication.

The words they use and their attitude clearly reflects that of adults. Some children have severe burn scars on their skin and other physical damage (loss of hearing, head traumas) that leave no doubt about the type of abuse they have been through. It is often coupled with worrying behaviors such as wanting to tie up other children, playing dangerous games, having sudden mood changes, hiding and eating inedible materials (tree leaves, stones or earth).

Sexual abuse can also be detected in the way the children play together – wanting to introduce objects into each others' genitals, inappropriately touching people's intimate parts or sudden and unexpected changes in behavior.

Many children show signs of street life and emotional distress by trying to steal anything – sometimes even food. Emotional blackmail is quite frequent: testing the carers to see how far they can go, threatening to kill themselves just to get a hug, running away to then hide by the main gate so that they can easily be found. Pushing adults' limits to ensure that people care for them are classic signs of fear of abandonment and the need for emotional reassurance.

Some of the challenges the orphanage has had to deal with are discipline (corporal punishment is forbidden which has created some issues for the staff who are culturally used to managing children through hitting); lack of knowledge about HIV-related issues; providing children with important values such as mutual respect; giving support to the staff and teaching them how to intervene and address the underlying issues every time a climate of tension, fighting and bullying arises; children's psychological support and counselling (it is hard to find competent psychologists in India, all the more so in a poor and rural state like Bihar); and HIV disclosure to the children.

In trying to assess how much the children knew about their medical status, the center came to realize that many had been stigmatized and had a total misconception of AIDS. A young HIV-positive girl explained that her HIV-negative sister had explained to her that she could 'contaminate' anyone through her mouth and the air people were breathing around her. For that reason she had always acted in a very shy manner, constantly protecting her mouth.

Misconceptions about AIDS are quite strong in India, especially in rural areas such as Bihar. Medical staff can be very ignorant and disrespectful, especially with regards to confidentiality of HIV status. The nurse or even the secretary in a clinic will publicly identify a patient by their HIV status: 'you, you are HIV-positive, no? Come here'. The Gaya ART center, on which the TCP depends, has a particularly bad reputation for corruption and neglect.

All the children at the TCP were abandoned primarily because of their HIV status. Some were abandoned in their cradles at train stations or police stations; others were left in orphanages by their extended families after both parents had died without giving any information on their background. For those who are brought to the orphanage by their extended families, background information is thoroughly documented, particularly as regards inheritance and land ownership, as sending a child to an institution can be a way for the other members of the family to get hold of the child's parents' wealth, especially in the case of boys.

The person who brings the child to the TCP is usually the only person who really cares for the child, an aunt or a grandmother but has no way of keeping the child with them, either because they fear that their husband, who is already cruel to the child, might find out about the child's HIV status or they are themselves too old to care for them. It also happens that families identify that the child will be better off in the TCP because they will have access to schooling, good nutrition and a better chance to get on with their lives. TCP refuses children on these criteria and only takes in those who would otherwise die because of neglect and important stigma.

Although there are many challenging issues within the TCP, there is no doubt that, as in DRC and Côte d'Ivoire, if they had not taken in these children, the children would not have survived.

Children would queue and wait for their turn to take their medicine, although efforts are regularly made to make this moment fun. It is a stressful moment for all: for children who are reluctant to take their medicines and for caretakers who are afraid of missing out on a child and sometimes need to run around to look for those missing. While this 'med time' might seem extreme, it ensures that children take their medicines in the prescribed regime to keep them healthy.

In addition, regular checks are conducted to ensure children are adhering to their treatment. In TCP it had been noted that at one point at least five children were developing resistance to their treatment. After investigation, it turned out that a rumor had been circulated saying that pills were making them ill. This served as an opportunity to talk about medicine, what they were for and their importance. This miscommunication issue has often been noticed in other residential care institutions (Abadıa-Barrero and Castro 2006). This is also due to the fact that most residential care workers learn as they go since no particular guidance is in place to support them.

Conclusion

There is little knowledge about what is happening within residential institutions caring for children affected by HIV. While most literature focuses on the reasons why children should not be placed in institutional care homes, little research has been conducted on the reasons why children have ended up there. Understanding the underlying reasons for abandonment and neglect of orphans living with HIV is key for appropriate HIV programing in communities.

It has been shown in this chapter that the reasons for abandonment and neglect from extended families are essentially structural: poverty, unemployment, lack of education, overcrowded houses and so on. In addition to these structural causes, families have to manage the stigma still associated with AIDS and the specific challenges of caring for children who are HIV affected – for example, demanding treatment regimes, caring for one's health, grief and low self-esteem. These are explosive factors contributing toward self-directed, collective and interpersonal violence.

Another important point of this study was to document the level of violence orphans living with HIV can face so that additional information and HIV-relevant support can be brought to families and to the children themselves. The ideal situation is that children could stop living in secrecy and could be provided with all the medical and psychological support they might need.

This chapter did not seek to demonstrate that children are better off without their families or communities, nor to encourage their placement into residential institutions. It simply describes a situation whereby children are rejected by their kin who cannot provide for their health needs, and the fact that these children end being cared for in institutions. That this care is often given by women living with HIV and is not supported by public funds is of relevance in the context of international HIV programing. While these institutions are being overlooked by the international community, there are nonetheless providing care and protecting children from violence on an ongoing basis.

Bibliography

Abadıa-Barrero, C. and Castro, A. (2006) Experiences of Stigma and Access to HAART in Children and Adolescents Living with HIV/AIDS in Brazil. *Social Science & Medicine*, 62, 1219–1228.

Akwara, P. A., Noubary, B., Ah Ken, P. l., Johnson, K., Yates, R., Winfrey, W., Chandan, U. K., Mulenga, D., Kolker, J. and Luo, C. (2010) Who is the Vulnerable Child? Using Survey Data to Identify Children at Risk in the Era of HIV and AIDS. *AIDS care*, 22 (9), 1066–1085.

Anand, U. (2012) Safer Anti-HIV Drugs to Replace Stavudine. *The Indian Express*. 4 September 2012. http://www.indianexpress.com.

Anglin, J. P. and Knorth, E. J. (2004) Competing Declarations on Residential Care for Children and Youth – Stockholm Versus Malmö. *Special Issue on International Perspectives on Rethinking Residential Care, Child and Youth Care Forum*, 33 (3), 139–235.

Bourgois, P. (1998) Families and Children in the U.S. Inner City. In N. Scheper-Hughes and C. Sargent (eds.) *Small Wars: The Cultural Politicsof Childhood*. Berkeley: University of California Press, pp. 331–351.

Bourgois, P. (2003a) *Search of Respect: Selling Crack in El Barrio*. 2nd edition. Cambridge: Cambridge University Press.

Bourgois, P. (2003b) Crack and the Political Economy of Social Suffering. *Addiction Research and Theory*, 11 (1), 31–37.

Butchart A. et al. (2006) *Preventing Child Maltreatment: A Guide to Taking Action and Generating Evidence*. Geneva: WHO and International Society for the Prevention of Child Abuse and Neglect.

Chase, E. and Aggleton, P. (2001) *Stigma, HIV/AIDS and Prevention of Mother-to-Child Transmission: A Pilot Study in Zambia, India, Ukraine and Burkina Faso*. UK: UNICEF/Panos Institute.

Dahl, B. (2009) The 'Failures of Culture': Christianity, Kinship, and Moral Discourses about Orphans during Botswana's AIDS Crisis. *Africa Today*, 56 (1), 23–43.

Deacon, H. and Stephney, I. (2007) *HIV/AIDS, Stigma and Children: A Literature Review*. Cape Town, South Africa: HSRC Press.

De Baets, A. J. et al. (2008) The Unique Features of Pediatric HIV-1 in Sub-Saharan Africa. *Current HIV Research*, 6 (4), 351–362.

Delpeu, M. (2011) Prendre en charge les enfants affectés par le VIH/sida en Inde du Sud: recommandations internationales et pratiques locales, In F. Eboko, F. Bourdier, and C. Broqual (eds.) *Les Suds Face au Sida*, Marseile: IRD Éditions Institut de Recherche pour le Developpement, Collection Objectifs Suds Marseille, pp. 179–204.

Desmond, C. (2009) Consequences of HIV for Children: Avoidable or Inevitable? *AIDS Care* 21(S1), 98–104.

Farmer, P. (2003) *Pathologies of Power: Health, Human Rights, and the New War on the Poor*. Berkeley: University of California Press.

Ford, K. and Hosegood, V. (2005) AIDS Mortality and the Mobility of Children in KwaZulu-Natal, South Africa. *Demography*, 42, 757–768.

Green, L. (1999) *Fear as a Way of Life: Mayan Widows in Rural Guatemala*. New York: Columbia University Press.

Hale, F. and Vasquez, M. (2011) *Violence against Women Living with HIV/AIDS: A Background Paper*. Washington, D.C.: Development Connections and the International Community of Women Living with HIV and AIDS (ICW Global).

Hejoaka, F. (Forthcoming, 2014) Chronicles of Suspicion in Time of AIDS: Ethnographic Perspectives on the Grey Zone of HIV Disclosure to Children and Adolescents in Burkina Faso. In M. Skovdal and S. K. Belton (eds.) *Children and Youth Services Review, Special Issue: Supportive Community Contexts for Children and Youths Growing up with HIV in Africa*.

IFRC (2009) *Plan 2010–2011 Democratic Republic of Congo*.

Knorth et al. (2007) Under One Roof: A Review and Selective Meta-Analysis on the Outcomes of Residential Child and Youth Care. *Children and Youth Services Review*, 30 (2008), 123–140.

Krug, E. G. et al. (eds.) (2002) *World Report on Violence and Health*. Geneva: World Health Organization.

Lockhart, C. (2008) Everyday Violence in the Time of AIDS: The Life and Death of a Street Boy in East Africa. *Medical Anthropology Quarterly*, 2 (1), 94–115.

Mann, G. et al. (2012) *Children Living with and Affected by HIV in Residential Care, Desk-based Research*. Everychild/Maestral International/UNICEF.

Meintjes, H. and Pinkerton, J. (2011) *Home Truths: HIV, Residential Care and Family Support for Children in South Africa*. Keynote at the Protecting Children through Family Support Conference, Child and Family Research Centre, National University of Ireland, Galway, 16 June 2011.

Ministry of Social Affairs, Humanitarian Action and National Solidarity (2009) *2010–2014 National Action Plan for Orphans and Vulnerable Children in DRC*. MINAS/UNICEF/USAID/PNMLS/Futures.

Morantz, G. and Heymann, J. (2010) Life in Institutional Care: The Voices of Children in a Residential Facility in Botswana. *AIDS Care: Psychological and Socio-medical Aspects of AIDS/HIV*, 22 (1), 10–16.

OAU (1999) *African Charter on the Rights and Welfare of the Child*. Monrovia: Organisation of African Unity.

Parker, R. and Aggleton, P. (2003) HIV and AIDS-Related Stigma and Discrimination: A Conceptual Framework and Implications for Action. *Social Sciences and Medicine* 57, 13–24.

PEPFAR (2012) *Guidance for Orphans and Vulnerable Children Programming*. http://www.pepfar.gov/documents/organization/195702.pdf.

Richter, L. and Norman, A. (2010) AIDS Orphan Tourism: A Threat to Young Children in Residential Care. *Vulnerable Children and Youth Studies: An International Interdisciplinary, Journal for Research, Policy and Care*, 5 (3), 217–229.

Scheper-Hughes, N. (1992) *Death without Weeping: The Violence of Everyday Life in Brazil*. Berkeley: University of California Press.

Smart, R. (2003) *Policies for Orphans and Vulnerable Children: A Framework for Moving Ahead*. Washington: Policy Project, Futures Group.

UN (2010) *Guidelines for the Alternative Care of Children.* http://ap.ohchr.org/documents/dpage_e.aspx?si=A/HRC/11/L.13.

United Nations General Assembly Special Session – UNGASS – (2007) Kinshasa: PNMLS.

UNAIDS (2013) Global Report: UNAIDS Report on the Global AIDS Epidemic 2013.

UNICEF (1989) *Convention on the Rights of the Child.* New York: United Nations.

UNICEF (2006) *Caring for Children Affected by HIV and AIDS.* Florence, Italy: Innocenti Research Centre.

UNICEF (2007) *Enhanced Protection for Children Affected by AIDS.* New York: UNICEF.

UNICEF (2011) *Taking Evidence to Impact: Making a Difference for Vulnerable Children Living in a World with HIV and AIDS.* New York: UNICEF.

UNICEF, UNAIDS, USAID (2004) *Children on the Brink 2004: A Joint Report of New Orphan Estimates and a Framework for Action.* New York: UNICEF.

Van Vilsteren et al. (2011) An Exploratory Study of Psychological and Developmental Issues Facing HIV and AIDS Affected Adolescents Living in a Residential Care Facility. *Journal of Child and Adolescent Mental Health,* 23 (1), 43–51.

von Linstow, M. L., Rosenfeldt, V., Lebech, A. M., Storgaard, M., Hornstrup, T., Katzenstein, T. L., Pedersen, G., Herlin, T., Valerius, N. H., and Weis, N. (2010) Prevention of Mother-to-Child Transmission of HIV in Denmark, 1994–2008. *HIV Med,* 11, 448–456.

Walter, N., Bourgois, P. and Loinaz, M. (2004) Masculinity and Undocumented Labor Migration: Injured Latino Day Laborers in San Francisco. *Social Science and Medicine,* 59(6), 1159–1168.

West, A. and Wedgwood, K. (2006) Children Affected by AIDS: Orphans and Impact Mitigation in China. In Kaufman, J., Kleinman, A. and Saich, T. (eds.). *AIDS and Social Policy in China.* Cambridge, MA: Harvard University Asia Center, pp. 243–264.

Yeap, A. D. et al. (2010) Factors Influencing Uptake of HIV Care and Treatment among Children in South Africa – A Qualitative Study of Caregivers and Clinic Staff. *AIDS Care: Psychological and Socio-Medical Aspects of AIDS/HIV,* 22 (9), 1101–1107.

Part III
Early Childhood

Erica Burman

Treatments of childhood and violence typically start from middle childhood onward, but in this book we begin much earlier in the lifespan. If childhood is typically portrayed as a life period or stage of incompletion and receptivity, then very early childhood – and especially infancy – is recognized as a period of maximal vulnerability and dependence. Babies and young children are intertwined in and dependent upon the lives, habits and habitats of others – their caregivers – and are understood to be most impressionable. Early childhood is also usually perceived as a period of exhibition of and demanding the indulgence or fulfilment of unquestionable, and presumed general, 'needs' – the deprivation of which constitutes significant violence or abuse. It is the intimacy of early childhood contexts that marks its significance and poses both the greatest methodological and ethical problems in terms of both investigation and intervention. It is also what frames the redefinition of violence. The question of how early influences and experiences relate to later outcomes exercises national and international policymakers alike, and – in particular – psychologists are called upon to arbitrate and evaluate the available material. However, the contributions in this book draw on the disciplines of anthropology and education, providing alternative resources for the reconsideration of definitions and approaches to the study of violence.

Chapters 6 and 7 relating to early childhood in this book offer striking contrasts in a number of ways, across institutional and cultural contexts, addressing rather different kinds of violence as well as different chronological periods. Both, however, pose key issues of interpretation as well as intervention. Alma Gottlieb's discussion of the Beng people of Côte d'Ivoire focuses on apparently 'violent' or 'violating' practices of mothers of young babies by force-feeding them with water before breastfeeding them and of administering enemas from the first weeks of the infants' lives (Chapter 6). Such practices could readily evoke pejorative evaluation and condemnation, as certainly qualifying as intimate and unwanted intrusions, but in her sensitive and nuanced exploration Gottlieb situates these practices within the life and labor worlds within which these mothers have to manage. Here questions of securing willing helpers with childcare in contexts of very scarce resources (in terms of payment, clothing, washing and time) help make sense of such practices as maximizing care rather than neglect. This is a challenging chapter which, as Gottlieb suggests, prompts reflection on the nature, the costs and the payoffs of 'violence' in disciplining bodies for a life in society. Gottlieb situates her analysis within wider frames relating to key concerns of this book, around the ways practices of violence articulate the relations between structural, material and interpersonal contexts – from the macroeconomic to the everyday – such that its evaluation requires an understanding of how their intersections moderate and modulate, as well as distribute, definitions and agencies of violence. Key dilemmas come to the fore that illustrate the contingent character and mutual configuration of interests and agencies at issue and that resist easy resolution. Would it not be worse for an infant to be shunned from care or even abandoned, while its mother is working in the fields, because it is 'difficult' and dirty? Where do we locate the violence in contexts of such economic constraints and gendered division of labor?

The rise of rights-based, rather than needs-based, discourses around childhood in International Non Governmental Organizations such as UNICEF has been associated with the shift of focus from under fives to older children. While earlier work focused on reducing infant and child mortality, the shift to focus on those who survived, as well as promoting greater survival rates, imported the discourse of resilience as well as connecting material and economic conditions with psychological ones (see, e.g., Myers, 1992). However, the two chapters on early childhood in this volume illustrate how the interpretation of resilience itself poses interpretive demands to understand contexts of early development better, including moving away from child-focused characteristics to addressing their interactional, social and institutional aspects, including – crucially – the socio-political context of debate in which such actions occur. Moreover, Gottlieb highlights further analytical questions arising from her ethnographic work. For consideration of the practices she documents surely goes beyond mere evaluation of being 'good' or 'bad' but rather invites further exploration of how such early experiences indicate profound cultural shaping of individual personality characteristics that can – she invites us to speculate – be set alongside the cultural attributes of the adult society they will join.

While perhaps we cannot know how such infants experience the violating intrusions into their bodily functions and appetites she discusses, it would appear that – contrary to modern and Western narratives regarding trauma and development – Beng babies grow up to be adults who are peaceful and cooperative in outlook and daily life practice.

Trefor Lloyd's chapter addresses a very different context, one that is perhaps more familiar, albeit nevertheless posing equally urgent questions (Chapter 7). Writing as a practitioner, working with groups of children in British schools, he is concerned with teaching children about conflict and conflict resolution. The focus of intervention here is interpersonal relationships between children in institutional contexts where children are expected to be compliant and cooperative with each other as well as with the staff and structure of the school. Lloyd's account starts by making an important point: that conflict is not necessarily bad and indeed is likely to be inevitable, and therefore the key issue is not to defuse or prevent conflicts (as perhaps teachers would prefer) but rather how best to support children to negotiate and resolve these. Here we see tensions between a whole-school, institutional, perspective that is understandably the focus of teachers and which sees conflict as a problem to be managed, and a skills development approach which works on and with individual children's repertoires and responses via group work. He discusses the current policy context and the theoretical rationale underlying the approach to working with children and young people to make them more aware of their responses to conflict and to widen their range. This is followed by a description of the conflict-resolution program 'Oy you', which he has developed, working with year grade three and four pupils (seven–eight year olds), and some evaluations of areas for further investigation and practice development.

Like Gottlieb, albeit in a very different environment and level of analysis, we see a redefinition of the problem of violence to shift away from the child as its focal or origin point and instead look at relationships and practices. The unspoken context is one of inner city social and intercommunity tensions, where public order and children's behavior come to be linked within a developmental discourse of prevention and early intervention. Lloyd discusses conflict as dynamic and, in particular, attends to gender dynamics – with boys more likely than girls to lack the negotiation skills to manage conflict, which is why his interventions include work with both boys and girls as classroom interventions. He notes the conceptual complexities but crucially how children can be sensitized to the differences between 'being mean' (aggressive) and 'being strong' (assertive). Through such means the children are less likely to resort to violence, and this appears to be because they feel more capable of engaging with conflictual situations with a wider set of responses. Through such child-focused work, we can perhaps begin to disaggregate social agendas of control from those of skills and knowledge development.

Bibliography

Myers, R. G. (1992). *The Twelve Who Survive: Strengthening Programmes of Early Childhood Development in the Third World*. London and New York: Routledge.

6

First Acts of Small Violence: Reflections on Breastfeeding and Enemas in West Africa

Alma Gottlieb

Introduction

In conjuring up acts of violence, many Westerners readily picture guns or other unyielding weapons that allow one person to use force against another – including projectile force (via bullets) or, even more, 'weapons of mass destruction', which have an enormous capacity to produce a great deal of violence with a minimum of effort. When we consider such acts of violence, many of us likewise readily picture strangers as their perpetrators. The government-funded initiative, Drug Abuse Resistance Education (D.A.R.E.) – which is now administered by local police departments in 49 countries – takes as its earliest goal the socialization of young children into fearing strangers as potential perpetrators of drug-motivated violence.[1] Through the program, police officers entering elementary school rooms instruct five-year-old children to shun strangers who might abduct them for unspeakable purposes. Other programs target even younger children for this lesson (Holcombe et al. 1995).

'Don't talk to strangers'; 'Don't get into a car with a stranger'; 'Don't take candy from a stranger' – these lessons become mantras that we hope our young children will memorize and internalize for their own protection. Through initiatives such as D.A.R.E. in post-industrialized and urbanized societies – reinforced by the more informal, daily teachings of parents and other adults – the notion of the *stranger* becomes synonymous with the notion of *danger* in general and *violence* in particular.

But the sociologists recount a different story. For many kinds of violence, it is not strangers but *consociates*, people we know either casually or intimately, who commit the majority of crimes. Statistics in the USA record a slight preponderance of known versus unknown assailants for crimes overall,[2] and this tendency is marked for certain crimes. For example, 'From 1993 to 2008, among homicides reported to the FBI for which the victim-offender relationship was known [by authorities],... between 73% and 79% were committed by offenders known to the victims' (2012). This trend is also highly gendered. For example, in the USA as in many other countries, women who are violently attacked are even more likely to be assaulted by someone they know than are men (US Department of Agriculture n.d.). In the USA, one study revealed that in 2008, 77 percent of all reported rape survivors knew their assailants either as husbands, boyfriends, relatives or dates (Catalano et al. 2009); in the UK, some estimates put the equivalent figure at 85 percent (Rape Crisis [England and Wales] 2012).

Many Westerners would doubtless consider these findings counterintuitive insofar as they challenge the widespread image of the stranger as the epitome of danger and the associated notion of danger as instantiated by strangers (Scott 2003). Yet anthropologist Clifford Geertz instructed us long ago that what passes for 'common sense' is often anything but common, inasmuch as it is constructed by cultural systems of logic that are highly localized (Geertz 1983). Could it be that the notion of strangers as inherently dangerous, and the twin notion of danger as instantiated by strangers, is such a 'common-sense' notion that bears further scrutiny?

In this chapter, I follow Geertz's simple but powerful reminder and destabilize a 'common-sensical' notion of danger by highlighting a very different kind of violence from that with which most Westerners usually associate the term. In fact, I explore acts of violence embedded within a relationship often taken to epitomize the essence of safety and reliability and enacted in the day-to-day lives of two people who normally have an intimate relationship with one another based on trust: the mother–infant duo. Unlike the advanced industrial technologies I have just mentioned, the two kinds of violence we explore in this chapter use simple and seemingly innocent technologies. And both acts are perpetrated by mothers on their babies day in and day out, as required by the dictates of their society, for reasons that we explore.

The Beng

Before we encounter these acts of violence, some brief background is required. The Beng people who form the subject of this chapter are a relatively small and, until the recent civil war, relatively obscure minority ethnic group in the West African nation of Côte d'Ivoire (Ivory Coast).

Subsistence farmers, the Beng, also hunt game in the forest on occasion to supplement their crops with animal protein sources. In a good year, farmers produce a modest surplus of crops that they plant to sell for cash, to buy some necessities (salt, soap, industrially produced cooking oil) as well as the occasional luxury (dried or canned fish, baguettes, candy, cigarettes, jewelry, beer). Yet even considering that they are somewhat self-sufficient, they are a severely impoverished population. Vaccines and other basic preventive care as well as effective Western medicines are rarely available; as a result, adults as well as children (especially infants and toddlers) die regularly of diseases that biomedical treatments might either prevent or cure (Gottlieb 2004, 236–305).

The discussion provided in this chapter is largely based on observations I made before the civil war that began in 2002 claimed the nation but is supplemented by updates obtained from phone and Internet conversations with Beng interlocutors when possible. With their homeland located along the border of the nation's north/south-oriented conflict,[3] most Beng responded to invading rebels and soldiers by fleeing their villages either to towns or cities or into the bush; only recently have they begun making their way back to the villages. The extent to which the practices analyzed here have been reinstated – or were maintained without interruption – has not yet been documented. If they have withstood the upheavals caused by the national conflict, it would be because of the ways in which the practices are embedded in gendered structures of labor, on the one hand, and in an overarching religious system, on the other – themes to which we now turn.

Exploring first acts of small violence

Among the Beng, babies' bodily orifices are manipulated by their mothers from their first moments *ex utero* in such a way that outsiders might feel justified in calling these manipulations a kind of 'violation'. Mothers violate their infants' bodies daily and in two ways. Let us examine them both.

First, as part of a lengthy bathing routine, Beng mothers administer an enema twice a day to their infants. The practice begins quite early in a child's life – on the day the umbilical stump falls off. Without explicit treatment, this event typically occurs some time in the first three weeks after birth. Beng mothers hasten the process by applying particular herbs to the dangling stump. The concoction must be biochemically effective, for Beng newborns' umbilical stumps tend to drop off within the first three or four days after birth.

Women offer several reasons for desiring the stump to fall off quickly, but one of them is to enable mothers to begin training their babies' digestive system via enemas.[4] Every morning and every evening, until such time that the baby can walk confidently, the mother puts the child through a lengthy bathing routine that includes an enema.[5] Traditionally the technology used was a small, round, long-necked gourd that women hollowed out and dried; nowadays, an industrially produced rubber syringe, or clyster, of the same shape takes its place. Consider this description of one enema session I observed, among hundreds:

> In the midst of scrubbing, baby Sassandra's mother reaches for the bulb syringe and inserts it into the little one's anus. Immediately, the baby squirms and whimpers – he seems resigned to his fate, yet not so docile that he doesn't indulge in waging a slight protest. Still, Sassandra's intestines oblige his mother. She continues to wash him, splashing herb water gently over her infant, who continues to defecate into the basin below while whining ever so slightly...

Beng mothers administer these enemas to their babies every morning and evening, day in and day out, through the first year of life – and often into the second year – until the toddler becomes, as we might say, 'potty-trained'.

The second violation we explore here involves the other end of the digestive system. When a young baby is obviously hungry, one might imagine, the first action a nursing mother might take would be to position the baby comfortably to allow for breastfeeding. In Bengland, this is the second action that a traditionally oriented, breastfeeding mother does. Her first action is quite different. The mother scoops up a small bowlful of cool water from her water pot, cups a small amount in her right palm and – with her baby lying or sitting in her lap – offers a small amount of water to her child. If she is faithfully following tradition, the mother offers two more small handfuls.

A cooperative baby laps up these mouthfuls of water willingly from the mother's cupped hand, well and good. But an uncooperative baby balks. Then, the mother of such a baby does what Beng women call *kami*: she forces her baby to drink at least a small amount of water. Depending on the baby's reaction, perhaps guided by the child's *sie*, his temperament or personality, the mother may feel compelled to force some water down the tiny throat in a somewhat violent fashion. A baby with a *sie grégré*, or 'difficult temperament', might start choking and gasping, trying desperately to spit out the liquid – that is not breastmilk – being sloshed into her mouth; perhaps such a child adds for good measure some dramatic thrashing about with tiny arms and legs that insist, 'Listen to me! I don't want this water, I want that liquid that comes from the breast!' But the traditional Beng mother is trained not to take pity on such a rebellious infant before she makes sure that at least a few drops of water go down her baby's throat. Then and only then does she guide her child toward her nipple. Beginning right at birth and continuing for several months, mothers force their infants to consume water in this way before allowing them to breastfeed.[6]

Most Westerners would likely view the two Beng infant training practices I have described as unacceptable on several grounds. First, let us explore the medical implications. In evaluating Beng toilet-training practices, cultural anthropologist David Lancy (2008, 53) finds Beng infant enemas 'deplorable' insofar as they leave babies vulnerable to diarrhea and dehydration – two conditions that prove fatal for at least 1.5 million children globally every year (World Health Organization). Additional medical risks of infant enemas have recently been identified in South Africa, where medical researchers have reported 'marked clinical deterioration [with a variety of symptoms] following enema administration' in children who are 'struggling with an underlying illness' (Moore and Moore 1998).[7]

Beyond these medical concerns, most Western pediatricians probably disapprove of trying to 'toilet-train' newborns for another reason: in their view, the training would be purely physiological, lacking any emotional or cognitive learning. In the USA, the current medical standard is to recommend that 'potty training' begins between loosely between one-and-a-half and three years of age; a recent study based on research with infants claims that toilet-training is best undertaken between the 24th and 32nd months to be most effective (Barone, Jasutkar, and Schneider 2009). These recommendations all assume that toddlers should be consciously involved in the decision to toilet-train and even that they have the *right* to be so involved, as many online advice givers make explicit (e.g., Greene 2001; Crowton 2005). In so doing, these studies imply an underlying cultural value privileging the individual's decision-making ability even at a very young age. By contrast, although most Beng mothers value their infants' ability to make *some* decisions (Gottlieb 2004), the question of toilet-training is typically deemed non-negotiable. Rather, Beng mothers judge that they alone have the right to regulate their infants' bowels, while infants lack this right.

As for the second practice I have described, most Western pediatricians would probably take an equally dim view toward the Beng practice of forcing water on newborns before breastfeeding. Lancy's point about regular enemas rendering West African infants vulnerable to potentially dangerous diarrhea might well apply to the Beng breastfeeding practice. This is because, as with so many rural communities across Sub-Saharan Africa, Beng villages do not always have access to a reliably purified water supply. The World Health Organization repeatedly warns women in such contexts against exposing their infants to water-borne pathogens (see WHO 2008). We may infer that force-feeding water to babies in the tropics risks introducing water-borne pathogens; thereby denying neonates the protection from infections and parasites that breastfeeding should otherwise ensure. Moreover, even in areas with access to safe water supply, pediatricians recommend no water supplements for the first several months to avoid filling up the child's small stomach with a substance lacking any nutritional value (see Greene 2009).

Beyond these medical issues lie emotional and cognitive questions concerning volition. Again, as with enemas, the practice of force-feeding water denies infants the ability to choose what, and how, they ingest. And again, Beng mothers see the issue of rights differently from how many Westerners would view the issue. Although they do allow infants to choose when to breastfeed (Gottlieb 2004, 185–219), Beng women do not allow babies the right to reject what they ingest when it comes to water. The right to choose water or breastmilk is reserved for mothers.

Explaining first acts of small violence

If Westerners might be inclined to condemn the two practices I have described here as dangerous, both medically and psychologically, why do Beng mothers engage in them? Here we enter squarely into Mary Douglas territory. Beginning with nuclear waste and other environmental risks, cultural anthropologist Mary Douglas taught us long ago to view all assumptions and claims regarding safety and danger as founded not only in biochemical realities but also in perceptual realities that amount to statements of cultural values (Douglas 1985, 1992; Douglas and Wildavsky 1982). Taking her insight as a starting point leads us to ask: Do Beng mothers view as risky the two acts of force against their infants that I have described here?

In fact, the response is quite the opposite. In the view of all Beng mothers I have known, both practices are beneficial to babies. Beng mothers feel certain that babies should become regular in their bowel habits from an early age, and they do not acknowledge any health risks associated with the practice of enemas. Indeed, mothers continue to administer enemas (with specific herbal components) to older children for a variety of ailments, as a medical treatment. Moreover, as adults, both men and women give themselves enemas with medicinal herbs whenever they contract digestive ailments (as well as some other illnesses). While living among the Beng, whenever I suffered from digestive troubles myself, my Beng neighbors – aware that I was not a devotee of this practice – often teased me that I would only recover with an enema, which they offered to prepare for me (Gottlieb and Graham 2012, 55). In acknowledging that Americans may not savor enemas as much as they do, my Beng friends' teasing nevertheless underscored a distinctive somatic reality for their own experiential world: enemas comprise a regular component of health maintenance across the life cycle of virtually all Beng people, and training infants to accept them is an important bodily discipline imposed on them by their mothers.

As for force-feeding water before breastfeeding, Beng mothers see this practice, too, as beneficial for their newborns. A linguistic inquiry reveals that at the conceptual level, Beng adults view water and breastmilk as somewhat equivalent. The Beng word for 'breastmilk' is literally 'breast-water' (*nyo yi*) and is etymologically unrelated to the Beng word for cow's milk (*nunu*). Underlying this semantic field lies a broader health model: Beng adults consider both water and 'breast-water' as life-giving substances. Indeed, water itself is often used in religious contexts, as an offering to ancestors (cf. Gottlieb 1993, 24; Gottlieb 2012, 80–81, 85–86, 92–93, 97–98, 101–103, 120–121). In the face of this cultural model, my husband and I found it difficult to introduce the notion of water-borne pathogens to Beng villagers, who preferred their view of water-as-quasi-holy to our model of water-as-potentially-dangerous (Gottlieb and Graham 1994, 259–262).

Complementing these conceptual factors, the economic issue of labor looms large in women's enthusiasm both for administering enemas and for force-feeding water to their babies. Given that both practices involve extra labor on the part of mothers, this might seem an odd claim. To explain it, we must back up and explore the world of women's work.

Although the nation's civil war and ensuing conflicts over the past two decades have had brutal effects on the Beng, life in the villages was already tough in all sorts of ways before the national conflict. When

I have lived among the Beng, everyone worked hard for meager material rewards. Those who are now returning to the villages have resumed their previous rigorous work schedules. Men typically work in the fields from about 8 in the morning until about 5 in the afternoon and may do some light village-based work in the evenings; women typically work far harder – as men acknowledge.

After waking at 5 or 5:30 every morning, the typical mother lights the fire to heat water for her family's baths, then she bathes her baby and toddler. Soon thereafter, she cooks breakfast for everyone, then washes the dishes and sweeps the compound. Either before or after breakfast, she joins the girls of the village to pump and head-carry water for the household from a village pump (or forest pool). On some days, she will then wash the family's laundry. After all this morning activity, she walks – up to several miles – to her fields in the forest, with her older children alongside of her and perhaps a toddler begging to be carried on her back if she is not already carrying a baby. Once arrived, she does a good six to eight hours of hard farmwork in the fields. Later in the afternoon she returns to the village. With her toddler probably begging to be carried, she typically carries a heavy head load, in addition (usually, either firewood that she has chopped in the forest or crops that she has gathered from her fields).

Arrived back in the village, she then lights a fire and proceeds to cook dinner for her children and husband and perhaps other miscellaneous relatives who stop by. Dinner preparation often requires demanding efforts to pound yams in a large mortar with a heavy, 4′-long wooden pestle. After dinner, she washes dishes, bathes the baby and toddler as well as herself, tidies up the compound and perhaps enjoys half an hour of gossip or storytelling around the fire, before tumbling into bed. Depending on the extent of her poverty, she may be further slowed or weakened in all this work from anemia or another vitamin or mineral deficiency; she may be afflicted by malaria, Guinea worms, intestinal parasites, miscellaneous fevers and other health challenges great and small. With or without such additional medical challenges, she will typically awaken early the next morning to begin her labor all over again.

To prepare, both physically and mentally, for this daunting work schedule, girls start learning many of these tasks from a young age. Depending on their motor development, at between one-and-a-half to three years they begin helping their mothers pound food and wash laundry; by five or six years of age, most girls carry babies on their backs for short periods of time; by 12, most girls can perform all but the heaviest components of adult women's labor effectively. Beyond their farming and household work, if they are lucky enough to be fertile and give birth to newborns who survive infancy and grow to adulthood, women spend much of their adult lives raising their children and grandchildren.

In effect, then, Beng women have three full-time jobs – as mothers (and, later, grandmothers), as household managers and as farmers. Often, two of those jobs overlap quite literally, as women frequently work with babies attached to their backs. With such a labor burden, it is not surprising that women are frequently exhausted and eager to catch naps in odd moments when they can. Here is where we can partially understand the two infant care practices I have described.

In order to survive the enormous demands for their labor, mothers buy themselves time and energy whenever they can by relying on a babysitter. Indeed, having access to one or more reliable babysitters is critical to a mother's ability to maintain her demanding work requirements. To minimize the time they must spend working with babies attached to their backs, Beng women especially seek relief from someone else who will hold or carry the baby while they chop wood, carry water and do agricultural work in the fields. In fact, the Beng word for a 'babysitter', *lɛŋ kũli*, translates literally as 'baby carrier'. Typically, though not always, these 'baby carriers' are female, including an older relative such as a woman's own mother or a young girl such as an older daughter or niece.

If she is lucky, a pregnant woman may identify one person who commits to being a reliable, daily 'baby carrier' for the first year or more, once the baby is born. In the absence of such a person, a new mother endeavors to identify a network of several girls and women who agree to carry the baby whenever they are available. Even if she has identified a single major 'baby carrier', the mother of a child under the age of two takes advantage of many other girls' and women's spontaneous offers to carry the baby when neither she nor a regular *lɛŋ kũli* is holding the baby. Without either one committed babysitter or a reliable pool of part-time babysitters, a mother of an infant finds life almost impossible. This is especially the case if she also has a toddler and another young child to care for.[8]

How does a mother identify babysitters? In effect, administering enemas and force-feeding water before nursing constitute two methods to attract a 'baby carrier' – however unorthodox these strategies appear by Western standards. In both cases, Beng women aim to make infants attractive to *lɛŋ kũli* in ways that allow the babysitters to take care of their young children without any undue stress or trauma to either of them. With enemas, as we have seen, mothers 'toilet-train' the babies from the first week of life so that they evacuate their bowels both regularly and minimally. Training infants to defecate only twice a day, once in the morning (at approximately 7 am) and again once in the evening (at approximately 7 pm), reduces the likelihood that they will evacuate their bowels during the day, between enemas.

Western child specialists doubtless point out that 12 hours comprise a very long period for an infant to last without defecating. Yet, with their meager cash supply coupled with their distance from a marketplace offering a wide supply of industrially produced goods, Beng villagers lack access to commercially made diapers, nor have they constructed any alternative technologies to reliably catch the feces of babies. Without any absorbent material for the purpose, unscheduled infants' feces produces an unsanitary mess.

And that mess would likely land on someone else's clothes. For a variety of reasons – economic, medical, sociological and emotional – babies are held by someone, either on a back or lap, for most of their waking as well as sleeping daytime hours (Gottlieb 2004, 136–184). Thus, were babies to defecate between the morning and evening enemas, it would be likely that they would do so on somebody's back or lap. That would be frowned upon in the extreme, and not just for sanitary reasons but also for moral ones. Conceptually, Beng adults classify feces as 'dirty'. In describing feces, they use the word for 'dirt' (*gbrégbré*), which describes both empirical dirt on the ground and a metaphorical notion of dirt that indexes a symbolically resonant condition that we might call 'symbolic pollution' (cf. Douglas 1966). This conceptual model suggests that feces are not just considered messy but are tinged with morally negative connotations.

Given this conceptual foundation, if a baby defecates on an adult's back, the adult would be so annoyed, even revolted, that she would immediately put the baby down, clean both of them off and probably never offer to carry that child again. There would be an implicit criticism of the mother as well. Why was the baby defecating between baths to begin with? The mother must have shirked her maternal duties and neglected to administer an enema. If word got out in the village that a particular baby were not fully trained and regularly defecated on anyone who carried him or her, the available pool of babysitters for that infant would probably dwindle to nil. This scenario could prove catastrophic, for it would significantly curtail the mother's work hours; in turn, this labor reduction could potentially threaten her household's food supply. In short, the technological factor of diaper deficiency, combined with the sociological factor of nearly continual carrying of infants by a variety of adults, impels mothers to administer enemas to regulate their infants' bowels.

If administering enemas twice a day renders infants attractive to possible *lɛŋ kũli*, force-feeding them water before nursing makes them appealing in another way. Beng mothers need to feel confident that when they leave a baby with a babysitter for more than a few minutes – say, to go chop wood, haul water or fetch harvested crops in the field – the baby will not cry unrelentingly from hunger. A *lɛŋ kũli* should be able to offer water to the baby as a way of sating the baby's thirst for a short while before the mother returns. If a newborn is not trained to accept and enjoy water from the first days, mothers judge it unlikely that their infants will imbibe water from a babysitter later on. Thus mothers train infants to drink water so that the babies can, in effect, tolerate short separations from them for the sake of the mothers' work demands (and emotional needs), the babysitters' peace of mind and the comfort of the babies themselves.

Conclusions

Among the Beng people of Côte d'Ivoire, babies' bodily orifices are forcibly manipulated by their mothers from their first moments *ex utero* in ways that violate bodily boundaries. In recent years, scholars have endeavored to expand the definition of violence from acts perpetrated directly by an individual or corporate group to 'structural violence' that derives from policies of exclusion and injustice and that causes material suffering (see Farmer 1996). In the latter case, rather than physical armaments, the weapons take the form of institutional decisions made by elite policy makers and grounded in values both implicit and explicit.

For example, some scholars and political commentators argue that in the USA, basing funding for public schools on property tax proceeds (the current policy across the nation) constitutes a type of structural violence insofar as it privileges the elite, who live in more expensive houses and therefore pay higher property taxes (Ladson-Billings and Tate 1995, Slavin 1999, Walters 2001). The taxes are then used to construct local schools with better equipment and to hire more teachers at higher salaries, who are likely to feel content in their workplace while happier instructing fewer students in better-equipped classrooms. By contrast, neighborhoods in which most or all residents are impoverished have a paltry property tax base, thanks to the low value of their housing combined with the reluctance of business owners to locate in these neighborhoods. Almost inevitably, the schools in those neighborhoods are likewise of poor quality. Shoddily constructed buildings contain discouraged and low-paid teachers, crumbling walls, broken furnaces, defaced desks, crackling loudspeakers, gyms that double as auditoriums, deflated soccer balls, canceled after-school clubs and activities, few or no college-bound-course options, inadequate college advising services and out-of-date computers and textbooks. Recognizing such conditions as the result of an invisible but potent form of 'structural violence' provides a conceptual breakthrough that allows lawmakers (as well as fellow citizens) to go beyond a 'blame the victim' mentality concerning the stigmatized category of 'high school dropout' and rethink not only educational policy but also tax policy.

The expansion of the notion of 'violence' to include structural violence has inspired me to think about violence in new ways. In this chapter, I have expanded the notion of violence in another direction. Looking at a small act by one person against one small body day in and day out highlights violence on a very different scale from either the criminal violence that Westerners typically envision at the urban level, the military violence that we easily invoke at the international level or the structural violence that we now acknowledge at the institutional level. And yet, I suggest that the two infant care practices I have outlined here can and should be considered a kind of violence – albeit enacted in a very different register and with very different results from those just mentioned.

The two practices I have described certainly violate the integrity of infants' bodies in ways that many babies clearly find painful and that medical science would not support. The result is twofold: first, to train the body and the mind of the infant into a kind of discipline; second, to free up labor time and energy for the full-time-working mother. These pragmatic effects are clear enough. But on what ideological basis do they rest? I suggest that the assumption behind the decision to perpetrate these two acts of violence on a daily basis rests on a cultural value that privileges the individual as part of a social matrix.

The notion of the individual as a freestanding unit with, as Westerners term it, 'free will' has a particular temporal and spatial history (Cary 2007, O'Connor 2010). Although few anthropologists today would endorse the erasure of the individual out of existence in non-Western societies, as previous generations of scholars sometimes (however unwittingly) did, abundant data do point to many non-Western societies whose members resist inevitably privileging the interests of the individual over those of the group. I suggest that the two Beng infant care practices I have outlined here index such a model of society. In effect, in administering an enema to her infant and in forcing her to drink water before breastmilk, the Beng mother makes a statement to her child from the earliest days outside the womb that the child's body is not his own, that his interests are subordinate to the needs of others – those of his mother, most immediately, and of the society at large, more generally. Being trained in two extraordinarily demanding body habits from the very first days of their lives *ex utero* distinguishes the somatic experiences of Beng infants from those of their Western counterparts who are, by contrast, trained to defecate into diapers at will, whenever they have the urge, and are never force-fed by mothers (at least not by those mothers whom our societies deem psychologically balanced). Both sets of babies learn critical lessons involving discipline and the formation of subjectivity.

In the case of Beng children, does their early training prime them to accept violence in the middle childhood years and to become violent or otherwise troubled adults later on? That is the lesson that we hear emerging from some recent research in the USA correlating early exposure to violence with later emotional disturbances (McCloskey et al. 1995; Dubow and Miller 1996; Huesmann and Taylor 2006; Afifi et al. 2012). Although I have not carried out a systematic study testing possible effects, I do not perceive evidence that Beng children become either violent or otherwise troubled adults as a result of the somatic violence perpetrated on them during their first year of life. For one thing, the Beng are ideological pacifists and have a taboo against physically killing another human being; the murder rate thus approaches zero. Beyond murder, two forms of interpersonal domestic violence that are common in men globally – wife-beating and child-beating – are not encountered commonly in Beng villages. Although neither is forbidden as such, they are subject to community sanction when practiced excessively. For example, a child who is beaten excessively by a parent will be critiqued harshly by relatives and neighbors; if the mistreatment continues, typically the child is removed from the household to be raised by a grandparent or another relative. Some specific contexts forbid physical violence. For example, no one may commit any acts of physical (or verbal) violence on the day of the traditional six-day week dedicated to worship of local deities (for discussion of a trial held against a husband who threatened to beat his two wives on such a day, see Gottlieb and Graham 1994, 214–216, 225–226, 287; Gottlieb and Graham 2012, 58), and a husband who beats his wife while she is pregnant is subject to immediate divorce.

Rather than physical violence, the suffering that most afflicts Beng lives is discursively linked to the mystical idiom of witchcraft, based in resentments of unequal levels of prosperity. But this pan-African discourse is hardly rooted in distinctive Beng infant care practices, not practiced elsewhere. (Regular use of enemas to maintain health in infants has been reported for some other groups elsewhere in Africa (Timyan 1988; Huygens et al. 2002), but the extent to which they are used systematically across the continent remains to be documented; as for the water force-feeding habit I have described here, I am unaware of reports for any other groups documenting this practice). In short, if early enemas and force-feeding of water produce later trauma and/or disturbed or violent behavior in Beng adults, I have not yet found the path to a causal correlation.

Given that early encounters with certain kinds of violence are now documented as statistically likely to produce later emotional disruptions and social failure in many US children but that the situation is not equivalent for Beng children, what might account for the striking difference in outcome? Without seeking recourse to hypothetical biological or psychoanalytic factors, I suggest that an anthropological perspective provides sufficient explanation. That is, sociocultural context determines the meaning of violence and either amplifies (in the US case) or mitigates (in the Beng case) its potential long-term negative effects. Simply knowing that the practices are normative rather than exceptional can go some way toward decreasing the likelihood of trauma, as some US researchers have discovered in comparing racialized differences in assessing the long-term negative impact of spanking in children (Taylor et al. 2010). When infants are socialized into body-violating practices that are viewed not as punishment for rude or sinful behavior (as violence toward children is often justified by parents) but rather as beneficial both to themselves and to their mothers, the outside observer must pause to consider the possibility that long-term emotional damage may be far from inevitable.

Although some unfortunate medical effects may result in some children from both practices described in this chapter, because of their effect on recruiting babysitters to help overworked mothers with childcare, the risks to the household food supply from limiting these practices (and, hence, eliminating back-up babysitting) appears to be worse. An anthropologist might acknowledge that in an ideal world, neither force-feeding water nor administering twice-daily enemas should be encouraged. But, without easy, affordable and safe access to infant formula and bottles on the one hand, or to absorbent diapers on the other hand, Beng mothers would be unable to recruit babysitters who would agree to carry babies who would likely defecate on their backs while being held and cry pitilessly from hunger because they were not used to accepting water as a short-term substitute for breastmilk. Making force-feeding of water and enforced twice-daily enemas into ordinary practices of infant care may appear abusive to the outsider; from the 'native's perspective', these practices are survival strategies critical in a world limned by poverty and pathogens.

Anthropology teaches us that life is about trade-offs. Rather than eliminating all risks in an ideal world, members of particular societies choose certain risks for the greater benefits they promise. When we consider the impacts of violence on children's lives in comparative perspective, the Beng case reminds us to be mindful of *local structures of violence*, to acknowledge that violence can come in many shapes and forms and to consider the morally challenging possibility that the known benefits of certain forms of violence may in some cases outweigh their potential risks. More broadly, we can observe from the practices discussed in this chapter that, working with economic and other structural constraints, culture provides the conceptual ground for defining the self.

Cultural norms of parenting that incorporate early forms of systematic violence go against much Western common-sense understandings of society. But the lessons of anthropology in urging us to attend to others' subjective realities are not always easy, nor easily palatable. Yet they are ignored at our peril. One might imagine well-intentioned NGO workers, for example, intervening in Beng villages to discourage the two infant care practices I have outlined in this chapter, for the sake of children's medical health. But such a hypothetical intervention would ignore the ways in which the two practices are embedded in gendered structures of labor, on the one hand, and broader conceptions of the value of community on the other hand. Were force-feeding of water to be prohibited in contemporary Beng villages, for example, mothers could not leave their nursing-age children with others for more than very short periods of time, and this restriction could have a serious impact on women's vital labor contributions to the household as well as on their mental health. With infants' well-being cybernetically tied to that of their mothers, their own well-being could in turn become compromised. Likewise, prohibiting mothers from training their newborns' digestive systems via enemas could well significantly restrict their access to babysitters. Again, this result could have a negative domino effect on the household economy and hence, ultimately, on the infant's life chances.

In sum, the Beng case challenges us to rethink two key assumptions that Westerners may take for granted. First, neonatal enemas and force-fed water practices alert us to the possibility that 'violence' may take forms unimagined by conventional social science. In particular, these two childcare practices present us with what we might term a 'violence of the quotidian' that is, moreover, enacted by a category of person whom Westerners frequently stereotype as the ultimate protector against violence. In that sense, the Beng case also challenges us to rethink our gendered stereotypes of the maternal as defined by nurturance. Some years ago, Rosaldo and Atkinson (1975) hypothesized that women rarely hunt animals because their nurturing role as mothers normatively teaches them to protect life rather than take it. Similarly, the contemporary 'ecofeminist' movement is implicitly predicated on a postulated nurturing instinct embedded in women's presumed nature (Sturgeon 1997). Such models bear rethinking (cf. Biehl 1991). Beyond the childcare practices described here that are ultimately meant to be nurturing while using violent means, evidence elsewhere provides examples of women who directly harm their children for a variety of reasons (Scheper-Hughes 1987; Tsing 1990). Although prisons tend to contain far more men than women who committed violent crimes, less obvious forms of violence done in the domestic domain by mothers may remain invisible to the statistics compiled of more publicly visible forms of violence.

Second, at the ethical level, Beng practices remind us to withhold judgment against seemingly immoral acts before evaluating the full range of their cultural meanings as well as their socioeconomic utility. As with other challenging practices, female genital cutting comes readily to mind here (Shweder 2000), the anthropological insistence on understanding 'other' practices in their local contexts before judging them proves critical. The converse point is also worth making. In Western contexts of middle-class parenting culture, for example, ordinary practices ranging from routine newborn boys' circumcision and infant girls' ear piercing to putting infants to sleep in cribs in their own rooms are accepted as normative, while they would be problematized as unnecessary violations of infants' bodily boundaries and emotional rights (respectively) by members of other societies.

Putting drastically different childcare practices into stark relief vis-à-vis one another offers the opportunity to rethink basic unquestioned assumptions that underlie all parenting decisions (cf. DeLoache and Gottlieb 2000). In the case discussed in this chapter, Beng breastfeeding and toilet-training practices suggest that the violence of the quotidian, as I am terming it, amounts to a new arena in which important scholarship has yet to be written. The remaining chapters in this volume provide further case studies that will help scholars forge creative new approaches to just such an endeavor.

Acknowledgments

An earlier version of this talk was presented to the workshop on 'Violence and Childhood in an International and Comparative Perspective' (Seminar 1: Violence and the Making of the Subject), at Birkbeck College/University College London (12 March 2010). Some material in this chapter appears in a different form in my book, *The Afterlife Is Where We Come from: The Culture of Infancy in West Africa* (Gottlieb 2004).

For sharing so much of their wisdom and their understanding of their world with me, I remain indebted to many more Beng individuals than I can name here, but I would like to single out two here for their extraordinary generosity with their knowledge: Véronique Akpoueh Amenan and Yacouba Kouadio Bah. Other Beng friends who have shared with me their wise understandings of Beng infant culture during summer 1993 include Kouakou Bah and the late Kouassi Kokora. For expert help with transcription and translation, I thank Bertin Kouadio and Augustin Kouakou; for careful observations of selected Beng infants, many thanks to Dieudonné Kwame Kouassi. For comments on this chapter, many thanks to Philip Graham, Bertin Kouadio and Erica Burman. Over the years, the research and writing of this material was supported by generous awards from the John Simon Guggenheim Memorial Foundation, National Endowment for the Humanities, Social Science Research Council, Wenner-Gren Foundation for Anthropological Research and several units at the University of Illinois at Urbana-Champaign.

Notes

1. The acronym stands for Drug Abuse Resistance Education. The program began in 1983 in Los Angeles and (according to its website) is now active in 75 percent of school districts in the USA (www.dare-america.com). At the international level, the program now holds 'consultative status' with the UN (http://www.dare.org/home/UN_endorses_DARE.asp) and is regularly expanding its activities in countries around the world (for a regularly updated list, see: http://www.dare-america.com/home/International/Story1d4d.asp?N=International&M=9&S=6).
2. Between 1998 and 2002, for example, 54 percent of all violent crimes in the USA occurred between individuals known to one another (Hessick 2007, 344).

3. For a map of the Beng region vis-à-vis the nation's conflict, see Gottlieb and Graham (2012, 154).
4. For another reason rooted in a local religious ideology oriented around a model of reincarnation, see Gottlieb (2004, 83–93).
5. For a description and analysis of the entire bathing routine, see Gottlieb (2004,105–136); for a brief video including an abridged enema session, see http://www.press.uchicago.edu/books/gottlieb/gottlieb_videos.html.
6. For a brief video of this routine with a one-month-old infant, see http://www.press.uchicago.edu/books/gottlieb/gottlieb_videos.html.
7. For an early patronizing but otherwise reliable medical discussion of the risks of diarrhea following infant enemas in South Africa, see van der Horst (1964); on medical risks from enemas for adults, see Segal et al. (1979), among others.
8. In Beng villages, birth control – in the form of herbal preparations – is tightly regulated by old women, who typically keep access to their knowledge from young women who have not yet given birth to at least several children; as of my last stay, condoms were actively rejected (cf. Gottlieb and Graham 2012, 116–117). Nevertheless, this is not the 'natural fertility' regime envisioned by demographers, as some intentional spacing of children is accomplished by a post-partum taboo on sex until the child can effectively walk. In this reproductive context, many Beng women bear children spaced two to three years apart. Thus if she is generally healthy, fertile, sexually active and does not suffer the tragedy of an infant or toddler dying, a Beng woman of reproductive age can normally expect to be responsible for her own baby, toddler and child of about five or six years old (as well as similarly spaced older children) for a good two to three decades of her adult life (and later, to varying extents, for grandchildren of all ages). Sadly, high child mortality rates often alter this profile.

Bibliography

Afifi, T. O. et al. (2012) Physical Punishment and Mental Disorders: Results from a Nationally Representative U.S. Sample. *Pediatrics*, 2 July 2012. http://pediatrics.aappublications.org/content/early/2012/06/27/peds.2011-2947.full.pdf+html.

Barone, J., Jasutkar, N. and Schneider D. (2009) Later Toilet Training is Associated with Urge Incontinence in Children. *Journal of Pediatric Urology*, 5 (6), 458–461.

Biehl, J. (1991) *Rethinking Eco-Feminist Politics*. Boston: South End Press.

Cary, P. (2007) A Brief History of the Concept of Free Will: Issues that Are and Are Not Germane to Legal Reasoning. *Behavioral Science and the Law*, 25 (2), 65–81.

Catalano, S. et al. (2009) *Female Victims of Violence*. U.S. Dept. of Justice. Bureau of Justice Statistics.

Crowton, D. (2005) Is It Time to Potty Train Yet? http://housesandgarden.com/story.aspx?id=784.

DeLoache, J. and Gottlieb, A. (2000) *A World of Babies: Imagined Childcare Guides for Seven Societies*. New York: Cambridge University Press.

Douglas, M. (1966) *Purity and Danger: An Analysis of the Concepts of Pollution and Taboo*. London: Routledge & Kegan Paul.

Douglas, M. (1985) *Risk Acceptability According to the Social Sciences*. New York: Russell Sage Foundation.

Douglas, M. (1992) *Risk and Blame: Essays in Cultural Theory.* London: Routledge.
Douglas, M. and Wildavsky, Aaron (1982) *Risk and Culture: An Essay on the Selection of Technological and Environmental Dangers.* Berkeley: University of California Press.
Dubow, E. F. and Miller, L. S. (1996) Television Violence Viewing and Aggressive Behavior. In T. M. MacBeth (ed.) *Tuning in to Young Viewers: Social Science Perspectives on Television*, Thousand Oaks, CA: Sage, pp. 117–147.
Farmer, P. (1996) On Suffering and Structural Violence: A View from Below. *Daedalus*, 125 (1), 261–276, 278–283.
Farmer, P. (2003) *Pathologies of Power: Health, Human Rights and the New War on the Poor*. Berkeley: University of California Berkeley Press.
Geertz, C. (1983) [1975] Common Sense as a Cultural System. In C. Geertz (ed.) *Local Knowledge*, New York: Basic Books, pp. 73–93.
Gottlieb, A. (1993) [1992] *Under the Kapok Tree: Identity and Difference in Beng Thought*. Chicago: University of Chicago Press.
Gottlieb, A. (2004) *The Afterlife Is Where We Come from: The Culture of Infancy in West Africa*. Chicago: University of Chicago Press.
Gottlieb, A. and Graham, P. (1994) [1993] *Parallel Worlds: An Anthropologist and a Writer Encounter Africa*. Chicago: University of Chicago Press.
Gottlieb, A. and Graham, P. (2012) *Braided Worlds*. Chicago: University of Chicago Press.
Greene, A. (2001) How and When Do I Potty Train? *Pediatrics Naturally*, Dr. Green.com. http://www.drgreene.com/qa/how-and-when-do-i-potty-train.
Greene, A. (2009) Is It Safe for Babies to Drink Water? *New York Times*, 19 August 2009. http://consults.blogs.nytimes.com/2009/08/19/is-it-safe-for-babies-to-drink-water/.
Harrell, E. (2012) *Violent Victimization Committed by Strangers, 1993–2010.* U.S. Department of Justice, Bureau of Justice Statistics. NCJ 239424. http://bjs.ojp.usdoj.gov/index.cfm?ty=pbdetail&iid=4557.
Hessick, C. B. (2007) Violence between Lovers, Strangers, and Friends. *Washington University Law Review*, 85, 343–407. http://lawreview.wustl.edu/inprint/85/2/Hessick.pdf.
Holcombe, A., Wolery, M. and Katzenmeyer J. (1995) Teaching Preschoolers to Avoid Abduction by Strangers: Evaluation of Maintenance Strategies. *Journal of Child and Family Studies*, 4, 177–192.
Huesmann, L. R. and Taylor, L. D. (2006) The Role of Media Violence in Violent Behavior. *Annual Review of Public Health*, 27, 393–415.
Huygens, P. B. et al. (2002) Hygiène et Socialisation du Nourrisson: Le Lavement Rectal en Milieu Urbain à Bobo Dioulasso. *Santé*, 12 (4), 357–362.
Ladson-Billings, G. and Tate IV, W. F. (1995) Toward a Critical Race Theory of Education. *Teachers College Record*, 97 (1), 47–68.
Lancy, D. (2008) *The Anthropology of Childhood; Cherubs, Chattel, Changelings.* Cambridge: Cambridge University Press
McCloskey, L. A., Figueredo, A. J. and Koss, M. P. (1995) The Effects of Systemic Family Violence on Children's Mental Health. *Child Development*, 66, 1239–1261.
Moore, D. A. and Moore, N. L. (1998) Paediatric Enema Syndrome in a Rural African Setting. Annals of Tropical. *Paediatrics*, 18 (2), 139–144.

O'Connor, T. (2010) Free Will. In E. N. Zalta (ed.) *The Stanford Encyclopedia of Philosophy* (Summer 2011 Edition). http://plato.stanford.edu/archives/sum2011/entries/freewill/.

Rape Crisis (England and Wales) (2012) *Common Myths about Rape. Rape Crisis (England and Wales)*. Women's Health and Equality Consortium. http://www.rapecrisis.org.uk/commonmyths2.php.

Rosaldo, M. Z. and Atkinson J. (1975) Man the Hunter and Woman. In R. Willis (ed.) *The Interpretation of Symbolism*, New York: Wiley, pp. 43–75.

Scheper-Hughes, N. (ed.) (1987) *Child Survival: Anthropological Perspectives on the Treatment and Maltreatment of Children*. New York: Springer.

Scott, H. (2003) Stranger Danger: Explaining Women's Fear of Crime. *Western Criminology Review*, 4 (3), 203–214.

Segal, I. et al. (1979) Ritual-Enema-Induced Colitis. *Diseases of the Colon & Rectum*, 22 (3), 195–199.

Shweder, R. A. (2000) What about 'Female Genital Mutilation'? And Why Understanding Culture Matters in the First Place. *Daedalus*, 129 (4), 209–232.

Slavin, R. E. (1999) How Can Funding Equity Ensure Enhanced Achievement? *Journal of Education Finances*, 24, 519–528.

Sturgeon, N. (1997) *Ecofeminist Natures: Race, Gender, Feminist Theory, and Political Action*. London: Routledge.

Taylor, C. A. et al. (2010) Mothers' Spanking of 3-Year-Old Children and Subsequent Risk of Children's Aggressive Behavior. *Pediatrics*, 12 April. http://pediatrics.aappublications.org/content/early/2010/04/12/peds.2009-2678.

Timyan, J. (1988) *Cultural Aspects of Psychosocial Development: An Examination of West African Childrearing Practices*. The Consultative Group on Early Childhood Care and Development. A Report Prepared for the Regional UNICEF Workshop: Toward a Strategy for Enhancing Early Childhood Development in the West and Central Africa Region, 18–22 January 1988.

Tsing, A. (1990) Monster Stories: Women Charged with Perinatal Endangerment. In F. Ginsberg and A. Tsing (eds.) *Uncertain Terms: Negotiating Gender in American Culture*, Boston: Beacon Press, pp. 282–299.

U.S. Department of Agriculture (n.d.) *Domestic Violence Awareness Handbook*. U.S. Department of Agriculture. Departmental Management. Office of Procurement and Property Management. Safety, Health and Employee Welfare Division.

van der Horst, R. L. (1964) The Enema and the African Child. *South African Medical Journal*, 4 July 1964, 465–466.

Walters, P. B. (2001) Educational Access and the State: Historical Continuities and Discontinuities in Racial Inequality in American Education. *Sociology of Education*, 74, 35–49.

World Health Organization (2008) *Guidelines for Drinking-Water Quality, Third edition, Incorporating the First and Second Addenda*. Volume 1: Recommendations. Geneva: World Health Organization. http://www.who.int/water_sanitation_health/dwq/fulltext.pdf.

World Health Organization (2009) *Diarrhoeal Disease*. Fact Sheet No. 330, August 2009. Media Centre, World Health Organization. http://www.who.int/mediacentre/factsheets/fs330/en/index.html.

7
Young Children and Conflict Resolution

Trefor Lloyd

Some children learn how to deal with conflict through the rough and tumble of family life and others do not. Schools, both across the United Kingdom and worldwide, are reporting that they have to deal with conflict between children, between teachers and children and even between parents and teachers. This chapter describes a conflict resolution program, targeting pupils in years three and four (aged seven and eight), which was delivered in eight schools in South London.

I write as the worker for the Boys' Development Project (hereafter the BDP). BDP is a social enterprise (note 1) that designs and develops programs targeting children under 11 (particularly boys), in a range of subject areas including conflict resolution and motivation. A social enterprise is a business that has a clear social mission, which means it knows what difference it is trying to make, who it aims to help and how it plans to do it. It operates as a charity, reinvesting 'profits' to further the social mission. While much of the BDP's work is targeted specifically at individuals and groups of boys, this conflict resolution program ('Oy You') has been delivered to whole-class groups.

Over the last few years, British primary schools have seen exclusion rates increase. Exclusion is what the British education system calls the suspension of children from school. Such exclusions may be temporary or permanent, depending on the severity of the action that precipitated it. While the numbers are still relatively small, some neighborhoods are seeing permanent and fixed term exclusions for children in reception and year one (aged four and five). Although the peak age for exclusions is still 13 and 14 years old, one in seven is now in primary schools (Department of Education 2012a). This is at least in part a reflection of an increase in aggression and conflict within an environment we traditionally think of for innocent children.

Some of the behaviors that are familiar within secondary (or high) school have crept into the top-end of primary schools. This is the case for boys in particular, with both physical confrontations and verbal aggression becoming more commonplace. Some of this of course comes in from the 'road', hearing 10 and 11 year olds cuss each other's mums, hearing girls say 'whatever' as though they have just walked off the set of a New York soap and seven and eight year olds trying to sound like their older brothers and sisters. This contributes to a changing atmosphere, where some children are overconfident and others intimidated.

This age is of course a time for experimentation, learning about relationships, but too often within the playground an accidental collision becomes a confrontation or a verbal mishearing escalates into an aggressive verbal exchange.

Schools we (at BDP) work in have become increasingly concerned about the limited options girls and boys seem to think they have, with fight or flight too often their default modes of response. Some schools are experiencing daily incidents where verbal aggression and intimidation are distracting too many children from their learning.

Our aim for this program was to impact on children's knowledge, attitudes, beliefs, skills and behavior toward conflict and conflict resolution. Within the class and wider school we also wanted to impact on the way in which conflict is handled. We wanted to move the responsibility for dealing with conflict (where possible) from teachers and other adults to the children themselves.

Managing conflict and the rationale for 'Oy You'

Conflict generally has a negative press. Not surprisingly, too often those exhibiting violent behavior are those with underdeveloped conflict resolution skills. However, most acknowledge that conflict is an essential part of growing up, from disputes over toys onward. Johnson and Johnson (1995) suggest that 'conflict can increase achievement, motivation to learn, higher-level reasoning, long term retention, healthy social and cognitive development, and the fun students have in school'. Cheong et al. (2011) makes the distinction between 'constructive and destructive' conflicts while Galtung (1969) argues that conflict is dynamic and constantly changing.

Within this conflict resolution program, we were not looking to create a conflict-free environment but one where children were able to manage and learn from the conflict they find themselves in. We were also acknowledging the dynamic nature of conflict, where the reaction is critical in determining whether the outcome is positive or negative.

There is a range of ways to understand conflict: as a basic element of socialization (Shantz 1992); a series of developmental stages (Piaget 1951; Kohlberg 1981); a set of problem-solving skills (Broadbear and Broadbear 2000); and, of most interest to us, skills and characteristics that underpin the ability to resolve conflict. Hoffman suggests that it is only when children get to six or seven that they are able to see situations from another person's viewpoint (Hoffman 1979).

In planning this intervention, we take from these authors that within any class of children, age will not be a guide to similar development or experience. This will also be the case for the development of characteristics such as empathy (that are thought to underpin problem-solving and conflict-resolving). While some children aged four and five have well-developed conflict resolution skills, others within the same class might not, and this will change the conflict dynamic. One implication of this is that our program will need to be delivered with the mixed abilities of children in mind.

Gender is a major theme within the literature, with studies finding distinct differences in the way boys and girls have responded to conflict and the strategies they use. These studies have focused particularly on boys, with talk of testosterone, gangs, 'warrior genes', hyper masculinity, anti-social personality disorders, competition, hierarchy, crime, organized violence and weapons (Lloyd 2009). Black (2000) found that adolescent males reported more conflict with friends than females and females used higher communication skills and less 'withdrawal' when carrying out a conflict resolution task. Shure (1982) suggests that boys experience more pressures and challenges from other boys that result in a higher number of conflict incidents, and Laursen and Hartup (1989) suggest that there are gender differences in the causes of conflict and also how boys and girls resolve these differences. In the light of this, we wanted a program that focused on both girls and boys and the interaction between the two.

In designing this program we were interested in a skills approach, in part, not only because we think this is most effective but also because there has been recognition that some children are not learning the conflict resolution skills they require (Department for Education 2012b). Johnson and Johnson (1995) found that children in 1st to 9th grade (USA, 5–14) had very limited skills too often relying on teachers to sort out conflict or using 'destructive strategies' (including physical force) that usually made the conflict worse.

What skills children need to enable them to resolve conflict effectively is a much more difficult question to answer. A list of skills and characteristics is important (such as compromise, empathy and negotiation), but we were much more interested in the dynamic contextual nature of conflict that can mean that an ability to compromise with one person in one setting does not necessarily translate into a new setting with someone else. So not only will children have to be in possession of a set of skills, but they will also have to be embedded to enable them to transfer and adapt them to a range of settings.

We are not of course the first to develop conflict resolution skills. Programs are common in the USA, although much less so in the UK. For example, Second Step is a classroom-based social skills program for preschool through junior high students (4–14 years old) and is designed to reduce impulsive, high-risk and aggressive behaviors and to increase children's social and emotional competence and other protective factors. Group discussion, modeling, coaching and practice are used to increase students' social competence, risk assessment, decision-making ability, self-regulation and positive goal setting. The program's lesson content varies by grade level and is organized into three skill-building units covering empathy, impulse control and problem-solving and anger management (Jones 2004).

Some of the US-developed programs have been imported to the UK. For example, the Promoting Alternative Thinking Strategies program has been rolled out in 30 primary schools in Birmingham (Birmingham City Council 2009). While the most established program in the UK is the Social, Emotional and Aspects of Learning (SEAL) delivered in primary schools and concentrating on 'social awareness, managing feelings, motivation, empathy, and social interaction'. Used as a whole-school, cross-curricular approach, SEAL aims to 'help children become successful learners, responsible citizens, and confident individuals'. Around two-thirds of UK primary schools use SEAL.

Humphrey et al. (2008, 7), in their evaluation of SEAL, found a small improvement across the main elements, including Getting On and Falling Out (where conflict resolution skills reside). In this element there were increases in staff-rated self-regulation, decreases in staff-rated peer problems and increases in pupil-rated empathy, self-regulation, social skills and overall emotional literacy.

'Oy You'

From our reading of the literature and our experience within primary schools, we felt that there was scope for a dedicated program targeting years three and four (developmentally appropriate and timely in terms of levels of conflict). We based 'Oy You' on the following assumptions:

1. If children lack the ability to resolve conflict effectively, this is likely to lead to time out of class, further conflict, the development of behavioral difficulties and a lowering of engagement in their learning. Conversely, children who have the ability to resolve conflict effectively are more likely to be engaged in their learning and in turn achieve.
2. Not all children learn conflict resolution within their families, and school provides a setting where a broad range of new potential conflict exists and therefore also provides a 'live' environment to learn strategies and skills. Conflict can be positive and negative and is certainly dynamic. This needs to be a critical part of any conflict resolution program.
3. Developmentally, children under eight years of age are certainly capable of understanding simple processes of conflict resolution. There is evidence that these simple foundations have to be learnt before more complex levels can be grappled with. We also think that these are not skills that are on the whole learnt naturally and also require regular reinforcement.
4. If taught simply, but practically, then all children can learn a set of foundation skills to which more complex skills can be added. We see this program as the first in a layered approach.

A number of issues have been suggested as contributors to conflict. These include the following: testosterone; genes (so-called warrior genes); additives in foods; poor communication skills; parents modeling poor conflict skills; violence within communities; peer pressure to act in certain ways; concerns about respect, status and area protection; and more 'boy-related' conditions such as conduct disorder, attention deficit hyperactivity disorder and general learning difficulties. We are not dealing with a simple cause and effect set of skills.

Neuroscientists looking at the 'plasticity' of children's brains have stressed that repetition, rehearsal and practice are all important when new skills are being learnt. This suggests that if children are to learn practical skills then an active learning style will be more important than a reflective or more cerebral approach, and this is particularly the case with our targeted group (age group) (Kolb 1995; Shore 1997).

Schools too often *manage* conflict rather than *teach* conflict resolution. When there is a playground incident, not surprisingly the overwhelming priority is to stop it and ensure that no one gets hurt. For young children, adults concentrate on finding out who did what and ensure that the one that started it is appropriately punished and a part of that is to say 'sorry'. This can lead to children offering 'sorry' just after a bout of conflict so that they can get back to their play.

A common difficulty for teachers is that their primary focus is on the whole-class learning, which means that conflict is usually resolved as quickly as possible, whereas the learning of conflict resolution skills requires a focus on both the conflict itself and the process of resolution. Even if teachers recognize the importance of this, they do not usually have the time to focus on children's learning of these skills.

When conflict resolution skills are taught, there can be an overreliance on verbal reflection and solutions. Many of those that struggle with conflict find that reflection and verbal skills are often the most difficult methods.

For young children, fairness can sit at the root of too much of the conflict they experience. If someone takes a toy then the cry is 'that isn't fair'. Young children's understanding of 'fair' is too often explained as being a matter of possession. This has come from our observations but is supported in the literature (Kowel et al. 2002; Almas et al. 2010).

We wanted to achieve some clear outcomes for both pupils and the schools. We wanted students to have an increased understanding of conflict (how it starts and how it can be dealt with effectively); a set of skills that will enable them to deal with conflict in and outside of school; and increased confidence and safety within the school environment.

For schools, we wanted the program to lead to a reduction in conflict within the school generally and the playground in particular and students being able to resolve conflicts and being more focused on their classroom work and less on playground matters.

The program

The program we delivered consisted of six, one-hour sessions over two to three weeks (two or three sessions each week), with additional individual support for those who found the skills harder to learn. The all-class regular sessions aimed to build more momentum than weekly sessions could. Our experience of this age group was that having weekly sessions risked losing the learning between sessions.

There were six underlying concepts we wanted all children to learn, rehearse and use. Some children too often rely on one or two of these, but we wanted them to understand that there was always more than one way of sorting out any problem. The six concepts were as follows:

Negotiate ('Talk out'): the ability to talk with confidence, yield when necessary and stand firm when needed.

Arbitrate ('Ask teacher'): the ability to know when they need outside help and how to get that.

Mediate ('Ask friend'): know when that outside help could be another child.

Legislate ('Make rules'): know when formalizing a rule that everyone operates within will help to reduce unnecessary conflict, so for example, only year 4's are allowed in the football cage on Wednesdays.

Litigate 'Class view' (jury): know how and when a broader classroom discussion and resolution is appropriate.

Cooperate ('Find solution'): know how and when someone needs to help others to find solutions to problems.

To illustrate these and provide concrete ways of dealing with conflict, we also introduced 12 strategies. Again we used the sessions to rehearse and let children see the impact of these and enable them to see when they would be appropriate to use.

Skill	**Description**
Negotiating	Talking out
Compromising	Finding agreement
Taking turns	Taking turns
Active listening	Listening hard
Threat-free explanation	Explaining
Apologizing	Saying sorry
Soliciting intervention	Getting help to solve it
Postponing	Dealing with it later
Distracting	Doing something else
Humor	Making a joke
Chance	Flipping for it
Sharing	Sharing it

The first session was on the concept of fairness. It included practical exercises that enabled students to reflect and understand what is fair. At the beginning of this session, a large sweet lollipop was shown to the class (with lots of ooohhhhs). They were told that I wanted to share this with all of them, but I wanted this to be 'fair' and I wanted their ideas about how we could share this lollipop between all 30 of them and still be 'fair'.

Usually the first one with a hand up was a boy who said 'Give it to me'. Others would follow responses usually going through 'Cut it into 30 pieces' (I asked them how we could make sure that the 30 pieces were the same size) to 'We hand it around and everyone gets a lick' (the class is usually horrified by this).

In between the suggestions, we talked about what was fair as this is a critical component for understanding conflict at this age. Some unexpected responses were offered. One came from a boy who was less able and said that the lollipop should be given to someone who was sick. His rationale was that if we didn't have enough to go around, then to be 'fair' we should give the more vulnerable what little there was.

This conversation usually takes us past 'fair' meaning equal, which is often a difficult but essential concept for children and enables them to consider a more complex notion of 'fair'.

In the second session, we did more work on fairness and then moved onto the causes of conflict. Three ways of responding to conflict were introduced. These were 'giving in', 'being mean' and 'being strong'. Children by this stage were asked to suggest conflict situations they found themselves in, which often ranged from fights over pencils to verbal comments made in the playground. There was never a shortage of these.

We took these conflict situations and acted them out with volunteers showing the three ways of responding. The two most common themes were that most children were reluctant to 'give in' and that there was difficulty in making a distinction between 'being mean' and 'being strong' (the difference between aggression and assertion). This was an important distinction, especially because the role-play allowed children to see the interactive nature of conflict and how easily responses could be misinterpreted, with a 'mean' response, often bringing a mean one back. We then moved on to the introduction of 'what makes matters worse' and 'what makes matters better'. These were again acted out allowing children to see how they could do both, although making matters worse was more common. In the third session, we did more work on the three ways of responding to conflict, particularly focusing on being strong (assertive).

In the fourth session, we addressed how to solve problems. The six concepts outlined above were introduced and acted out with role-play.

It was clear in this session that many students often read far too much into conflicts. In the final session, we introduced the process of resolving conflict. The 'problem-solver' role was introduced. One of the outputs of this project was to provide a method for the children to use with each other to resolve conflict (thus enabling the learning and rehearsal to continue long after the six sessions were over). Each child in the class got the opportunity to be the 'problem solver' for the day. They were given a laminated sheet, which had the following problem-solving steps:

FOUR STEPS TO PROBLEM-SOLVING	
1. What is the problem?	Red
2. So the problem is	Amber
3. What can you do to solve the problem?	Amber
4. Is the problem solved?	Green

This was adapted from the Highscope (preschool) method (Evans 2002) where designated young children approached a conflict, first asking 'What is the problem?' While the response might be 'he took my pen', the problem solver's next task was to identify what the problem really was. This is different from who was to blame or who started it, which is often what is offered or what adults might ask, which too often leads to a claim of unfairness. The problem solver, having found out that the pen belonged to the school and that the person making the complaint had wanted that particular pen, might say, 'So, the problem is two children and one pen'.

If this was agreed as the problem, then they could move to stage three, which asked the question: 'What can you do to solve the problem?' The expectation was that those involved came up with a suitable solution, and once the problem solver had ensured that the problem was indeed solved she or he would move away. Children were also helped to grasp what was an appropriate conflict for them to deal with and what was not. If emotions were high or if violence occurred if the children involved were not listening, then Plan B was to get an adult.

The problem-solver role and the process of clarifying the problem gave children the experience of resolving conflict, increasing their confidence in dealing with conflict and consolidating the learning from the sessions.

For many of the children, they were on the cusp of being able to reflect on ideas, concepts and other people's views that might be different from their own. Verbal skills within the classroom varied hugely, with a significant number of girls and fewer boys being verbally strong and usually one or two girls and up to seven of the boys finding this more difficult.

While reflection and thought were an important part of the sessions, drawing from their own experience (conflict situations) and role-play was core to the delivery methods. For many of the children, acting out and seeing others act out conflict situations helped them recognize differences in sometimes subtle responses and how others could perceive these. Role-play and rehearsal enabled children of this age to learn through doing and observing. The immediacy and tension often led to similar pressure to conflict itself – enabling children to see the interaction and recognize what made matters better and worse. So, for example, most children were very surprised at how effective humor could be in making matters better and how ineffective 'being mean' could be. Discussion, reflection and asking questions are important parts of the process, but they arise out of the role-play. This adds a dynamic that often raises the tension, excitement and enthusiasm for the subject matter.

To evaluate the program's impact, we used four mechanisms: a critical reflection form completed by the person delivering the session; a 'quiz' for children to complete at the end of the program, which tested their knowledge of conflict resolution by offering a number of scenarios for them to work out the best response to the questions such as: 'You are in the playground and someone badmouths your mum. Give three ways you could deal with that situation?' The teachers were also asked about the general impact of the sessions – a detailed questionnaire for the class teacher to complete, asking for their views on the impact of the course and what changes she or he had seen as a result of the program; we also returned to the class four weeks after the program had been delivered to ask pupils about the role of 'problem solver' and how well this had worked.

Conclusions

Most children attending this program reported an increase in their understanding of conflict and how to deal with it. This was also supported by observations of teachers and reports of children adopting the language and concepts introduced in the program. The 'problem-solver' role enabled children's learning to continue after the course had been delivered.

On reflection, more visual representation and structured exercises (initially) may well have increased this further. We are also of the view that we could have layered the learning more (some concepts such as complex views of fairness and the distinction between being mean and being strong are critical foundations for other concepts to be built upon).

A majority of children reported that the course had broadened their skill sets, and this also allowed for a more relaxed view of conflict for some. The more options they had, the more their anxiety reduced. Body language, tone of voice and the use of humor were revelations for some, and the core method of acting out conflict with all its complexities allowed children to see what differences subtle changes in reaction could bring.

In one class prior to the course, the teacher reported that children would tell tales on each other and show irritation toward one another very easily. This teacher said that this kind of behavior had changed as a result of the course. Previously she felt that they had been very quick to assume the worst of each other. The increased understanding of actions determining reaction (if you smile then you are more likely to get a smile back, if you look angry you can expect this to be mirrored) and other opportunities to reflect on communication generally seemed to have made a difference. Again the problem-solver role took the course out into the playground and other parts of the school less 'policed' by staff. Some children reported changes at home, especially with brothers and sisters.

At times we were uncertain about reflecting on the more complex interactions, but found that most of the children (and especially many of the girls) were both able and willing to discuss the interaction between verbal, physical and emotional responses.

We think their age (seven–eight years), enabled many to be more reflective and we believe this is the right time to deliver the program. Younger children may not be able to reflect on their behavior. There were of course some children who struggled to engage at this level, but they were still able to benefit.

In terms of increased understanding of concepts and strategies, this is the area we think we had least impact on, although about half of the children reported change. Both gender and academic ability played a part in this. Those girls and more able children who were used to conceptual and strategic thinking were very able to engage. For those less able, or less complex in their level of communication (often boys), it was more of a struggle. However, we also think that this element stretched and engaged the more able children, while the more practical and lively parts engaged the less able and communicative. There may be a question of balance to ensure that the program as a whole does not become either too practical or conceptual.

Generally, teachers reported that there was less conflict in the classroom and the playground, and less being reported to them. When we returned to see whether the problem-solver role had been effective, those who had taken the role later reported there was less conflict to deal with. Sometimes children would complain that on their problem-solving day, there was 'nothing to do'.

Initially (at the planning stage), the problem-solver role was an add-on to continue the learning. Now we are of the view that this might have a more important place within the wider learning. This was offered to the schools as an added extra (only one school did not take this up as they felt their mediation program already had it covered).

As already indicated, teachers reported less conflict as a result of the program, and this was particularly true in the case of conflict brought into the classroom from the playground. Time lost with reported incidents and conflicts rolling on within the classroom are common distractors for children and for a teacher's time. For most of the schools, this was a significant element of the program. Overall, we were very pleased with the results and think that this provided a good foundation for children to learn conflict resolution skills.

Bibliography

Almas, I., Cappelen, A. W., Sørensen, E. O. and Tungodden. B. (2010) Development of Fairness Preferences in Children. *Science*, 328 (5982), 1176–1178.

Birmingham City Council (2009) *Promoting Alternative Thinking Strategies (PATHS)* www.birmingham.gov.uk/paths.

Black, K. A. (2000) Gender Differences in Adolescents' Behavior during Conflict Resolution Tasks with Best Friends. *Adolescence*, 35 (139), 499–512.

Broadbear, B. C. and Broadbear, J. T. (2000) Development of Conflict Resolution Skills in Infancy and Early Childhood. *The International Electronic Journal of Health Education*, 3 (4), 284–290.

Cheong, Y.-G. et al. (2011) *A Computational Approach towards Conflict Resolution for Serious Games Foundation of Digital Games*. 29 June–1 July 2011, Bordeaux, France. Available at: http://www.itu.dk/~yannakakis/Cheong_FDG11.pdf.

Department of Education (2012a) A Profile of Pupil Exclusions in England Research. Report DFE-RR190, Department of Education, February 2012.

Department for Education (2012b) Pupil Behaviour in Schools in England. Education Standards Analysis and Research Division. Research Report DFE-RR218.

Evans, B. (2002) *You can't come to my birthday party: Conflict resolution with young children*. Ypsilanti, MI: High/Scope Press.

Galtung, J. (1969) Violence, Peace, and Peace Research. *Journal of Peace Research*, 6 (3), 167–191.

Hoffman, L. (1979) Maternal Employment: 1979. *American Psychologist,* 34, 859–865.

Humphrey, N. et al. (2008) *Primary Social and Emotional Aspects of Learning (SEAL) Evaluation of Small Group Work.* Department for Children, Schools and Families.

Johnson, D. W. and Johnson, R. (1995) Why Violence Prevention Programs Don't Work and What Does. *Educational Leadership,* 52 (5), 63–67.

Jones, T. S. (2004) Conflict Resolution Education: The Field, the Findings, and the Future. *Conflict Resolution Quarterly,* 22 (1–2).

Kohlberg, L. (1981) *The Philosophy of Moral Development, Essays on Moral Development* (Vol. 1). San Fransisco, CA: Harper & Row.

Kolb, B. (1995) *Brain Plasticity and Behaviour.* New Jersey: Lawrence Erlbaum Associates.

Kowel, A., Kramer, L., Krull, J. L. and Crick, N. R. (2002) Children's Perceptions of the Fairness of Parental Preferential Treatment and Their Socio-Emotional Well-Being. *Journal of Family Psychology,* 16 (3), 297–306.

Laursen, B. and Hartup, W. W. (1989) The Dynamics of Preschool Children's Conflicts. *Merrill Palmer Quarterly,* 35 (3 July), 281–297.

Lloyd, T. (2009) *Young Men and Violence – Literature Review.* Belfast: Centre for Young Men's Studies, Ulster University.

Piaget, J. (1951) [1914] *Judgment and Reasoning in the Child* (Trans. M. Warden). London: Routledge & Kegan Paul.

Shantz, C. U. (1992) *Conflict in Child and Adolescent Development.* Cambridge: Cambridge University Press,

Shore, R. (1997) *Rethinking the Brain.* New York: Families and Work Institute, pp. 15–27.

Shure, M. B. (1982) Interpersonal Problem Solving: A Cog in the Wheel of Social Cognition. In F. C. Serafica (ed.) *Social-cognitive Development in Context,* New York: The Guilford Press, pp. 133–166.

Part IV
War and Everyday Violence

Alison Watson

Many of the images of war most permanently seared into our memories involve children and young people. Thus if we try to conjure up a visual image of war, probably what most often comes to mind is the face of a child: Kim Phuc desperately running toward the camera in Nick Ut's iconic photograph of the aftermath of a South Vietnamese napalm attack; 12-year-old Muhammad al-Durrah crouching beside his father against a concrete wall near Netzarim in the Gaza Strip moments before he was killed by Israeli forces; the little girl crawling for food in a Sudan decimated by civil war and famine as a vulture waits behind her; or the children with hollow eyes staring through the barbed wire surrounding a concentration camp. Children are perhaps our most searing image of the horrors of war, something that the media does little to undermine. When journalists cover conflict, their aim is to make us, the public, sit up and take notice. In our hyper-mediated world, violence has become commonplace and many of us inured to the suffering of others. For this reason, the power to shock is often what is required, and pictures of children do just that. The way in which they are represented, however, also conditions our response to them. The child is an emotive subject, their representation guaranteed to bring forward a response. Such images often cast children in times of war as only victims – a class of actor that leaves no room for their present agency or for their future potential. Children, however, are much more than that, and must be considered in this way if there is to be any hope for a long-term settlement in a post-conflict setting.

Violence is an everyday reality for so many children around the world and in Claudia Seymour's chapter we see the significance of such violence in a conflict that has been described by some commentators as Africa's First World War. In the Democratic Republic of Congo (DRC), more than five million lives have been lost. The recent decision to establish an 'intervention brigade' in the eastern DRC is unparalleled in the history of UN peacekeeping, Yet despite this, the eyes of the world remain elsewhere. For Claudia Seymour, the issue of children and youth in the Kivus – arguably the region that lies at the heart of conflict in the DRC – is paramount. Drawing on her experiences both as a researcher and as a practitioner, she aims to contribute toward child protection interventions 'which can more effectively support the actual needs of young people living in contexts of violence'. In particular, Seymour discovers that 'structural violence was . . . a defining aspect of their everyday life' and charts 'the interface between political and structural violence' that is so clear in the narratives of the young people whom Seymour interviews and that often leads to them taking on the role of 'victim' as a coping mechanism, within the context of the continual threat of violence. Such positioning, however, can actually prove to be counter-productive both in terms of children and on the potential for the roles that they may play in the international security system. For rather than seeing children as victims, if we instead consider them to be agents in their own right we must consider whether our perception of what they may be able to achieve, and in turn what the post-conflict process is able to achieve, would be altered. Of course, this issue is not only one that affects children in the international system. The mechanisms of the liberal peace have been constructed in such a way that anyone classified as 'victim' finds it difficult to claim agency as the event that has resulted in their being cast as victims, has had an emotional and psychological impact that may be perceived as impacting upon the potential to act rationally and hence claim agency. Thinking that those who have been hurt cannot have the strength to respond makes the words of one interviewee in the Kivus, that Seymour quotes, self-fulfilling: '(f)or me it's the same. It will always be the same, nothing changes . . . .'.

This issue of violence and conflict in everyday life is picked up in Chapter 9 that focuses on war and how 'conflict and violence impact upon children and their education, experiences and learning from the field and the humanitarian sector'. It's an important analysis considering education both within its global context and as a 'positive relationship that can aid in the building of peace'. Deborah Haines is a practitioner, her chapter reflecting her 'work experiences in Liberia, Kenya, Lebanon, West Timor and Timor L'Este'. In her experiences in these countries, she has come to realize the significance of education in the search for peace and thus once again recognizes that in the post-conflict environment the roles that children and youth play are vital to the possibilities for long-term peaceful settlement. Her work here is particularly concerned with notions of movement and of how displacement impacts upon education, but in many ways she too is examining the notion of 'everyday life', recognizing that in conflict and post-conflict environments, those affected seek normalcy and may channel their feelings about their situation into acts of play – drawing, singing, dancing. They may also find themselves in situations where education – at that particular point in time – is not in their best interests, an important point that recognizes that there is nothing straightforward in a conflict or post-conflict environment. Whether a person is an adult or child, making sense of everyday life in a conflict or post-conflict environment is both a challenge and a requirement. It is also an act of resistance and an opportunity to demonstrate agency in an environment in which there may be few opportunities to do so. In this way, even the smallest acts of a child may, when taken together, be viewed as a practice that precipitates political change.

8
Everyday Violence and War in the Kivus, DRC

Claudia Seymour

Introduction

This chapter has two main objectives: the first is to explore young people's experience of political and structural violence in the context of eastern Democratic Republic of Congo (DRC) through their narratives of everyday life; the second objective is to critically examine dominant international child protection interventions in the context of eastern DRC. The chapter considers the structures of violence that dominate life in the Kivus today, by briefly overviewing the historic rootedness of violence in eastern DRC, its manifestation in contemporary political and structural violence and how young people live within and experience these forms of violence. It examines how the valorization of vulnerability and the disconnect between rights-based discourses and lived realities can contribute to weakening young people's coping capacities and strengthen structures of violence.

The data used in this chapter draws on a larger interdisciplinary doctoral research project on young people's experiences and means of coping with violence in the provinces of North and South Kivu, eastern DRC. The fieldwork for this research was conducted between 2010 and 2011. In South Kivu, an intensive data collection period took place over a period of four months with 44 young people between the ages of 14 and 24 years of age, based on mixed qualitative methods which included participant observation, weekly discussions and semi-structured interviews. In North Kivu, approximately 200 young people between the ages of 12 and 22 years participated in this research through less-intensive but broader-based methods which included focus group discussions and individual interviews; in 2011 the field research in North Kivu was conducted with the support of Save the Children, UK, and in 2010 the research was conducted with the support of War Child, UK. My affiliation at the time of data collection, as an independent doctoral researcher or as associated with an international non-governmental organization (NGO), is clearly noted in the narratives included in this chapter.

The analysis presented in this chapter is also informed by my own previous experience as a child protection actor in the Kivus, where I first began working in 2006. Serving first as a Child Protection Advisor with the United Nations (UN) Department of Peacekeeping Operations between 2006 and 2007, with the UN Group of Experts on the DRC in 2009 and subsequently with various international NGOs, these experiences provided me with access to many hundreds of young people who were directly affected by violence. Through my interactions with these young people, I came to see that the child protection interventions in which I was involved were inadequate in responding to the actual needs of young people, and in some cases doing more harm than good. These professional experiences thus guided my doctoral work toward gaining greater understanding of young people's actual experiences of and means of coping with violence and questioning the dominant assumptions of the child protection regime. The aim of this work is to contribute toward interventions that can more effectively support the actual needs of young people living in contexts of violence.

Structures of violence

Looking at history to understand how the present comes to be is an essential step toward making sense of contemporary violence (Farmer 2004). While aware that there is a risk in placing too much importance on the violence of the colonial past or of making the living 'victims of their own history' (Jackson 2005, 371), the lasting impact of former Belgian rule in the DRC requires attention. The 'founding violence' (Das 2007) on which the Congolese state was built dates back at least to the 1885 Berlin Conference, when the delineated Congo Free State was placed under the rule of King Leopold II of Belgium. Governed as a personal fiefdom for the extraction of rubber and copper wealth, the extreme brutality of King Leopold's reign eventually led to the assumption of control by the Belgian state in 1908 (Hochschild 1998). For the Belgian Congo, the eastern region of the Kivus offered highly fertile land and great natural resource wealth. Laborers forcibly displaced from neighboring Rwanda worked the farms and mines extensively. Between 1920 and 1955, an estimated 100,000 people from Ruanda-Urundi were displaced into the Kivus (Jackson 2007). Labeled 'non-native' by the colonial authorities and considered 'foreign' by the 'autochthonous' populations, these newly settled Banyarwandans or 'people of Rwanda' were denied legal access to land and protection by the colonial Native Authority (Mamdani 2001). It is this policy of exclusion that laid the foundation for the contemporary identity-based conflict over land, citizenship and belonging in the Kivus.

The land–citizenship–identity complex formalized during the colonial period was transposed into Congo's independence era, serving as a highly effective tool for political and economic manipulation. President Mobutu Sese Seko, who ruled Zaire[1] from 1965 to 1996, used competition over land and contentious identity and citizenship politics as key strategies to maintain influence over the restive eastern provinces. Throughout the 1970s, these policies led to heightened discontent among the 'autochthons' Zaireans who considered themselves to be the only legitimate owners of the land (Jackson 2006). Identity-based manipulations continued to escalate throughout the 1980s, with tensions spilling over in the late 1980s and early 1990s as a result of the 'democratic' opening imposed on Mobutu by Western governments (Nzongola-Ntalaja 2002).

Land conflicts that had simmered and occasionally erupted from the early 1960s exploded in the early 1990s, leading to the killing of up to 10,000 people and the displacement of an estimated 250,000 others in North Kivu alone (Mamdani 2001). It was into this highly charged dynamic that, in the wake of the 1994 Rwandan genocide, an estimated one million Rwandan Hutu refugees arrived in the Kivus. As a result of the preexisting and tenuous ethnic balance, the resource-rich provinces of North and South Kivu became the launching grounds for what would become 'Africa's World War' (Prunier 2009), involving nine countries and lasting for the seven years between 1996 and 2003. The war resulted in the toppling of Mobutu in 1996 by the Rwanda-backed *Alliance des Forces Démocratiques pour la Libération du Congo* (AFDL). The AFDL, led by Laurent Kabila, eventually disintegrated and subsequent fighting effectively split the country – with the eastern provinces coming under the control of the *Rassemblement Congolais pour la Démocratie* (RCD), essentially a proxy government for Rwanda (Prunier 2009; Stearns 2011).

In the ensuing years, allegiances and enmities continued to shift violently. While formal peace was negotiated at a national level in 2003, violent conflict continued in the Kivus. The presidential elections in 2006 officially ended the 'post-conflict transition' period but resulted in renewed political violence in the east. Assuming a new configuration, Rwandan-backed Tutsi militia took control of large areas of the Kivus as the *Congres National pour le Défense du Peuple*, while the *Forces démocratiques de libération du Rwanda* (FDLR) – a Hutu-based rebel force emerging from the 1994 Rwandan genocide, still locally called *Interahamwe* – assumed control of others. At the same time various Mayi-mayi (local militia) groups re-emerged, ostensibly fighting to protect local interests, while the national Congolese army, the *Forces Armés de la Republique Démocratique du Congo*, struggled to assert any form of territorial control with a badly organized, poorly paid and largely demoralized force (Eriksson Baaz and Stern 2010).

This situation has largely prevailed in the Kivus since 2006 and roughly describes the militarized configuration that dominated throughout the time I lived, worked and conducted research in the Kivus (2006–2011). During these years, political violence was no longer expressed as all-out war but rather manifested as generalized insecurity and sporadic battles over key mining and resource-extraction zones. The situation was largely dictated by political and economic elites (Congolese, Rwandan and others) who successfully mobilized political violence in order to gain or maintain control of natural resource extraction and trade routes, while continuing to foment identity-based discourses of hatred and distrust. The conflict dynamics were additionally complicated by a large presence of international aid actors and a UN peacekeeping mission.

In contemporary international discourse, the DRC is commonly referred to in terms that emphasize the extremes of violence experienced there. It is a place where storylines of violence (Eriksson Baaz and Stern 2010) form a complex web of suffering, hardship and adversity – described by some as 'the world's deadliest humanitarian crisis' (Coghlan et al. 2006) and by others as 'the rape capital of the world' (BBC 2010).[2] These accounts usually describe the evident expressions of political violence, the 'targeted physical violence and terror administered by official authorities and those opposing it' (Bourgois 2001, 8). Yet political violence represents only one of the expressions of violence prevailing in eastern DRC.

My initial research aim had been to understand how young people experience and cope with this political violence, but my research participants were quick to guide me to look beyond the most obvious or 'subjective' (Zizek 2009) expressions of violence. According to them, 'violence is everywhere' (doctoral focus group discussion, Bukavu, April 2010), and they easily identified the multitudes of violence which affect them each day. Insecurity, assassinations, rape and theft were only the first of what would become a long list of everyday violence, which was continued with injustice and impunity, unemployment, hunger, poverty, sickness and children not being able to afford school fees. It was through their assertions and accounts of the dominant influence of these forms of violence in their lives that structural violence thus became a central frame of analysis for my research.

Structural violence is defined as 'chronic, historically-entrenched political-economic oppression and social inequality' (Bourgois 2001, 8), often described as that violence which 'does not show' (Galtung 1969, 173). Yet for my research participants, structural violence was anything but invisible; it was a defining aspect of their everyday experience. It defined their perspectives and prevented them from realizing any aspirations they might have for a better future in what they termed to be 'this dead Congo' (doctoral focus group discussion, Bukavu, June 2010). By imposing profound limitations on possibilities for human self-realization (Galtung 1969), structural violence in contemporary DRC has created a situation in which young people are aware of the limitations proscribing their lives, yet are unable to do anything about them.

Accounting for both political and structural violence, the 'structures of violence' analytical framework used in my research and in this chapter builds on Bourdieu's assumption that there exist 'objective structures independent of the consciousness and will of agents, which are capable of guiding and constraining their practices...' (Bourdieu 1989, 14). Borrowing further from Bourdieu, this research considers how young people who live within these structures of violence develop a habitus, the 'schemes of perception, thought, and action' (Bourdieu 1989, 19), which guides their lived experiences. The 'habitus of violence' developed by young people in eastern DRC allows them to live within and cope with the structures of violence which circumscribe their everyday lives. As advanced by Bourgois (2001, 29) in his ethnography of violence in El Salvador, 'people do not simply "survive" violence as if it somehow remained outside of them'. Rather, the social, economic and political processes of violence that originated in the past are lived in the present and define the future, becoming an integral part of young people's everyday lives.

Young people's experiences of violence

Examining in greater depth young people's experiences of the 'structures of violence' is a fundamental first step toward gaining a deeper understanding of how they cope with this violence. The structures of violence in the Kivus constrain and define young people's lives in profound ways, as shown through Emile's narrative.[3] Emile, 22 years old when I first met him in 2010, was a key informant to my doctoral research. He recounted his biographical narrative as follows:

> I'm the third child of my family. My mother was killed in 2004, my father in 1997. My father used to work at the Kavumu airport [near Bukavu] as a pilot. At the start of the war, soldiers from the FAZ [*Forces Armés Zairoises*] tried to force him to fly a plane from Bukavu to Kisangani; he told the soldiers it wouldn't be possible, that the plane wasn't in good enough condition to fly. Then the AFDL arrived at the airport, they took him hostage, we didn't see him again. We heard this story from others who had been there.
>
> We stayed only with our mother then. During the RCD war, soldiers came to our house, accused us of having worked for Mobutu, of hiding Hutus in our home. They demanded money from my mother. She said we had none, but she gave them our sewing machine. They locked us [the children] into one of the rooms. They were going to rape my mother. We heard her screaming. I was the oldest boy. I forced the door open and saw my mother on the floor. The soldiers told me they'd kill me. One of them hit me and I spat on him. Then they forced me to come with them into the forest.
>
> They gave me a weapon, taught me how to use it. In the forest, we fought against the *Interahamwe* [FDLR], there was a lot of gunfire. Then there was a cease-fire. We walked to Lulingu, Shabunda. For one week we walked. We didn't eat anything except ugali [manioc-based paste]. I was so hungry, I asked a soldier about getting food, he replied: 'Do you see anyone of us eating meat? Are you so hungry?' He took his knife and held my arm. He cut off the flesh from my arm. He made me grill my flesh, and then he forced me to eat it. I pretended to, but I couldn't. I spat it out when he wasn't looking.
>
> Then there was more fighting against the *Interahamwe* in Lulingu. I got shot in the leg in a few places. I woke up later in the hospital in Bukavu. They told me I had been brought there by the ICRC [International Committee for the Red Cross]. I was in the hospital for a month. One day, people I knew from church found me. They told my sisters where I was, and they came to find me. How they cried. I had left my mother when she was still alive…

> [Emile fell silent here and looked down at his hands folded in his lap. After a few moments, he continued.]
>
> That's how it is.

In the DRC, the experiences of extreme and terrible suffering are generalized. Variations on themes of brutality and loss, these experiences have either been directly lived or at least witnessed and are thus woven into the texture of every day. While the details of political violence – which Emile clearly articulated in his biographical narrative – would rarely emerge in subsequent discussions, his experience of violence was incorporated in his physical self, his conception of the world and his way of being in it. The bullet wounds in his leg had healed badly and continued to cause him significant pain, while the wide and smooth scar running down the length of his forearm served as a constant physical reminder of what he had lived. Beyond the direct consequences of the political violence, Emile struggled to survive the structural violence of being an orphan, without a secondary school degree and with no prospects for earning a stable livelihood.

The interface between political and structural violence also emerged clearly in the narrative of another doctoral research participant in Kalehe Territory, South Kivu. B- was 21 years old when I first met him. His village had been attacked in 2003 and many of the villagers had been killed, including his parents and his sister. He and his older brother had fled to the town center where they had since lived. B- would often express his frustration of having to depend on his older brother who supported his education and in whose home he continued to live. He was eager to move out on his own, to prepare himself to begin his own family, but his lack of financial independence made this impossible:[4]

> I eventually want to have children, to have the means to feed them and educate them. But now my only priority is my schooling. If I have any luck, it would be to get a job. I'll probably be a teacher when I finish secondary school, though I really dream of going to university. As a teacher, maybe the government will pay me 30,000 Fc (Congolese francs, approximately US$30) plus the 25,000 Fc from the school fees, but then 10% of what I earn I'd have to give back to the church that runs the school, plus more for the school's functioning. This would never be enough money to live on, not at all.
>
> (doctoral interview, Bunyakiri, April 2010)

The structures of violence permeated and controlled so many aspects of my research participants lives. Testifying to the ways in which 'inequality is structured and legitimated over time' (Farmer 2004, 309), young people involved in this research were deeply aware of the ways in which violence defined their present and their future. As evident in the narrative of M-, a 17-year-old mother of a six-month-old girl, also a key doctoral research participant in Kalehe Territory, South Kivu:[5]

> I'm the youngest child of my mother – she died soon after I was born. My father is extremely ill, he can't take care of me. After my mother died, his second wife never accepted me. Now I live in my older brother's house. I don't get along well with my sister-in-law, but I have to stay there with them. My brother is also chronically ill; he can't use his hand, and can't work, but we have no means of paying for him to go to the hospital in Bukavu.
>
> Every day we work, *c'est penible*. I go to the field with my sister-in-law, we cultivate manioc and peanuts. Every day we have to make the choice: do we eat what we've cultivated, or do we sell it? It's never enough for both and we have to choose. Each day the decision is difficult.
>
> (doctoral interview, Bunyakiri, May 2010)

M- and her family lived in conditions of abject rural poverty. Her older brother was responsible for ensuring the livelihood of his own wife and children as well as his large extended family, but he suffered from a debilitating undiagnosed condition that had paralyzed his left arm, making manual work impossible. On the day I visited M- in her house, her brother had received a 'convocation' from the local authorities demanding that he report to them to explain his absence at the previous days' communal labor effort, a formality which would inevitably result him having to pay a fine or face the risk of imprisonment. The money that M- and the entire family had been working to save up in order to send him to Bukavu for medical tests and treatment would instead be used to pay the fine to the local authority.

The gruelling conditions of each day did not prevent M- from imagining a very different kind of life. Among her dreams was to become one day a woman selling fish in the market, a dream that was partially a way of avoiding the physical exhaustion of cultivation and partially a way of escaping the insecurity which plagued each of her walks through the hills to the fields. M-'s daughter had been born as a result of a rape by an unknown armed man when she had been working in the fields in 2009, and she continued to feel herself at risk of attack each day. After establishing herself as a market woman, her biggest dream would then be 'to be married, to have a stable home of my own. I want to be able to take care of my daughter'. Although M- was capable of imagining a better life for herself and her daughter, she remained deeply pragmatic; she knew that having been raped and having had a child from that rape dramatically reduced her chances of being considered a desirable wife. If she ever did marry, the physical abuse that she expected she would receive from her husband would never give her the freedom of which she sometimes allowed herself to dream.

Agency and young people's capacity for coping with violence

Although dominant perspectives among child protection actors consider young people to be vulnerable and passively victim to the structures and processes of violence, this research instead conceives of young people as being active agents within the structures in which they live (Boyden 2000; Utas 2005; Vigh 2006; Hart 2008). An agentic perspective examines how young people construct and determine their own life outcomes (James and Prout 1997), negotiating the highly uncertain and often deeply proscribed conditions of violent conflict. Defined as the capacity one has to act within and influence established social structures and relations (Bourdieu 1977), agency involves an ability to adjust to and take advantage of new and changing circumstances (Arnfred and Utas 2007) as well as the capacity to constructively engage with one's environment and society (Boyden and Mann 2005); these skills are especially important in the uncertain conditions dominating contexts of violence.

Agency is thus a central component of young people's coping mechanisms. Yet given the overwhelmingly powerful structures of violence and the limited range of possibility within which operation is possible, young people's agentic capacity is highly conscribed in eastern DRC. In this sense, de Certeau's (1984) elaboration of the concept of tactical agency is more useful – a perspective which considers how individuals who live within the established structures become reliant on tactics to 'use, manipulate and divert' the spaces that have been determined for them (de Certeau 1984, 30). Although individuals within the system are unable to change the structures, they are able to 'find ways of using the constraining order' (de Certeau 1984, 30) to their advantage, of seizing any possible opportunities to subvert it and to reappropriate those aspects which may be considered useful.

Utas (2005) has used the concept of tactical agency in his research with young people living in war-affected Liberia, showing that the ways in which individuals use their tactical agency depends not only on the structures in which they are embedded but also on the social environment in which they live. Young people in the Kivu's also use their tactical agency in responding to the threats, risks and possibilities they face – relying on what they describe as their capacity for intelligence at surviving the harsh conditions imposed on them. According to their definition, intelligence is

> [t]he capacity to look for one's livelihood [*chercher la vie*]. We don't cross our arms, we look to others for help...Intelligence requires the ability to change behaviours...to think about solutions and to know how to realise them. It's knowing how to use what we've been given...Intelligence comes from experiencing difficulties, if one isn't hungry, one won't learn intelligence.
>
> (doctoral focus group discussion, Bukavu, April 2010)

Through their intelligence, they are able to navigate the structures of violence:

> We live despite it all...We depend on our intelligence – the capacity to know how to exploit our potential, to seize possible opportunities....
>
> (doctoral interview, Bunyakiri, May 2010)

Among my research participants, their tactical agency and intelligence in coping with the structures of violence was demonstrated through three dominant coping mechanisms: *la débrouille*, submission and 'victimcy' (Utas 2005). These are expressions of agency that are simultaneously individual, social and political, expressing tactics which allow young people to cope as effectively as they can within the structures of violence.

La débrouille is a ubiquitous concept throughout the DRC and throughout much of Francophone Sub-Saharan Africa – a term which is derived from the French verb *se débrouiller* (see Olivier de Sardan 1996). *Se débrouiller* can be translated as 'to find a way', 'o make arrangements', 'to use one's own means' or 'to be satisfied with'. It is a specific way of coping that has come to dominate discourses on survival in the DRC

(MacGaffey 1986), while at the same time serving as an epithet to justify the absence of government services and control (Eriksson Baaz and Stern 2010). In eastern DRC, *la débrouille* allows young people to survive and to make the best of difficult circumstances, evincing how people are able to cope with adverse conditions. Strategies of *la débrouille* among my research participants included daily wage labor (e.g., carrying goods from the fields or the port to the market, or working on the fields of someone else), searching for financial handouts from friends or relatives, or for the girls engaging in transactional sex. These strategies are used on a daily basis to ensure their material survival, and while displaying their tactical agency to ensure the best possible short-term outcomes, in the long term can lead to weakening young people's capacities for effective coping.

The second dominant strategy which young people in eastern DRC adopt to cope with the structures of violence is submission. As demonstrated by my research participants, submission is an essential mechanism for coping with violence, which can be life-saving when dealing with conditions of uncertainty and insecurity. The prevailing and generalized sense of helplessness for young people to challenge the structures of violence in which they are entrenched was often rationalized as: 'that's just how it is' (multiple interviews and focus group discussions). This defeat not only permeates young people's conceptions of the present but also colors their perspectives for the future. For example, in a discussion about hopes and dreams for the future, a 20-year-old man who had lived in the streets of Goma since he was seven years old stated: 'Why should I have thoughts about my future? I'm already dead' (focus group discussion on behalf of War Child UK, Goma, July 2010; also quoted in War Child UK 2010, 30). Young people in eastern DRC have submitted to the structures in which they live, demonstrating how 'the dominated, often unwittingly, contribute to their own domination by tacitly accepting, in advance, the limits imposed on them' (Bourdieu 2000, 169). Contrary to Bourdieu's conception of unwitting submission, however, my research participants demonstrated their active choice in submitting to the violence in their lives. Having learnt firsthand that resistance would not make a difference in their lives, my research participants explained: 'If we try to liberate ourselves or if we aim to be heroes, we'll just be killed. So it's better just to suffer' (doctoral focus group discussion, Bukavu, June 2010).

The third dominant coping strategy adopted by young people in the DRC expresses what Utas (2005) has termed 'victimcy' in his work with young people in Liberia. Utas (2005, 403) defines victimcy as 'a form of self-representation by which a certain form of tactic agency is effectively exercised under the trying, uncertain, and disempowering circumstances that confront actors in warscapes'. Through the presentation of oneself as a victim in order to gain access to assistance, young people actively negotiate their survival outcomes in highly rational ways. Victimcy is a complex and highly interactive coping strategy that depends on portrayals of weakness in order to increase the chances of accessing assistance. As I experienced countless times in the DRC, as well as throughout my research, accounts of suffering and helplessness were shared in the hope that I might offer material support or some other form of patronage. These accounts were often shared with me on the basis of the perceived differential of power and access to resources that separated me from the people I would interact with, a historically derived, racialized and nationality-based perception that is unavoidable in the context of the DRC. Self-conscious of the spaces and possibilities presented by the structures of violence, victimcy is thus a clear expression of tactical agency used by young people as their attempt to make the most of available opportunities. While victimcy can often allow young people to gain access to support, the reliance on it as a coping strategy ultimately valorizes vulnerability, leading to weakened capacities for coping in the longer term. As will be discussed in the next section, victimcy is also a key tool for coping within the global political economy, as represented by international actors working in eastern DRC.

International child protection interventions in the Kivus

International child protection actors have been dominant players in the theater of international aid in eastern DRC since the mid-1990s. Their actions have focused on a range of interventions which tend to be standardized across contexts affected by war or natural disasters, from family tracing and reunification of children separated from their families, to disarmament, demobilization and reintegration of children associated with armed groups to the provision of psychosocial support. Building on a well-established literature critiquing the dominant approach to child protection interventions (Boyden 1997; James and Prout 1997; Pupavac 2001; Mann 2004; Hart 2006; Macmillan 2009; Hart and Lo Forte 2010), this chapter now critically considers the relevance and appropriateness of child protection interventions in eastern DRC from two perspectives. The first examines the potentially damaging role that the child protection's focus on vulnerability can play in weakening young people's capacities for coping. The second critique addresses the disconnect between the rights-based discourse and young people's actual experiences of violence, introducing the concept of denial to analyze why child protection interventions may remain so ill-adapted in responding to the actual coping needs of young people in the context of DRC's violence.

Valorizing vulnerability

The first critique of child protection interventions discussed in this chapter is their tendency to target categories of children who are considered to be a priori vulnerable. Categorizations of vulnerability for selected groups of children, such as 'child soldier', rape victim or street child, are imposed without considering the individual experience of each young person or the conditions which led to their joining an armed group, being a victim of rape, or moving to the streets in the first place, conditions which are themselves defined by the structures of violence in which young people live. In many cases, young people who join armed groups or move to the streets do so not in a position of weakness, but rather as it presents the best possible coping strategy available to them.

As demonstrated by my research participants, young people in the Kivus are well aware of these categorizations of vulnerability and the accompanying material benefits that can come with them. Practicing the 'very ancient art of "making do"' (de Certeau 1984, 30), young people thus use the child protection system to their advantage; subverting the order from within (de Certeau, 32) by emphasizing their weakness and vulnerability. My research participants demonstrated how they had reappropriated and successfully incorporated vulnerability as a key coping response, aware that certain kinds of violence will be more likely to receive a response from child protection actors than others. Young people would thus portray their weakness, in narratives of orphanhood, experiences of rape and histories of mobilization, to child protection actors in the hopes that these defined conditions of vulnerability might accord them access to material support, such as the payment of school fees or enrolment in a vocational training program. For example, one of my research participants in Bukavu had learnt the value placed on militarized rape by international actors in eastern DRC. N-, who was twenty-two years old when we met, easily shared her story during our first meeting:

> I'd like to tell you the story about my life, even if it's sad. I try to forget things, but it's not easy... In 2007 I started at [a local NGO] where

> I was trained in tailoring. [The same NGO] pays my school fees now. I'm a student of law at the university. I dream of becoming a lawyer, to defend women and children. Girls here suffer too much. My role is to be a messenger for all the girls, all the women, all the young people who have suffered like me...
>
> Look at me, I was born of rape. My mother didn't love my father and I didn't know my father. My mother had 6 children in all. When I was 11 years old, we came to Bukavu...
>
> In 2003, during the fighting, I was taken away by the *Interahamwe*. They took me hostage with another girl, into the forest. It was a Tuesday that day. We were taken to the forest not far from Minova. It's hard for me to talk about this... I was a slave for 6 men, always the same men. I had to do sexual acts for them, it was so difficult. I couldn't eat, it was such suffering.
>
> One day, after two and a half years, they went to a battle, I was left guarded by only one soldier. I asked the soldier if I could go to bathe; he said I could if I had sex with him first. After I did, I managed to get far from him, and then I escaped, I hid in the forest for two days, I didn't know where I was. Eventually I found the road, and a car stopped to pick me up and took me to Goma.
>
> Eventually I became very sick... and I learned I was pregnant. Now I have my 5 year old daughter with me. Like me, she was born of rape...

N- is an impressive person – intelligent, articulate and courageous. She had lived through incredibly difficult life experiences, surviving in ways that defied expectation. Having since been provided all the opportunities on offer by the child protection system, material support, education, training and even international travel, she had turned her experience into something positive and hoped to use her access to Congolese leaders and international audiences to advocate for the needs of other young people:

> Since 2007, I've travelled four times to speak to officials and leaders. I've been to Nairobi, to Kinshasa and to Kigali twice. Next week I'll go to Norway to tell my story. My priority now is to advocate for the rights of children born of rape and for those who became mothers against their will (doctoral interview, Bukavu, April 2010).

Yet N-'s narrative and the way she projected herself left me questioning if there might not be negative consequences of all the support she was receiving from the child protection system around her. While she was thriving with all the attention, it was attention that was based primarily on her status as a rape victim. Through her narrative, it was evident that her personal identity was now anchored in her experience of abduction, violence, rape and unwanted motherhood. Because of her gruesome experience of suffering at the hands of the rebel forces, she was deemed an appropriate target of aid and could therefore benefit from unprecedented opportunities. She was being supported through her education, even continuing on to university – which is an exceptional privilege for a young person in the DRC, and was repeatedly invited to speak at international conferences. More cynically, it was clear that N-'s experience and her public accounting of it was especially useful in the fund-raising efforts of the local and international NGOs who supported her and invited her to speak during meetings with potential and current donors.

N- had lived through a brutal human experience and the assistance she was getting from the child protection system was helping her to gain access to opportunities that she would never otherwise have been able to access. However, N-'s experience also shows other young people that in order to gain access to aid and assistance, one must portray one's victim status. This focus on victimhood espoused by the child protection system demonstrates how processes by which 'the weaker party conforms to the same rationality as the dominant party' (Marriage 2012) can become entrenched. By conforming to the child protection regime's rationality of vulnerability, young people reinforce their position of victimhood and dependence and thus contribute to the weakening of their capacities for coping in the long term.

Disconnect and denial

The second critique of international child protection in the DRC discussed in this chapter is its tendency to be disconnected from the realities experienced by young people living within the structures of violence. Although there can be merit in holding standards regarding the primordial nature of children's rights toward which states may aspire, the space between that which is enshrined in child protection conventions and protocols – for example children's 'full and harmonious development' in 'peace' and 'dignity' (United Nations Convention on the Rights of the Child 1989) and the realities actually lived by children on a daily basis – raises questions about the relevance of the rights-based discourse. Absolutist discourses about 'inalienable rights' in contexts of structural and political violence are advanced by child protection actors, yet, as described elsewhere with regard to rights-based approaches more generally, 'the same words are used to describe something that happens, something that should happen, and something that does not happen' (Marriage 2006, v). Such cognitive dissonance between discourse and reality (Marriage 2006) often results in the avoidance, denial or obscuration of the structures of violence that so powerfully constrain the lives of young people.

The disconnect between child protection approaches and the actual protection needs faced by young people is striking: while loudly proclaiming the values of universal child rights, the underlying causes of those very rights being violated remain unaddressed. For example, in the Kivus, dominant child protection actors tend to either provide palliative and short-term project-based solutions that do not respond in any way to the structural causes of violence, or they focus only on extreme and overt expressions of violence through monitoring, documenting and denouncing of child rights violations. The UN Monitoring and Reporting Mechanism (MRM), for example, is a key child protection activity in the Kivus – a mechanism initiated through UN Security Council Resolution 1612 (2005) established to monitor and report on six grave violations of children's rights in contexts affected by violent conflict. The MRM compiles regular reports that are used in advocacy efforts at the national and international level. While this system of reporting has raised awareness on the grave violations of children's rights occurring in the DRC, the end result is a system of reporting which serves to enumerate violations without responding to or preventing them. The lack of analysis of the political and historical roots of the violence and the lack of mention of the structural violence leading to the violations in the first place contributes to obscuring the causes of violence and to perpetuating interventions which do not respond to young people's actual protection needs.

To make analytical sense of the obscuration of the disconnect between child protection discourse and the reality lived by young people in the Kivus, the concept of 'denial' as elaborated by Cohen (2001, 79) is helpful toward explaining that which is 'known and not known at the same time'. As examined by Nordstrom (2004) in her ethnographic work in war-affected contexts, denial can be used to explain the incongruence of selected narratives of violence being accepted in public discourses – such as narratives of militarized rape in eastern DRC – while 'daily realities of life under extreme violence are erased' (Nordstrom 2004, 28). In another examination of denial, Marriage (2006) shows how the standard practice of selectively targeting only some 'beneficiaries' of humanitarian aid in a context of extreme and widespread material needs 'passes for pragmatism, but conscripts the idealism (or surrealism) that significant impact can be made with insignificant contributions' (Marriage 2006, 225).

Denial thus allows child protection actors to ignore the cognitive dissonance of 'doing protection' without actually protecting young people. This is especially dangerous as it consequently leads to obscuring the structures that create and maintain the conditions of violence with which young people are struggling to cope. As critiqued in other humanitarian contexts, well-intentioned international interventions can create and reinforce a 'false sense that something was being done, preventing discussion and analysis around what really needed doing' (Levine and Chastre 2004, 19). The structures of violence continue to operate without restriction, as international child protection actors scramble to decry and denounce abuses against young people without engaging in the deeper political, economic and strategic dynamics that allow such abuses to continue.

Conclusion

International child protection work is highly political, yet the dominant approach to child protection in contexts affected by violence tends to ignore this fact. Rather than engaging with the structures of violence, most international child protection activities remain simplified and superficial, offering short-term interventions which do little to engage in the necessary change in the structures of violence which conscribe and constrain so many aspects of young people's lives.

Dominant child protection discourse in contexts affected by violence tend to focus on the extreme experiences of violence lived by young people; driven by media interest or donor funding potential interventions remain focused on predetermined categories of vulnerability such as 'child soldiers' or victims of militarized rape. While there are certainly children who have suffered experiences of sexual violence or forced recruitment who need medical and psychosocial support, presumptions of vulnerability and avoidance in dealing with the causes leading to actual vulnerability do little to make long-lasting and positive change. By ignoring the structural violence which young people are faced with, child protection actors inadvertently contribute to reinforcing the structures of violence. As explained by one research participant:

> My life is difficult. Both of my parents are poor, we haven't been able to study. I don't have much to do. I work for whoever offers a job, carrying loads, cultivating in their fields. I try to find whatever work wherever I can. I'm the eldest of 7 children, I'm 17 years old now... Even though war has finished here, life isn't easier. I see how hard my mother works. For me it's the same. It will always be the same, nothing changes....
>
> (doctoral interview, Mushinga, May 2010)

If nothing changes for the young people whom the international child protection system has mandated itself to protect, then it is long past time for the international child protection system to more critically reflect on its role and relevance in responding to the actual needs of young people living in contexts of violence.

Notes

1. The DRC has repeatedly changed its name. Under King Leopold it was called the Congo Free State, which eventually became the Belgian Congo under colonial rule. At independence it was named the Democratic Republic of Congo, a name that it regained in 1996 following the end of Mobutu's rule. From 1965 to 1996, it was called Zaire.
2. "UN official calls DR Congo 'rape capital of the world'" http://news.bbc.co.uk/1/hi/8650112.stm Last accessed 29 April 2010.
3. Emile explicitly asked that his name always be used when I write about him, rather than changing or concealing his name as I have done with most other research participants.
4. This narrative is also written in Seymour (2012).
5. This narrative is also written in Seymour (2012).

Bibliography

Arnfred, S. and Utas, M. (2007) *Re-thinking Africa: A Contribution to the Swedish Government White Paper on Africa*. Uppsala: The Nordic Africa Institute.

BBC (2010) UN Official Calls DR Congo 'rape capital of the world'. http://news.bbc.co.uk/1/hi/8650112.stm.

Bourdieu, P. (1977) *Outline of a Theory of Practice*. London: Cambridge University Press.

Bourdieu, P. (1980) Le Capital Social: Notes Provisoires. *Actes de la Recherche en Sciences Sociales*, 31, 2–3.

Bourdieu, P. (1989) Social Space and Symbolic Power. *Sociological Theory*, 7 (1), 14–25.

Bourdieu, P. (2000) *Pascalian Meditations*. Translated by Richard Nice. Stanford: Stanford University Press.
Bourgois, P. (2001) The Power of Violence in War and Peace: Post-Cold War Lessons from El Salvador. *Ethnography*, 2 (1), 5–34.
Boyden, J. (1997) Childhood and the Policy Makers: A Comparative Perspective on the Globalization of Childhood. In A. James and A. Prout (eds.) *Constructing and Reconstructing Childhood*, 2nd edition. London: Falmer Press, pp. 190–215.
Boyden, J. (2000) Children and Social Healing. In L. Carlson, M. Mackeson-Sandbach and T. Allen (eds.) *Children in Extreme Situations Proceedings from the 1998 Alistair Berkley Memorial Lecture*. London: London School of Economics, pp. 58–91.
Boyden, J. and Mann, G. (2005) Children's Risk, Resilience, and Coping in Extreme Situations. In M. Ungar (ed.) *Handbook for Working with Children and Youth: Pathways to Resilience across Cultures and Contexts*. Thousand Oaks, CA: Sage, pp. 3–26.
Coghlan, B. et al. (2006) Mortality in the Democratic Republic of Congo: A Nationwide Survey. *Lancet*, 367, 44–51.
Cohen, S. (2001) *States of Denial: Knowing about Atrocities and Suffering*. Cambridge: Polity Press.
Das, V. (2007) *Life and Words: Violence and the Descent into the Ordinary*. London: University of California Press.
de Certeau, M. (1984) *The Practice of Everyday Life*. Berkeley: University of California Press.
Eriksson Baaz, M. and Stern, M. (2010) *The Complexity of Violence: A Critical Analysis of Sexual Violence in the Democratic Republic of Congo*. Uppsala: Nordiska Afrikainstitutet.
Farmer, P. (2004) An Anthropology of Structural Violence. *Current Anthropology*, 45 (3), 305–325.
Galtung, J. (1969) Violence, Peace and Peace Research. *Journal of Peace Research*, 6 (3), 167–191.
Hart, J. (2006) Saving Children: What Role for Anthropology? *Anthropology Today*, 22 (1), 5–8.
Hart, J. (2008) Displaced Children's Participation in Political Violence: Towards Greater Understanding of Mobilization. *Conflict, Security & Development*, 8 (3), 277–293.
Hart, J. and Lo Forte, C. (2010) Protecting Palestinian Children from Political Violence: The Role of the International Community. *Forced Migration Policy Briefing*, 5. Oxford: Refugee Studies Centre.
Hochschild, A. (1998) *King Leopold's Ghost: A Story of Greed, Terror, and Heroism in Colonial Africa*. Boston: Houghton Mifflin.
Jackson, M. (2005) Storytelling Events, Violence, and the Appearance of the Past. *Anthropological Quarterly*, 78 (2), 355–375.
Jackson, S. (2006) Sons of Which Soil? The Language and Politics of Autochthony in Eastern D. R. Congo. *African Studies Review*, 49 (2), 95–123.
Jackson, S. (2007) Of 'Doubtful Nationality': Political Manipulation of Citizenship in the D. R. Congo. *Citizenship Studies*, 11 (5), 481–500.
James, A. and Prout, J. (1997) Introduction. In A. James and A. Prout (eds.) *Constructing and Reconstructing Childhood: Contemporary Issues in the Sociological Study of Childhood*, London: Routledge-Falmer, pp. 3–9.

Levine, S. and Chastre, C. (2004) *Missing the Point: An Analysis of Food Security Interventions in the Great Lakes*. London: Overseas Development Institute.

MacGaffey, J. (1986) Fending-for-Yourself: The Organization of the Second Economy in Zaire. In G. Nzongola-Ntalaja (ed.) *The Crisis in Zaire: Myths and Realities*, Trenton, NJ: Africa World Press, pp. 141–156.

Macmillan, L. (2009) The Child Soldier in North-South Relations. *International Political Sociology*, 3 (1), 36–52.

Mamdani, M. (2001) *When Victims Become Killers: Colonialism, Nativism, and the Genocide in Rwanda*. New Jersey: Princeton University Press.

Mann, G. (2004) Separated Children: Care and Support in Context. In J. Boyden and J. de Berry (eds.) *Children and Youth on the Front Line: Ethnography, Armed Conflict and Displacement*. Oxford: Berghahn Books, pp. 3–22.

Marriage, M. (2006) *Not Breaking the Rules Not Playing the Game: International Assistance to Countries at War*. London: Hurst & Company.

Marriage, Z. (2012) 'Tactics!' *Capoeria & Security*, Weblog Post 22 June 2012. Accessible at: http://capoeira-security.blogspot.com.

Nordstrom, C. (2004) *Shadows of War: Violence, Power and International Profiteering in the Twenty-first Century*. London: University of California Press.

Nzongola-Ntalaja, G. (2002) *The Congo from Leopold to Kabila: A People's History*. London: Zed Books.

Olivier de Sardan, J.-P. (1996) L'économie morale de la corruption en Afrique. *Politique Africaine*, 63, 97–116.

Prunier, G. (2009) *Africa's World War: Congo, the Rwandan Genocide, and the Making of a Continental Catastrophe*. New York: Oxford University Press.

Pupavac, V. (2001) Misanthropy without Borders: The International Children's Rights Regime. *Disasters*, 25 (2), 95–112.

Seymour, C. [2014, forthcoming] Ambiguous Agencies: Coping and Survival in Eastern Democratic Republic of Congo. *Children's Geographies*.

Stearns, J. (2011) *Dancing in the Glory of Monsters: The Collapse of the Congo and the Great War of Africa*. New York: Perseus Books.

United Nations (1989) *Convention on the Rights of the Child*. Available at http://www2.ohchr.org/english/law/crc.htm.

Utas, M. (2005) Victimcy, Girlfriending, Soldiering: Tactic Agency in a Young Woman's Social Navigation of the Liberian War Zone. *Anthropological Quarterly*, 78 (2), 403–430.

Vigh, H. (2006) *Navigating Terrains of War: Youth and Soldiering in Guinea-Bissau*. New York: Berghahn Books.

War Child UK (2010) *Strengthening Community-Based Child Protection Mechanisms in Uganda and the Democratic Republic of Congo*. Available at http://www.warchild.org.uk/sites/default/files/Community-based-child-protection-mechanisms.pdf.

Žižek, S. (2009) *Violence: Six Sideways Reflections*. London: Profile Books Ltd.

9

How Does Conflict and Violence Impact upon Children and Their Education? Experiences and Learning from the Humanitarian Field

Deborah Haines

Introduction

This chapter shows how conflict and violence affect children and their experiences of school and access to quality education. I draw upon my work experiences in Liberia, Kenya, Lebanon, West Timor and Timor L'Este as well as further research that has put education and conflict, including attacks on education, on the global agenda.

Education is a basic human right that is firmly established in humanitarian and international law, including the United Nations Convention on the Rights of the Child. It has been associated with development and improving life opportunities as well as the health and well-being of children and their families. When disasters and crises have occurred, humanitarian organizations work together with communities and governments to restore and ensure access to quality education for all children.

This chapter shows that conflict can cause massive disruption to children's lives by damaging or destroying education systems and communities. Because of conflict, children can experience loss, displacement and can enter further into a cycle of poverty, violence and exclusion. However, despite the challenges, children can benefit from schooling during and after conflict. Valuable learning occurs in places where education systems have been severely damaged; where major adaptations have taken place to establish learning spaces and routines;

and where children face significant barriers in just getting to school. Children and young people also learn important and relevant skills and information outside of school. Many children and young people choose alternative ways and learn. Finally, this chapter reflects on some of the negative experiences for children of attending school post-conflict. Schools are not always as protective and safe as they should be.

Why education in conflict?

There are several strong arguments for providing education for children during and after conflict. First, if children's education is crudely interrupted, there is a greater chance they may not have the chance to resume and complete it. This can have poor outcomes for the child, community and in the longer term, society. Providing education to children and families during or after crises can help restore a sense of dignity, and children can feel a sense of belonging and normality when going to school along with peers. Education is also widely recognized for its role in restoring and sustaining peace when lives have been interrupted by conflict and violence. It also is generally agreed among education and humanitarian practitioners and scholars that quality education can protect and promote the well-being of children.

Education in crises can provide vital, sometimes life-saving information (e.g., advice about prevalent diseases, landmines or unexploded ordnance or other risks and threats). Education is also widely believed to be as essential for a nation's economic, social and political development. These points underpin efforts to ensure that all children, including those affected by crisis, enjoy their right to education.

Since Graca Machel's first report, *The Impact of War on Children* (1996) and her reviews of the same issue (2001 and 2009), there has been increased recognition of the plight of children across the world whose lives are affected by conflict, including their right to education. Despite increased awareness of the right to education and the fact that it is firmly situated in international and humanitarian law, access to quality education is still challenged and prevented in many countries. As Machel points out 'International standards and their enforcement are the strongest defense against impunity for child rights violations in armed conflict. Yet they will only be effective if and when they are widely known, understood and implemented by everyone' (Machel 2009, 58).

The impacts of displacement

One of the greatest impacts of conflict on children's education occurs as a result of displacement. Globally, there are at least 27 million children and youth who are affected by armed conflict and who lack access to formal education, 90 percent of whom are internally displaced people (IDP) (Bethke and Braunschweig 2004). Many displaced people live in camps, although most do not. They live across a variety of places outside a camp arrangement – relatives or friends, rented or abandoned homes within migrant communities (Ferris and Winthrop 2010).

When communities are displaced, their chances of gaining access to and completing a basic quality education can often be threatened. Children and families are likely to face greater poverty and hardship. Due to their loss of livelihood and with constraints and restricted movement, it is difficult to re-establish a means of making a living and so basic survival can be much harder. In addition, not only have the displaced left their home, they often have no time to take useful items with them; many leave everything behind. Children are often forced to leave their school books, bags and school uniforms. To people driven into a situation of loss and poverty under chaotic conditions, such items can prove to be vital when settling into a new yet challenging environment and looking to restore or develop a routine and sense of belonging.

One of the most distressing issues for the displaced is the uncertainty of what will happen now and not knowing how their future will be affected. Some children and their families live in protracted displacement for a number of years (UNESCO 2011, 153). The average length of displacement for refugees or IDP is approaching 20 years (Milner and Loescher 2011). This can mean children spend their entire childhood and years of schooling in a displaced and uncertain situation.

Lebanon 2006

During the conflict in Lebanon in 2006, thousands of people were displaced having been driven by rocket attacks and shelling in the south of the country. They fled to places in and around Beirut and locations along the coast. The attacks were intense. One-third of the 1,183 people killed were children, 4,054 people were injured and 970,000 displaced (Amnesty International 2006). During the conflict, 40 schools were completely destroyed and a further 300 partially damaged. Despite the intensity of the violence and massive upheaval, many were hopeful they would be returning home within a week or less. Children articulated very clearly their desire to return to school and were positive about the possibility of having some temporary education activities in the meantime. Some parents however saw the provision of temporary or emergency education as an indication that displacement would be prolonged and were not forthcoming in discussing and planning for it (Graham and Haines 2008).

Dadaab Camp, Eastern Kenya 2006

Dadaab Camp was established at the outset of the Somali civil war in the early 1990s. It hosts more than 300,000 refugees who have fled from ethnic conflict and natural disasters. The camp was originally designed to host 90,000 people and is now home to 300,000. Most have arrived from Somalia although the camps also accommodate people from Rwanda, Democratic Republic of Congo, Tanzania, Sudan, Ethiopia and Somalia. It is divided into three separate camps, each of which has established primary and secondary schools. I visited the camps in 2006 as the displaced community of the overcrowded Hagadera camp was being relocated due to floods. While primary and secondary schools operate throughout all three of the Dadaab camps, there is insufficient capacity and more than half the children are not enrolled in school. Classes are large and crowded and very few teachers are formally trained. Many have only a secondary school certificate. Violence and insecurity pervades the camps where crime, including sexual violence, is not uncommon.

A huge concern is the children who do not go to school. The limited opportunities for the young to develop their interests leave them frustrated. The minority who manage to complete secondary education also become frustrated with the limited opportunities to build a livelihood in the restrictive camp environment. The United Nations High Commision for Refugees estimates that primary school participation in the Dadaab camps is 69 percent and secondary school 30 percent (Dryden-Peterson 2011). As a result, there are large numbers of young people out of school. Some try to develop their own means of livelihood in the restrictive, limited, closed camp environment. Video shops (showing films) and small private schools were becoming popular businesses.

More recently, Kenyatta University of Nairobi has opened a campus beside Dadaab which will facilitate higher education. While there can be positive outcomes for the education of some IDP and refugees, completing a full course of education is still a major challenge for many.

Schools themselves can be directly affected by displacement. When masses of people seek refuge schools can be an attractive option and quickly be occupied. In crises, the displaced sometimes may see a school as offering the best place for refuge. Schools can accommodate large numbers of people offering places to sleep, wash and cook but with so many often living in chaotic conditions under stress, they can be wrecked very quickly and while they are occupied also leave local children without school to go to. In Kenya, 2008, a primary school accommodated more than 80 families but soon almost half of the desks and chairs were damaged with some burned for firewood and latrines were left in a state of disrepair.

Kenya 2008

When conflict erupted as a result of the elections in Kenya in 2008, communities fled and as many as 660,000 people were displaced, taking refuge in camps and among host communities across the Rift Valley. Although displaced and living in tents, with friends and relatives, both parents and children wanted schooling to be available for children as soon as possible. One of the greatest fears of displaced children in Kenya 2008 was that their education would suffer. Some expressed concern that they might have to repeat a year of their education or they may never return to school again. Non-governmental organizations (NGOs) worked with the local and national government to ensure those displaced did not miss out on their education, especially those who were shortly due to take national examinations. Temporary tent schools were established in the camps and other local schools expanded their classrooms to accommodate thousands more children. Strategies were quickly developed to help integrate new children in a delicate, political climate where children of opposing tribes or political groups may be mixed within classes. One school started the idea of a 'buddy system' where particular children of the host school looked out for the well-being of an IDP child. Children of the host schools also gave a displaced child uniform items, so they wouldn't feel out of place or different.

After the violence of the post-election crisis in Kenya, many children feared that without income their families would be unable to meet the basic costs. Many families spoke of the dramatic change shifting from a comfortable home life into insecurity and uncertainty. The poorest children are more likely to be deprived of education by conflict than wealthier children (Novelli and Cardozo 2008, 478). There are always costs of schooling, even in countries where free education is provided. After the crisis in Kenya, many children worried about how they would pay examination fees, buy new exercise and textbooks and school uniforms. Some started petty trade selling things like corn, bread or oil before or after school hours to help contribute to the family livelihood.

Teachers were among the displaced so some of the camp schools were able to draw upon their expertise although many classes were resourced by unqualified, volunteer teachers, initially learning on the job while the Ministry of Education developed a fast track, emergency teacher training for them. The volunteer teachers needed to quickly learn teaching methodologies and management techniques in order to teach effectively in precarious, difficult conditions, some managed classes of 60 children or more – carpenters, secretaries, shop assistants – all stepped forward to help run the emergency school. The Ministry of Education also helped displaced teachers to transfer to new schools. One teacher told me he had lost his family in the conflict but that despite being displaced he would continue to teach.

The Ministry of Education also adapted the curriculum allowing time and space for psychosocial interventions to help alleviate tensions and support emotional healing. Although furniture (desks and chairs) arrived for the older children preparing for their examinations, some classes worked creatively without them, sitting on mats and pieces of tarpaulin in the tents during the initial weeks of displacement. To facilitate education in the emergency environment the government waived examination fees for the displaced and school uniform policies were relaxed in the schools within camps. With these initiatives and combined efforts, despite the massive upheaval caused by the conflict, disruption to children's education was minimized.

The impact on education infrastructure

Conflict can have sudden or gradual impacts on education systems. During the post-election crisis that startled the people of Kenya in 2008, the most severely affected schools were stripped of all their resources overnight. The perpetrators removed everything possible. Tin roofing was entirely removed, leaving classrooms open to the sky. Desks, chairs and blackboards were stolen and burned for firewood while school materials, including children's exercise books and work were left torn and sprawled on the floor of deserted classrooms. They were left deserted. Such swift and direct attacks were strong political statements regarding power and opportunities and while they happened in a moment, the impacts on children, young people and their families are indelible. Another difficulty, for girls and female teachers, in particular, is the lack of sanitation facilities. In Liberia, inadequate numbers of latrines forced girls to share with boys and teachers and menstruating girls were placed in awkward and embarrassing situations which sometimes affected their attendance or resulted in them dropping out of school. Liberia was ravaged by protracted war, which eventually ended in 2003. During the war, schooling had mostly ceased for children in Liberia. Hundreds of institutions including schools, colleges and universities across the country were badly damaged or completely destroyed and abandoned. Many were left derelict, deserted and scarred from bullets. A reported 80 percent of the country's 2,400 schools were destroyed (Shriberg 2008 cited in Stromquist et al. 2013) and left without basic infrastructure including desks, chairs and textbooks. Pages of children's work were left strewn across the classrooms, pitiful evidence of brutal attacks on the schools. For years, armed groups with child soldiers used empty and derelict schools for their own refuge. Teachers colleges were completely stripped bare of their resources and left with no attention from national administration for more than a decade.

My work in Liberia was to assess the capacity of stakeholders to provide quality education post-conflict. Despite the terrible impact that was evident at the time, including obvious traces of trauma in the physical environment, there was also determination and will among communities to reconstruct the country and maintain peace. The restoration of education and achieving free, compulsory primary education for all children was a national government priority.

Temporary schooling and conflict

Sometimes, schools and communities that have not been affected by conflict are able to assist, support and absorb children and teachers from conflict zones. In 1999, an overwhelming majority vote in Timor-Leste led to independence from 24 years of Indonesian rule. The response from the pro-Indonesia militias was one of sudden, brutal violence and terror. Thousands of people were killed and mass destruction swept the country in frenzied attacks. Homes, water systems, health institutions, schools and universities, banks and shops were destroyed within hours. This had profound impacts on education with schools specifically targeted for destruction. Schools were burned, dismantled and looted. Thousands fled across the boarder into West Timor where camps absorbed large numbers of the refugees.

With people flooding into West Timor, the Government of Indonesia immediately facilitated provision of education for displaced children. Some teachers and school principals reported to NGOs that the number of children in schools was growing dramatically; with a school roll of 300 children increasing to 900 over night. NGOs worked with the local government to expand the system, to increase the capacity of teachers and to foster integration between the communities.

A strategy was developed to facilitate resumption of their schooling. Children could attend the schools that had the capacity to absorb them. Some schools doubled their capacity by operating a shift system. Temporary tent schools were set up, mostly in the refugee camps but also using available spaces such as the market space. Over time small satellite or outreach schools were also constructed to relieve those that were overburdened.

With simmering tensions fueled by ethnic and political differences, strategies were needed to help foster peace and cooperation between the groups. A hub of the community, schools provided a space for activities that would help build and sustain relationships. NGOs worked with the local government and schools to design sports and recreational activities for children and adults to help relieve tensions and also build relationships between communities.

Impacts on the quality of education

Conflict and violence can have serious and sustained impacts on the quality of education affecting how and what children learn, their achievement and attendance. Poor quality can also result in children choosing not to go to school and dropping out altogether. The quality of education is determined by many interrelated factors, but teachers play a key role in determining the quality of education.

Teachers do not go unscathed in times of violence and conflict. The impact of the conflict and neglect of the Liberian education system resulted in a massive shortfall of experienced and qualified teachers countrywide. An approximate 60 percent of teachers were unqualified in 2005. In the post-conflict environment, teachers needed not only pedagogical skills but also the skills to support the psychosocial healing of children and young people. Many younger children entering the classroom had grown up in a very fragile and insecure environment defined by conflict and violence.

Conflict can produce gender inequalities in education. It is well documented that parents are less likely to send girls to school in conflict (Kirk 2004). The gender imbalance in Liberia is evident in the low number of girls enrolled and completing school and also the lack of female teachers. Teaching is perceived as a masculine profession in Liberia. A huge gender imbalance persists in the education system in post-conflict Liberia, which continues to be dominated by male teachers. Almost ten years on, there remains a serious shortfall of female teachers in Liberia. This gender imbalance results in limited role models for girls in education and also contributes to issues of insecurity for girls and women (Shriberg 2008).

In a post-conflict environment, teachers can have limited resources to aid teaching and learning. The most basic resources might not be available. In post-conflict Liberia, teachers in rural schools created classrooms and teaching aids with whatever was available. In some villages, teachers fashioned blackboards out of flattened out cardboard boxes and used cassava for chalk, and while it was not very effective, it made some impression that children could make some sense of to aid learning. I came across many communities making their own bricks to build new, small schools while others operated in spare spaces. Some classrooms were so dark and bare that one wondered whether children were better off outside in the sunshine. Children in many schools across Liberia would carry their own chair so a hundred or more children striding toward school in the morning carrying chairs, stalls or planks of wood to sit on was not an uncommon sight. Poor quality can lead to children dropping out of school where their contribution to the family income and survival is viewed as more important. In countries affected by conflict, it is not uncommon to see the poorest children working; some having dropped out of school, some never having been at all. When education is of such poor quality, the choice between sending the child to school or contributing toward the family income is easier to make. With few or uncertain rewards, perhaps not even becoming literate, education is not seen as a worthwhile investment. In Liberia, many children had made this choice, especially in the rural areas where quality of education was generally poorer. Instead of going to school, children went to work on the family farm. The urban areas also offered opportunities for work although the rewards were small in relation to the difficult work. Some children were able to both attend school and work. I met many children who worked breaking rocks into small pieces, filling sacks for the tiniest wages. Paid by the sack, they would break the rocks with a small hammer, fill the sack and carry the heavy load to a truck. Some spent more than eight hours a day on this job. Some of the same children were there when I returned to Liberia almost a year later. Others roamed the streets selling small bags of coal, bottles of oil, bread buns, bags of peanuts and bottles of cooking oil. Some collected and delivered gallons of water, pushed through the city streets on carts that carried more than six cans at a time. These chores were often alternatives to receiving quality education while some children worked in order to pay for their school expenses.

Child soldiers and school after conflict

For some children in countries ravaged by conflict, chances of education in school are denied as they join armed groups or military forces, either through forced or voluntary recruitment and become child soldiers. Child soldiers include the thousands of girls working as cooks, cleaners, porters (carrying equipment), kitchen staff, 'wives' (of commanders) as well as combatants. While there are numerous reasons why children join fighting forces, some child soldiers report having chosen the option because their education system was failing them and the economy showed no promise or prospects for the future. Some child soldiers felt that a military life in an armed group offered a better life than staying in the community where education and work opportunities were poor and limited. In addition to having an identified role, sometimes defined with a uniform, they would also have regular meals and maybe healthcare. For some child soldiers, more certainty, even if it involved violence, was more attractive than a life without education, opportunities and means for survival. Life in an armed group may be fraught with danger, risk and fear, but it also offers a sense of identity and purpose.

Many child soldiers who returned to civilian life after membership in one of the many armed groups in Liberia clearly articulated their views on the importance of education and the value of learning new and relevant skills, in the environment of reintegration and reconstruction. In 2005, after the process of disarmament and demobilization (part of the DDR – Disarmament, Demobilization, Rehabilitation – process that began in 2004) child soldiers in Monrovia and Gbanaga felt that education would help them to earn a legitimate and respected place within the community. Some were returning to communities where they or the groups they were associated with had committed grave atrocities. After a life of violence, becoming a student again would help them to feel they were moving on to positive things and help them feel like their peers, accepted within the community and like they were normal young people with a promise of a future. Some learned a trade, some joined literacy classes while others returned to school.

Learning in a positive and normalized environment provides a form of healing and psychosocial support for child soldiers. It enables them to build upon the skills they have and learn new skills. Education is a critical part of building a sustainable, peaceful society. As many said, they want to contribute toward building peace in Liberia. This was critical in an environment where child soldiers may be viewed with suspicion and doubt after conflict.

Ensuring high quality, relevant educational opportunities for child soldiers after war can be a tremendous challenge for the government and humanitarian community in countries like Liberia where 21,000 children joined the fighting forces and where the education and industry infrastructures were severely weakened. The process must be carefully designed and should aim to transform rather than rebuild communities and nations affected by conflict (Novelli and Cardozo 2008).

UNICEF in Liberia oversaw vocational skills training programs which aimed to ensure the full technical competence in a skill area particularly focusing on the skills needed in postwar reconstruction. Care was taken to ensure there was an existing and continuing market for all the skills, but some ex-combatants were anxious about the lack of market for their new trade. Some girls felt there were too many soap makers and tailors while others wondered how the electricians would cope where mains electricity was a long way off. Some teachers and mentors believed that building softer social skills with ex-combatants was more important – building confidence and collaborative skills so they would be able to cope with the potential social problems when reintegrating within communities.

Accelerated learning programs

In countries affected by protracted conflict, there can be extraordinary numbers of children who have missed years of formal education opportunities. Thousands of children and young people may have completed only a few years of education while others may have never been to school. Those that have left armed groups often learn valuable life skills while with warring factions but may lack literacy and the recognized qualifications gained from formal education.

During the civil war in Liberia, personal survival took precedence over education. Ten years on after the cessation of conflict, only 58 percent of the population is literate. A generation of children lost their opportunity for education and as a consequence are now entering and completing school much older than the traditional school age. This means there are now classes with mixed age groups, including children and young people as much as ten years or more apart in age. This situation can be difficult for children (particularly the older child in a class with much younger children) and also the teachers who must adjust their teaching and classroom environment to suit different levels of maturity. Liberian children and young people who had missed years of school enrolled in primary school. In some schools, young people of 22 years of age sat beside seven and eight year olds. Facing embarrassment when peers are more than ten years younger can result in school dropout (Stromquist et al. 2013).

To address this problem, large accelerated learning programs have been implemented in a number of countries affected by protracted or large-scale conflict including Afghanistan, DRC, Liberia, Sierra Leone, South Sudan and Uganda. These condense six years of schooling into three years. The programs are usually flexible, enabling the most disadvantaged groups of children and young people, including girls, children with disabilities and child soldiers – including ex-combatants to progress with their education while fulfilling other duties important in their lives, for example, they may have domestic responsibilities, do petty trade or other work.

Play and conflict

Article 31 of the UN CRC says that children have the right to play, creative expression and recreation. For children experiencing or recovering from the effects of conflict, play and recreation can help accelerate and facilitate the recovery; although, it is important to recognize that not all children respond in the same way. Children are affected by and have different ways of responding to the same violent experiences.

More certain are the impacts of conflict on children's play environments. In places of conflict, the resources – including the people, materials and structures that support children's play – can be weakened and sometimes completely destroyed or lost or unavailable to access. Spaces where children have played in the past might not be safe or used for other purposes (as when schools are sometimes occupied by displaced people). Nurseries or preschools may not function. Teachers and other adults who would normally support and promote children's play may be stressed or need to divert their attention and focus on other priorities. Parents may have less money and children may have greater responsibilities to help their families meet basic survival needs. When children's usual carers are unable to supervise or care for children, organized play and recreation in school and those for whom school is unavailable should have some means of accessing positive shared experiences that play and recreation can foster.

In the years following the peace agreement in Liberia, some children spent time before and after school to perform chores to support the family – fetching water, cleaning, preparing things to sell, buying or collecting firewood, breaking palm nuts and caring for younger siblings. Other children worked all day, missing out on school. Although it would be difficult to determine whether they played more or less than before the ceasefire, it was clear that for many children, much of their time was occupied with chores. In the camps amidst the post-conflict displacement, children helped with securing and organizing the new settlement, fetching firewood and water.

Children have a natural drive and propensity to play and can continue to find opportunities to do so regardless, even in times of conflict and instability. Given the space, time and opportunity most children will seek others to play with and will try to create their own resources and ideas for play. Despite the lack of materials for children's play in post-conflict Liberia, children showed resourcefulness and the will to play creating their own no-cost play materials. They made string and rope from palm tree bark, played with hoops from old rubber tires, made small vehicles to pull from an old wire, tin cans and other discarded materials and short-lived footballs from collections of paper bound with bits of rubber or any materials which would hold it together. In West Timor, children in the camps played football with old vegetables until they fell apart. They played five-jacks and other games with shells and stones and, like children in Liberia and Kenya, boys made slingshots from sticks, pieces of rubber, seeds and stones. In countries where the bicycle is a popular mode of transport, children skillfully roll and chase old tires along the street for miles.

During the 2006 Middle East Conflict, displaced Lebanese communities were keen to see children enjoy play and recreation in the IDP camps and settlements that had sprung up in and around Beirut in public spaces including colleges, parks and squares. Despite the temporary, crowded, volatile and unstable situation, many parents and children wanted to find spaces and opportunity to support children's play for those who were well enough. Within a few days and amidst the conflict, entire football tournaments were organized where children and youth played in confined spaces, on terraces, small gardens and other spaces dedicated to children's sports for certain periods of the day. Girls tended to play together, in enclosed areas with shelter and closer to their families. They said play helped them to forget what was happening. Many older girls preferred to read and involve themselves in more quiet, academic activities as boys played football. Mothers and grandmothers spoke of the terrifying experiences of fleeing amidst rocket attacks and the effects this had on their children. Mothers and siblings observed the emotional changes in young children. One grandmother in a congested IDP site in Beruit explained how her grandson had not spoken at all since they had left their home when the violence had begun. The attacks continued during the night, a reminder that despite having traveled far from home, they were still not safe. During this time, the streets of Beirut were deserted and people were advised to stay in. The displaced families settled together in their camps, each having claimed a spot to keep a few belongings, hang clothes to dry, spend the day and sleep at night in congested spaces – in classrooms, hallways, on landings and balconies. Among all of this most children found some space and time to play. A challenge in supporting the children was to facilitate play to help relieve tension while others were grieving for their loss.

When the ceasefire occurred, thousands immediately began the journey home. This sudden exodus from the IDP sites may have indicated the strong resilience and will to rebuild – to salvage and revive what is valued, as quickly as possible. Within three days of the ceasefire the majority of the displaced had returned home to areas that had undergone massive destruction. One of the priorities articulated was the immediate resumption of children's education. Children also spoke of their desire to play once back at home.

Facilitating children's play was also a priority for institutions and agencies supporting IDP arriving from East Timor into West Timor, after the conflict in 1999. As thousands of children and their families poured across the borders into West Timor, the tensions among both the host and displaced communities were strained. Some children had witnessed the atrocities. They had also endured difficult times leaving their homes and relocating across the border, mostly in IDP camps. Tensions also rose in some of the host communities as resources were distributed despite attempts to distribute equitably among both host and IDP populations.

Although the physical impacts were most obvious, the impact on children's social well-being was also recognized very early. Agencies worked with the communities and government to design games and play kits, relevant for both the displaced and host communities – activities that would encourage interaction and cooperation, rather than competition. Children were given the time and space and resources to play together during and after school time. Cooperative games kits contained popular, local traditional games and play resources to foster both solitary and also group activity. It was important that children had space and time for physical, energetic activities that fostered collaboration and cooperation as well as the quiet and calm play that would allow children time to reflect, share experiences and also build new friendships.

Facilitating children's artistic expression during and after crisis is also recognized as a way to foster emotional healing. One teacher in Atambua, a place close to the East Timor border that absorbed great numbers of displaced families, spoke of how pictures drawn by two of the displaced children in her class consistently depicted violent scenes for months after they had arrived despite them appearing to be well adjusted and emotionally stable when playing among their peers. Artistic expression through drawing can reveal or give expression to tensions or worries that are otherwise suppressed.

One month after they had fled from home and settled in the large camps for the displaced in Rift Valley, Kenya, some children were given art materials for creative or free drawing activities while adults were consulted about the situation. The drawings, however, revealed the memories that the children carried. Children who had witnessed violence drew pictures of people running away from home, chased by others wielding machetes, with houses on fire and their livestock left in pools of blood in the garden. Others drew pictures of their home the way they liked to remember it, brightly tiled structures with children playing in a yard flanked by animals feeding in the sunshine, even though it had been looted and burned. Some children drew themselves as they were before the violence – going to school dressed in a uniform, carrying their school bag, smiling and walking with their friends. These kinds of drawings show that such ordinary events of everyday life are important for children and their sense of normalcy, security and belonging. Children spoke of running with their parents and siblings as the home was left burning and everything was left behind. Some children mentioned their dreams and how the same experiences frequently appear in them.

Dreams and drawings need to be sensitively received and carefully interpreted. While these methods often used in humanitarian situations tend to lead to positive outcomes for children, they could be viewed as originating from Western approaches. How dreams, are interpreted is dependent upon the cultural perspective. For example, dreams may be viewed as important events with particular significance in some cultures while in others they may be of little consequence (Bracken 1998). In considering the impacts of conflict on children therefore, it is important to recognize that conclusions may not be relevant or applied to all children (Hyder 2005). There are likely to be local beliefs, traditions and approaches to healing and recovery that should be explored with people affected by violence and conflict. In Liberia, for example, communities saw their own rituals, sometimes involving traditional song and dance as an essential part of the healing and cleansing process without which there could never be complete acceptance and integration. This is particularly important where children have been directly implicated or involved in violent activity.

Depending upon the culture, dramatic arts and singing can also be an appropriate way to support children's psychosocial well-being. Singing and dancing to familiar and loved songs with others can be comforting and joyful – diverting thoughts away from insecurity. This can be especially important for the recovery and progression of child soldiers while they move through the transition from disarmament and demobilization toward reintegration with their communities. Moving away from a life of domination, obedience and harsh routines under the command of others, enjoying the freedom of joyful expression is important part of their journey toward normalcy and civilian life. Boothby, Crawford and Halperin (2006) suggest that the longer children were soldiers, the more strongly they will have been affected (Wessells 2005). Some agencies in humanitarian situations facilitate more organized play opportunities through children's clubs and providing resources for schools and community groups.

Areas designated and organized for children's play can be an important resource in IDP camps. They can help relieve mothers and carers for planned periods of time, enabling them to focus on other family priorities without worrying what children are doing and where they are in the camp. Young children can be exposed to more hazards in the camp situation like fires, boiling water and cooking posts outside tents, and there may also be no clear boundary of where children are safe to wander. In the earlier days of settling in the unfamiliarity can be distressing for some, although other children will enjoy the opportunities for exploration and making new friends. Children will play even in the most difficult circumstances and those that have chores will also integrate play opportunities into their work.

Establishing play areas for young children requires careful planning with the consideration of the patterns established (such as schedules for food distribution, health and nutrition visitors, etc.) as well as adequate materials and human resources. A well-resourced and well-run center where children can play can help build confidence, regain a sense of routine and also maintain or develop relationships with other children and trusted carers.

Violence in schools

Although schools can be protective and may even provide life-saving experiences and information for children, it cannot be assumed that going to school is always good for children. Their social, emotional and physical well-being is not always assured and safeguarded while at school. Conflict can result in the breakdown and erosion of the systems and structures that protect children. Family members may need to divert their attention, perhaps securing food and a safe home environment. Legislative systems can become less effective or break down altogether. Governments can have less capacity to enforce laws. Intense or protracted conflict can render countries lawless. The complex effects of degeneration due to conflict, a weak economy, unemployment and the breakdown of family structures have contributed to the large numbers of young people supporting siblings or living independently in difficult circumstances. During and after conflict, family structures are often fragmented and weakened and the economic pressures are great. This can render children vulnerable to exploitation.

In the immediate years following the war in Liberia, I heard many accounts from girls who had experienced abuse from their teachers. Girls reported accounts of sexual encounters with teachers in exchange for grades or passing exams. Some described having exchanged sex for study-note pamphlets which others might purchase from the teacher for a few Liberian dollars. It was not uncommon for girls to have a Sugar Daddy, Pa Uncle or God Pa. Some men gave the girl a place to live independently, which could be quite lavish depending upon the economic status of the man. In exchange for sex, he would pay a girl's school fees and other associated costs of schooling. Some Liberians described this as so common that it had become normalized, almost acceptable or at least something that was no longer shocking. There was a difference between the sex trade in urban and rural areas. In urban areas, material gains are sought as well as money for education and the means of survival for the girl and her family. In the rural areas, transactional sex is a means to get education and not to go hungry. Young students were dissatisfied – there were as many as 40 teachers in some schools, but we know that only few of them were paid and as a result the students suffer because teachers struggled to meet their own needs. Students felt that teachers needed the money while the students needed the grade. Others felt that some men preferred younger children as they could pay them less. There is a prevalent belief that younger children are not HIV positive. The full extent of the issue was not clear; although, six years later, researchers Stromquist et al. (2013) claim that it remains a problem for child protection in Liberia.

The government of Liberia has since led the development of a teachers code of conduct, designed to safeguard children and young people, providing preventative and protective measures for both teachers and students and criminalizing rape.[1]

Even when a child has secured a place within school, his or her protection and well-being is not always assured. Violence can become more normalized or acceptable in societies affected by war and violence, impeding recovery, restoration or realization of peace, harmony and stability. Children learn how to respond to stressful or demanding situations from others around them, including teachers, parents, their peers and carers. Some children experience or witness violence through the institutions they use every day on a regular basis – for example when harmful methods of discipline are exercised in schools. By promoting aggressive, negative and hurtful solutions to problems in school, teachers can play a role in fueling or perpetuating a culture of violence as opposed to peace and harmony.

In Liberia, while children described some of the positive methods of discipline that teachers use, they also describe more harmful methods. Children in Liberia spoke of a number of ways teachers discipline children – for example, being made to stand outside looking at the sun, being ordered to stand on ones toes in a squatting position with arms outstretched for long periods of time or washing the latrines with bare hands. Harmful methods of discipline are not only confusing for children, as the teacher is often seen as a figure they should be loyal to and respect, but they are also emotionally and physically hurtful and damaging. Children internalize the experiences. Children who feel badly affected by harmful school discipline may also drop out of school. In West Timor, children reported that teachers punished children by making them kneel for prolonged periods in response to not completing homework. Children were also reported that beating was a regular punishment for fighting with other children, not attending class or arriving late. Verbal abuse is also a common form of punishment in school – children are called names, such as dog or pig and are mocked in front of their peers.

In countries affected by conflict, teachers need to know and practice respectful methods of discipline, classroom management and know how to communicate well with children who have experienced or been affected by war.

Conclusion

When communities are affected by conflict and violence, education systems can be dramatically affected, disrupting children's access to and experience of education. There is growing recognition of the importance of providing education during and after conflict. When children are displaced through conflict, school provides a zone of stability and normalcy. While it is often difficult to re-establish schooling or to compensate for lost years of study, NGOs and governments have worked together to provide temporary schools, accelerated learning and to develop study resources with whatever is available. School is not only about learning, it is also about a space for play, drama and art, and these are valuable resources for working through the impact of violence and loss on the child's psychosocial well-being. Children also make do, developing their own games and play materials. However, despite the promise of school as a site of peace and rehabilitation, schools are also often a place of continuing violence in which corporal punishment is practiced and sexual violence is not uncommon. This may particularly be the case during and after conflict and urgently needs addressing.

Note

1. CEDAW (2009), 'Responses to the list of issues and questions with regard to the consideration of the combined initial, second, third, fourth, fifth and sixth periodic reports Liberia', CEDAW/C/LBR/Q/6/Add.1. New York, CEDAW.

Bibliography

Amnesty International (2006) *Lebanon: Deliberate Destruction or 'collateral damage'? Israeli Attacks on Civilian Infrastructure*. London: Amnesty International.

Bethke, L. and Braunschweig, S. (2004) *Global Survey on Education in Emergencies*. New York: Women's Commission for Refugee Women and Children.

Boothby, N., Crawford, J., and Halperin, J. (2006) Mozambique Child Solider Life Outcome Study: Lessons Learned in Rehabilitation and Reintegration Efforts. *Global Public Health – An International Journal for Research, Policy and Practice*, 1 (1), 87–107.

Bracken, P. (1998) Hidden Agendas: Deconstructing Post-Traumatic Stress Disorder. In P. Bracken and C. Petty (eds.) *Rethinking the Trauma of War*. London: Free Association Books.

Dryden-Peterson, S. (2011) *Refugee Education: A Global Review*. Geneva: UNHCR.

Ferris, E. and Winthrop, R. (2010) Education and Displacement: Assessing Conditions for Refugees and Internally Displaced Persons affected by Conflict. Background paper prepared for the Education for All Global Monitoring Report 2011, The Hidden Crisis: Armed Conflict and Education. UNESCO.

Graham, S. and Haines, D. (2008) *Education in Emergencies*. London: Save the Children.

Hyder, T. (2005) *War, Conflict and Play*. Maidenhead: Open University Press.

Kirk, J. (2004) Promoting a Gender-Just Peace: The Roles of Women Teachers in Peace Building and Reconstruction. *Gender and Development,* 12 (3), 50–59.

Machel, G. (1996) *Impact of Armed Conflict on Children*. New York: UNICEF.

Machel, G. (2001) *The Impact of War on Children*. New York: Palgrave.

Machel, G. (2009) *Machel Study, Ten Year Strategic Review: Children and Conflict in a Changing World*. New York: UNICEF.

Milner, J. and Loescher, G. (2011) *Responding to Protracted Refugee Situations: Lessons from a Decade of Discussion*. RSC Policy Briefing Paper No. 8.

Novelli, M. and Lopes Cardozo, T. A. (2008) Conflict, Education and the Global South: New Critical Directions. *International Journal of Educational Development,* 28 (4), 473–488.

Shriberg, J. (2008) *Fractured Help: Social Justice and Teacher Well-Being in Postwar Liberia*. Teachers College, Columbia University, 296 pp.

Stromquist, N. P., Ling, J., Corneilse, C., Klees, S. J., Chopti, T. and Haugen, C. S. (2013) Women Teachers in Liberia: Social and Institutional Forces Accounting for their Underrepresentation. *International Journal of Educational Development,* 33 (5), 521–530.

UNESCO (2011) *Education for All Global Monitoring Report 2011: The Hidden Crisis: Armed Conflict and Education*. Paris: UNESCO.

Wessells, M. (2005) Child Soldiers, Peace Education, and Post-Conflict Reconstruction for Peace. *Theory into Practice,* 44 (4), 363–367.

Index

Note: Locators with letter 'n' refers to notes.

Printed and bound by CPI Group (UK) Ltd, Croydon, CR0 4YY